How to Build a Profitable Business

A comprehensive guide to starting

and managing a business

Séamus Caulfield

Many thanks to Angela for her help and support,
to Ríona for her inspiration and patience over the years
and to Anna for her smiles and motivation.

Published by Metamorphosis Publications.

Enquiries regarding training to info@seamuscaulfield.ie

www.seamuscaulfield.ie

ISBN 978-0-9567080-0-7

Printed and bound in Ireland by Gemini International.

Foreword

My motivation for writing this book came from providing training to people who transformed their lives by starting their own business. Many had delayed starting because they didn't feel they had the skills, whilst others had struggled in business because of a lack of management experience.

The idea for a book evolved through much discussion and debate with students about the issues and obstacles facing anyone starting a business. I want to say a huge 'thank you' to all who have contributed their insights and experiences. May they continue to enjoy much business success and personal happiness.

The book provides practical advice and tips for anyone new to self-employment and explores a wide range of key topics not normally available in a single publication. It aims to stimulate thinking, as well as give clear guidance on how to avoid many of the pitfalls and mistakes involved during the early years in business.

Given the changing nature of employment, starting a business has become an increasingly attractive option for a growing number of people. If you have recently started a business or are actively considering it as an option, I hope you find this book useful.

Séamus Caulfield.
December 2010.

Contents

Chapter 1   Business Basics

The Golden Rule

If you're new to the business world, the first basic rule you need to understand is that business is first and foremost about money. Money is a form of trapped energy, and generating this energy is the reason any business exists (including charities).

"The people who get on in this world are the people who get up and look for the circumstances they want, and if they can't find them, make them."
- George Bernard Shaw

The 'golden rule' in business is that you must take in more money than you let out. If you don't do this, you will eventually go out of business. Begin by concentrating on how you can earn maximum money with minimum investment, not on what you need to spend to get fully set up. You can get 'fully set up' when you've earned the money to do so.

Check the 'golden rule' every week by counting all the money you have taken in, counting all the money you have paid out, and making sure that 'money in' exceeds 'money out'.

The KISS Principle

KISS stands for 'Keep It Simple Stupid'. It implies that the most efficient way of getting things done is to avoid unnecessary complications. Some people put progress just a little bit beyond their reach by over-complicating things to the point that they can no longer fully understand and control what's going on. This causes chaos and poorer results, not better ones.

Keep things simple, understandable and manageable.

Build your business one step at a time, and get activities in the proper order. Watch out that you don't get 'too far ahead of yourself' by trying to do tomorrow's work today. Don't take a complicated approach when a simple one will do, and focus on results, just getting things done.

When dealing with professional advisers (e.g. accountants or solicitors) keeps things simple enough for you to understand, and insist on clear explanations, because it's you that must understand how things work. After all, it's you that must manage the business profitably, not them, and they that work for you, not the other way around.

Three Steps to Creating a Business

One of the key realisations in life is that the future is not just something that happens to us – it is something we play a large part in creating ourselves. You will create a business if you take the three steps to creation:

1. **Thought** is the first step. Nothing was ever created by a human being that didn't first exist as a thought in someone's mind. The chair you are sitting on, the building you are in, the gardens outside, the cars in the carpark, the food you will eat for dinner, the business that ties it all together – they all exist because someone thought about how to create them. But many people stop there. They just think about things but they never actually do anything further.

2. **Word** is the second step. Word takes the form of written words, figures, calculations, drawings, sketches, etc. In business this step is represented by a Business Plan, which you can present to any relevant party as evidence that you are 'real' about your idea. But many people stop there, they just think about things and even write a plan but never do anything further.

3. **Action** is the final step. Action involves doing things, and getting results; it is the critical final step in creation. Action without sufficient thought or word will be rather wasteful as it's much cheaper to make your mistakes on paper than on the job itself.

Parkinson's Law

Parkinson's Law states that 'expenses rise to meet the income available'. Likewise work expands to fill the time available. You control your business from swallowing up all of your scarce resources of time and money by setting a budget for both. A badly managed business is a greedy thing, and failure to control it means Parkinson's Law will automatically apply.

Maintaining Boundaries

'Good fences make good neighbours' goes the saying, and you need to erect a boundary between your business life and your home life. A household has a completely different job to do than a business has. These two separate agendas need to be kept separate or one will end up dominating the other.

If the household (or the extravagant lifestyle of the owner) undermines the business by drawing too much cash, there's a danger of killing the goose that lays the golden egg. Don't place too many cash demands on a young and fragile business. Because owners' drawings are usually the biggest cost, keep them as low as possible initially.

It is important to maintain healthy boundaries between your business and other aspects of your life, otherwise issues from one will spill over to the other and cause harm. You have to be able to separate your personal feelings and difficulties from your business. You may be going through personal difficulties but it's important that they don't affect your work, because if they do you'll soon have both personal and business problems to deal with. There is a direct link between the way you feel, e.g. fed up, overworked, depressed, the way you look, e.g. untidy, tired, worried, and the way your business performs. This is particularly so in the service sector, e.g. pub, hairdressing, coffee shop, etc. It is important to maintain an optimistic attitude of happiness and helpfulness as this will be reflected in your business affairs and will win favour with your customers.

As a businessperson you must wear two hats – a hard hat when necessary for your business life because business is often hard and competitive, and a soft hat for your social and personal life, which requires more gentle treatment. Whilst not suffering fools gladly, business is also about people and relationships, so good people skills and a reputation for decency, integrity and respect will bring you a very long way. If your general attitude to life is that the world should be a little better because of your being here, this will come through in your business. Remember that while cash is king, and profit is the lifeblood of business, life itself is the supreme gift.

Three Categories of Business

Anyone can start a business but not everybody can start a profitable business.

Regardless of the many different types of business that there are, they all fall into three broad categories:

1. **Loss making/struggling businesses**. These businesses are a heartbreak, and are the most difficult to run. They are more common than people think, and even once-profitable businesses go through this stage before they eventually close down. Their owner will generally have worked all hours and borrowed money to keep them going. They will work hard for a further few years to repay any outstanding debts. This type of business situation is to be avoided like the plague.

2. **Break-even businesses**. Quite a lot of businesses fall into this category. Your break-even point is the point at which the amount of money you take in is equal to the amount you let out. It is often achieved by working every hour God sends, and scrimping and saving every penny. It's far better than incurring losses, but it's not good business.

3. **Profitable businesses**. A profitable business is able to make profits. It's the kind of business you want. Your business is only partly built until you achieve profits, so don't stop until you achieve this situation.

Before you go into business you need to be prepared to go the full distance through to profits. Falling short of this target means you'll get most of the pain of business without getting the financial gain you deserve. An absolute determination to reach profit is required, as half-hearted efforts cause cash shortages, hours of struggle, and generally end in failure.

Risk Taking

'Nothing ventured, nothing gained' is a well known phrase that emphasises the need to take risks. Before taking on any major project always ask yourself 'What's the downside?' If you stand to lose more than you can afford then you are taking a gamble rather than a calculated risk. If the downside of any undertaking is too serious then don't take it on, and try a different or smaller one that won't destroy you if it fails.

Let's be clear what we're talking about: risk is the degree of probability of loss; gambling is engaging in wild financial speculations. Calculated risk taking leaves you with a good amount of control over the outcome, whereas with gambling you've none, it's purely a game of chance. Be willing to stretch all your abilities, but don't overstretch yourself past breaking point.

In assessing the downside look at both the severity and the probability. Firstly, assess the severity of the worst possible outcome – what damage will it do to you? Might you lose a lot of money? Will it put you out of business? Secondly, assess the probability – how likely is this worst-case scenario? 50/50? 60/40 in favour of success? 70/30 in favour of success? Now it's looking better! If you have a 70/30 probability of success on ten separate decisions of equal value, then for each ten such risks you take, you'll lose on three and win on seven, winning overall.

Thoughts transform into reality with action.

Be aware of the need to eliminate as much risk as possible. If there are no major borrowings or major investments that will overstretch you, then there should be no major financial loss, but you still stand to lose your valuable time.

The Japanese have a saying: 'Only a fool learns from his own mistakes; a wise man learns from others.' Try to learn from others by observing or talking to people who know what they are talking about rather than only through direct experience. Use the mentors and professional advisers that are available to you from the County Enterprise Boards and other support agencies.

Organising a System

Organisation involves thinking things through, and putting a system in place so that you get the best results on a consistent basis. Organisation for record keeping requires folders, and a press/shelf/filing cabinet in which to store records; organisation for keeping a room tidy involves something as basic as a dustbin; organising your time properly requires a diary. Organising yourself is simple, but it does take the right attitude and a little time and effort.

Why organise a reliable system? To **S**ave **Y**our **S**elf **T**ime, **E**nergy & **M**oney. Bad organisation for a job, particularly when away from the workshop or office, wastes an awful lot of time, energy and money.

The best systems require minimum maintenance. e.g. direct debits for paying regular bills (electricity, telephone, rent, tax, etc.), organising trade accounts, maintaining sufficient stock of regularly needed materials, developing an efficient method for producing your goods and services, and creating efficient quotation and debt collection systems. All of these in turn depend on having organised sufficient working capital, which is the money needed to keep the various systems working as planned.

Organising a system is one thing, keeping it is another. Remember there are two parts to it – putting a system in place, and then using it.

Supply and Demand

Some types of business will be more profitable than others. This is based on the law of supply and demand which states that if there is greater demand for a product than the supply of it, the price will increase; if there is over supply, the price will fall.

Keen observation and customer feedback will give you a good feel for the supply/demand situation, and you must either reduce prices or increase product specifications to maintain demand in a falling market; you can do the opposite in a rising market.

Strengths, Weaknesses, Opportunities Threats (SWOT)

Strengths are the things you are good at, so build your business on these, particularly the ones you are naturally good at and enjoy doing.

Weaknesses counterbalance your strengths, so work to reduce these either by doing them better or getting someone else to do them for you.

Opportunities are occasions when you have an advantage and can move your business forward, so seize these quickly. Know that 'There's no such thing as a missed opportunity, because if you miss it the competition won't.'

Threats are the dangers that face any business. You must avoid these; 'Prepare for the worst and hope for the best' might help you avoid them altogether.

It is important to carry out a combined SWOT analysis both on your business and on yourself as promoter of the business. Start by dividing a blank page into four quarters with a pen. Give each quarter a separate heading (Strengths, Weaknesses, Opportunities and Threats) and conduct the analysis as honestly as possible.

Your natural strengths are the things you enjoy doing. Your weaknesses are the things you dislike doing. For instance if you enjoy bookkeeping, or selling, it's probably because you have a natural strength in these areas. If you hate doing them then they are weaknesses, and will probably need extra attention or delegation.

When it comes to opportunities there are loads flying around waiting for someone to grab them, but make sure that they suit your strengths; if they don't, or if you cannot afford them, then pass on them. And threats are everywhere, like potholes on a bad road, so learn to spot them early and avoid them.

Luck

If you agree with the statement that 'good luck is better than early rising' then it's important to set yourself up for good luck. Don't confuse luck with fate (e.g. being born when, where and who you are) which is largely predestined and thereby outside of your control.

Luck can be defined as when opportunity meets preparation, so it is not something that just happens to you out of the blue, it is something you can create for yourself. Did you not have a part to play in some of your bad luck? Likewise with your good luck – were you doing something which helped make it happen?

We sometimes hear a begrudging remark that the main reason a person got on was because he was lucky. Other people could have taken advantage of the same breaks, but they were not big enough to. 'The harder I practice, the luckier I get' is a famous quote from Gary Player, one of the world's best golfers. This supports the view that luck favours those who are prepared. Therefore you make your own luck. How? By looking out for an opportunity with a receptive, expectant mental attitude and grasping any opportunities that present themselves.

There is no shortage of opportunities to be productive and make money – there's actually a shortage of good people to take them. Prepare yourself mentally, spiritually, physically and emotionally to seize many of the opportunities that will inevitably cross your path. Others may call you lucky, but you know you will have played a large part in creating your own luck.

Getting Started

You start to really move forward when you stop making excuses.

'Where do I start?' The only place you can start is where you're at right now. It's you that put yourself there either directly or indirectly, so it's where you are meant to be. 'But it takes money to get started, and I don't have enough' I hear you say. Very few people have the money they wish to have, either to get started or to expand at a later date. Wherever you're at is where you're at, and there's no point wasting time wishing you were elsewhere.

Business Basics

Talk to the state agencies and other public bodies who are involved in helping small business – Department of Social Protection, Small Firms Association, Irish Small and Medium Enterprises (ISME), County Enterprise Board, FÁS etc. First Step has a loan facility for good business plans (not just good ideas). Sell stuff you don't need. Get a part-time job. Save money on shopping or lifestyle spending. Start as you mean to continue by making money at anything, but just get started. You'll gain in confidence with each new job.

But the best starting point of all is deciding on what businesses or business people you want to model yourself on. Find out who has done what you want to do and use them as a guide, just as if you had paid to buy a franchise from them. Visit their premises and note all the good things, get their price lists, observe how they do things, read a book about them if they are high profile, get to know them if they aren't. They may be relatives, or friends, or strangers; they may be in a similar business or a totally different one. If they're not close competitors they will most likely be glad to help you if they think you're serious. Try to learn from their attitudes, their work rate, their good business practices, their presentation – everything that will help you get started on the road to success.

But get started now. Do something to prepare yourself for business, strike with enthusiasm while the iron is hot, knowing that it only stays hot for so long.

Overtrading

If you try to grow too fast you may end up crashing the business. Overtrading is where the amount of business that is taken on outstrips the business' resources in terms of equipment, manpower, and money. It is foolish to keep taking on more and more work and not be able to pay the wages on Friday, but that's exactly how many profitable businesses go broke.

A small business needs to stay within its limits, with a few thousand euro put aside as soon as possible to save it when things get tight. Overtrading is a bit like speeding; you may hit a speed wobble and lose control of the business. So don't overtrade – don't take on more than you can do.

Three Keys to Profitability

Profit for sanity, turnover for vanity.

Your ability to produce profits (your profit-ability) requires work on the three parts of the 'Formula for Profit' which are:

1. **Reduce costs**. You must keep costs to a minimum by eliminating unnecessary costs and reducing necessary costs. By operating on a very low cost base you contribute greatly to your profitability.

2. **Optimise prices**. The better the price you get for anything, the better chance of profits. Anyone can give their products or services away, but it takes skill (and courage) to get a good price.

3. **Sell more stuff**. The more sales you make at the right price, the more profit you make.

Keep working on your profitability by working on each of its three parts. You will need to be good at at least two of the three if you are to be profitable.

Profit is the money left over for yourself after you have paid all your bills. It is the lifeblood of business, and any business that is drained of its lifeblood becomes unhealthy. Without profits you cannot save money to tide you over in lean times, or to invest in equipment for future growth.

The saying 'profit for sanity, turnover for vanity' underlines the fact that profit takes priority over turnover. Indeed, the best foundation for healthy growth in turnover is having a profitable operation in the first place.

Business Vision

Want to know an important secret? Knowing where you want to get to is one of the best kept secrets of success. How can you hope to get somewhere if you don't know where it is? 'Without a vision the people perish' states the Bible. To progress without a vision is difficult because there's nothing to work towards, just work for the sake of work.

You could just put your head down, work long and hard, and hope things work out. This approach has a certain merit – it's honest and hardworking – but it's not good enough. Before you rush into action the best work you will ever do is to think about where you want to get to, and about how to get there.

As we have already stated, we are constantly creating the future through our thoughts, words, and actions. From a practical business point of view, what vision is inspiring this process of creation? What do you really want to achieve? The clearer this vision, the better the chance you have of achieving it. It will give you direction and keep you on course during times when you get frustrated and lost.

Don't expect to be able to see everything that will crop up – it's an adventure! Like any journey having a good roadmap (i.e. a business plan) is a good help, but more important than any of that is really knowing where you want to get to.

Another aspect of vision you need to develop is double focus. Your main focus is obviously needed for the work in hand at present, but keep part of your focus on lining up work for two to three months ahead.

Finally, you need to develop your foresight to try to predict what will happen, and it will improve with practice. Too much time spent looking back at past glories or past difficulties means less time developing your foresight. How can you drive forward if you're constantly looking through the rear view mirror?

Attitude and Business

If you intend to succeed in your new venture then you will need to change a certain amount of your attitudes (an attitude is an habitual mode of thought or feeling). You always do what you're programmed to do by your habits. As you start to adopt new habits and attitudes you will come up against a certain amount of 'push/pull' conflict, i.e. you're trying to push through to new attitudes but old attitudes keep pulling you back and tripping you up. How do you drop these old attitudes? The same way you would drop a hot piece of coal if you found it in your hand – just drop it! Simple, no magic, no counselling, just drop it if it's hurting you.

"If all the money in the country were divided out equally in the morning, most of it would be back in the same hands within five years."
- Paddy Healy

Some new habits of thought relating to business will have to be developed, because business success is primarily dependent on being able to combine a good business attitude with good skill at your trade; you need both. If you have a negative attitude to business people, how can you possibly hope to commit your full efforts to becoming one? It's simply not possible, so you will need to engage in a mental brainwash to clear out some old attitudes that will block your path forward. Otherwise you will stay stuck where you are, and that will cost you.

Attitude and Money

'Money isn't that important' is a throwaway remark you've often heard. Except when you get to the checkout in the supermarket, or at the petrol pumps, or when it's mortgage time – in other words it's very important. That's the truth of the matter, so get to grips with it. Business is all about money; money is the lifeblood of business.

Many people have a huge hang-up about money. They will tell you about their health, relationships, loves, hates, but not about their money. Why is this? Money is just a form of energy, and of itself it is neutral, it will go into anybody's pocket. But people put a positive or a negative charge on this energy by the way they think about it. That's why it is important to develop the right attitude to money – in order to put a positive charge on it.

Money is a medium of exchange that replaced the awkwardness of the barter system, and a store of value that you can save up for a rainy day. It is a form of trapped energy, it has power. Without electric power you would be at a disadvantage, but who has a hang-up about electricity? Without money power you would also be at a disadvantage, so why have a hang-up about it either? Choose to be financially powerful, not powerless and hopeless with money.

If business is about money, and you have a negative attitude to money, this will cause huge problems both for yourself and those who deal with you. Imagine a runner that doesn't like running or a boxer who doesn't like boxing – will they go far? Likewise with you as a business person if you don't like money! Develop a healthy respect for money and what it can do to make your life more fulfilling, and you'll find yourself accumulating more of it because of the magnetic power of thought, which attracts to you what you respect and value.

Management

Management is about getting results; thus a good manager is someone who manages to get things done. Managing not alone to get things done, but done within the time and money budgets you have worked out are key tasks if you are to turn a profit. Sometimes this will be hard and will put you under pressure, so you must focus on the positive gain, not on the negative pain. 'It doesn't matter how hard you need to work, it's what's in your pocket at the end of the year that counts' is a bit of advice I was given when starting off.

Progression is a natural law.

The job of any manager is to think as well as to do. There are many opportunities to focus your thinking on your business, such as working out your costs and pricing on a job, putting together a business plan, or doing out a set of projected accounts. Research, observe, research again, listen, and research again, using your common sense for the ideas, the information and the people that will help your business become successful. Good management is an ongoing exercise in using your common sense to get a true sense of what to do.

In management there are two broad categories of work you need to get through: the everyday maintenance tasks needed to keep the show on the road and the cash flowing in; and the development tasks needed to take your business to the next step on the ladder. The job of management is to think strategically about creating the future as well as to think practically about the present, and this double focus is best described as working *on* the business as well as working *in* the business. This represents a subtle yet key shift in thinking, and will determine whether or not the business moves forward or becomes stagnant, leading to eventual decline. The ability to free up and invest scarce time and money working on the business is the hallmark of progressive management.

Get it Done

Building your business is not based on genius, but on getting things done. Not thinking about them in clever ways, but getting them done! Not putting them off, but getting them done!

Putting things off means that they build up. It's usually not the big problems that cause the trouble, but the little ones you let build up. Try to be efficient, get things done straight away rather than keep shuffling them around. This brings freedom from stress and clutter, freeing you up to do other progressive things. Freedom is born from discipline, the discipline of getting things done.

The question remains, are you good at getting things done? Remember Parkinson's Law: 'expenditure rises to meet the income available'. Likewise with work: 'work expands to fill the time available'. If you want to get things done you must assess the amount of time required to do them, set a deadline, and simply get them done within this time.

There's Never Enough Time

There is only so much time available to all of us; it is the one thing that is given out equally. Along with money, it is one of our

---

scarcest resources. In fact, in the world of work we can clearly argue that time is money. We buy people's time for money (at the going rate per hour) and we sell our time for money (at a price per job, having figured out how long it will take us). Therefore it is essential that we manage it carefully, and budget our time between our private lives and our working lives. An important issue is how much time we allocate to each.

Keep your costs as low as possible, and your spirits as high as possible. This spirit will feed your vision, your courage, and your determination.

The best method I have come across for getting the best return from the available time is the following, developed by a man called Ivy Lee.

The Ivy Lee Method

1. At the end of the day make a list of all the jobs you want to get through the next day
2. Number that list in order of importance
3. Start at number one on the list, and stay at it until it's completed; then move to number two, and stick with that until completed, and so on for the whole day. Then back to number one, and set a new prioritised list for the following day

If you don't get it all done at least you get the most important things done, and you still get more tasks completed than if you were skipping from task to task. (Remember you can only do one thing at a time). It's a simple method, and it makes perfect sense.

It is important to work this system in its three parts. Some people just do part one, but never bother separating the important work from the time-wasting, unimportant stuff. They may satisfy themselves that they are busy, but they may be busy at the wrong thing.

You cannot save time; you can just spend it wisely. You spend it the same way you spend money. Don't waste it. Are you getting value for your money? Are you getting value for your time? Keep working on the most important things (not the most enjoyable ones) and it is likely that your time will be well spent.

Decision Making

The mental creation precedes the physical.

On one occasion I was pondering how to do something when I met an old acquaintance, who has built up a fine business. 'Don't think too much about it or you'll only frighten yourself' was his common sense advice, and it illustrated the concept of 'paralysis through analysis' (i.e. doing nothing but thinking and worrying).

An ability to trust their best judgement and make decisions quickly is an important characteristic of the best business people. Why? Because it saves time, and allows them to take on the next opportunity or problem. They do not wait for complete information to be on board, because it never will be; neither do they rush headlong into something without considering it properly. Decision making is a delicate balance between the two, usually based on intuitive judgement.

There is no known method of always making the correct decision, so the most that you can expect is that your decision will probably be correct. A lot of people waste much precious time unable to make up their minds on anything because they are afraid they will make the wrong decision. The worst decision is not to make any decision, and merely let things drift on, undecided. Your business will suffer if you cannot make decisions quickly.

If you devote yourself to making small decisions promptly, you will find it much easier to be decisive when the stakes are much bigger. More importantly, you'll find making decisions and acting on them far easier if you act promptly. The person who doesn't reach decisions promptly when they have all necessary facts in hand cannot be depended on to carry out decisions after they make them. Thus slow decision makers are usually slow doers also.

A final word of caution about some well-intentioned advisers who will rush to give you their opinions, oftentimes quite forcibly: ask yourself is their advice based on their own fears and baggage, or is it based on a sound track record of achievement? Remember that 'too many cooks spoil the broth' and it is you who will have to live with the consequences of lost opportunity, not them. In the final analysis you must decide for yourself.

Managing Your Scarcest Resources

For most people their scarcest resources are their time and their money. A home and a business will compete for both, so each needs to be given the space in which to operate without unfair interruption from the other.

Money management accounts:

1. A **business account** for all your business expenses
2. A **personal account** for all your personal/household expenses
3. A **savings account** or accounts (pension, holidays, equipment, etc.) for your profits

If you don't keep your business and personal finances separate they will become confused on the one bank statement, and there'll be no savings.

Time management accounts:

1. A **work time account** for all work-related activities (including quotations and debt-collection)
2. A **family time** account for family
3. An **own time** account for hobbies, social activities, etc.

Your time in any day is limited; so if you don't keep separate time accounts some area of your life will suffer, dominated by the others.

Recession

Should you start a business during a recession, or should you wait for the good times to return? According to some people, the best time to start a business is during a recession. Why?

Firstly, because you have to build a lean, keen, money making machine, with none of the costly padding and inefficiencies that the good times can cover up.

Experience is a hard school, but a fool will learn no other way.

Secondly, because the established competition may have grown lazy during the good times and have difficulty cutting back on bigger outlays, luxuries and non essential expenses.

And finally, if you've built a low cost system and developed your business skills in bad times you will prosper when the economy picks up. A bit like planting a garden, you cannot wait till the summer sun – you have to have the groundwork done and the seeds planted in the springtime if you want a good harvest.

Think Like a Business Person

Thinking like a business person is slightly different to thinking like a working person. Why? Because business people must think more about money. They have to; it's a large part of their job, and if they ignore it for long they will go bankrupt. If you want to become successful in business you have to spend more time thinking about money; how to price your work, collect it, save it, invest it, account for it.

You also have to think more about your time. Time is money, particularly in business. If you're working for a wage, you can afford to be Mrs. Helpful or Mr. Nice Guy with your spare time, doing cheap or unpaid jobs. You cannot do that in business: you must get properly paid for your work, and give free time only to projects you really value. That means learning to say 'no' to time wasting requests and moving goalposts – the 'while you're there would you mind doing a few extra little jobs (without extra pay!)'.

An old neighbour of mine, Paddy Healy, used to say, 'If all the money in the country was divided out evenly today, in five years time most of it would be back in the same hands. Those without it now would have spent it all and be without it again, and those that have it now would have earned it all back again.' He's dead for many years, but was what he said true then, and is it still true? I believe so, which suggests that the reason people find themselves either with money or without it is because of the attitude they have towards it. A poor attitude will keep you poor, and a richer attitude will make you richer.

The business world can be tough, and is not based on fairness. Business is largely based on the rules of the animal kingdom – survival of the fittest.

When people whinge about unfairness it usually takes the form of 'But I wouldn't do that to them, I'd pay them on time' etc. So what? The world doesn't play by your rules. Read people as they are, not as you would like them to be. Applying your own standards to others can be a serious mistake. And wasting time in self-pity because other people don't act accordingly is another.

There is a lot of fairness in the world and you should treat people fairly. But don't be surprised if it isn't always returned in a similar fashion.

Innovation

Innovation can be defined as 'making changes to something established by introducing something new'. When looked at from a business point of view we can say that this 'something new' must be something that adds value to customers. Customers look for the best value, so if we add more value we'll add more customers and (hopefully) more profit.

There is a difference between innovation and invention. Invention is defined as 'creating something new that has never existed before'. Something new can be invented, but if it doesn't add value to the customer then it never becomes an innovation.

So we can further define innovation as follows:

Innovation = Invention + Exploitation (Roberts, 1988)

To be innovative in your business you don't need to invent anything, just figure out new and better ways of doing things that add value (lower cost / better quality / faster service) to your customer. An innovative approach to business is essential because if your way of doing business stands still whilst your competitors improve, you'll be left behind, and eventually get left out altogether.

How do we develop our innovation? Rather than just respond to the competition, we can also develop our innovation in order to get ahead of them by spotting and developing new opportunities. In times of change, gaps open in the market and a cheaper solution, a better service, a faster response, a new way of delivering a product to your customer (e.g. sold through your website and delivered directly to their door) would be examples of innovation in action.

What's in it for Me?

At a subconscious level all humans ask the question, 'What's in it for me?' One could say it's hardwired into our genetic coding.

An enterprise culture is one in which every individual understands that the world does not owe him or her a living.

Children are taught to share and not to be selfish – very worthwhile social values. However, business is business, which implies that a slightly different standard is used. You have a responsibility to get your financial needs met, and for some people that means making a shift from 'doing favours' to assertively asking 'what's in it for me?'. Don't confuse this with being selfish – it is an assertion of your right to have your own needs met.

Business success is about making money. 'Fools make feasts and wise men eat them' is a truism, so don't end up doing all the work while somebody else gets the benefits. The benefits must be shared and it's up to you to make sure you get your fair share.

Our first duty is to ourselves, and if we don't meet this duty then we're not much good to anybody else either. If we give to others from a depleted state then we are giving from our lacking, and our giving is tainted with negativity as a result. We need to look after ourselves first – it's called 'proper selfishness'. Over-selfishness is of course not a particularly nice trait, but neither is under-selfishness; it also creates negativity. Avoid people and deals that don't meet your needs. As a business person you need profits, not losses.

Exercise

Business Tasks to be Completed

Plot the various tasks you need to complete over the next 15 weeks. Try to get them in the correct sequence, and tick ✔ the number of weeks you think will be required to complete each task. List only **progression** tasks (i.e. tasks that move the business forward), not ongoing **maintenance** tasks (i.e. day-to-day jobs).

Tasks	Weeks 1 – 15														
	1	2	3	4	5	6	7	8	9	10	11	12	13	14	15
1. Aspirational business plan	✔														
2. Business bank account		✔													
3. Promotional materials				✔	✔	✔									
4.															
5.															
6.															
7.															
8.															
9.															
10.															
11.															
12.															

Chapter 2   Personal Preparation

Why Bother?

Why bother with all the hassle and effort involved in starting a business? This is one of the most important questions you have to ask yourself. If you are not clear about exactly why you are starting a business, then when times get tough and you come under a lot of pressure, you are more likely to quit.

If it's just because 'it seems like a good idea', or because 'I can't get a job at anything else', then you may quit when the going gets tough. If you are absolutely clear about why you are starting you will be harder to throw off course, because a strong enough 'Why' will bear almost any 'How'; in other words regardless of how tough it gets, if you are clear on why you are doing it you will survive the inevitable temporary setbacks.

"The real act of discovery consists not in finding new lands but in seeing with new eyes."
- Marcel Proust

In Victor Frankl's book 'Man's Search For Meaning' he describes how he survived the Nazi concentration camp at Auschwitz. He kept in mind being reunited with his family, his wife and his children – this was his reason 'Why'. He drew the conclusion that a strong enough reason 'Why' is sufficient to withstand any hardship, or any 'How'. Similarly in business it doesn't really matter how difficult the circumstances, it's the reason why that matters. Maybe it's to give a good example or education to your children, to provide a more comfortable home, or to have more flexibility in your working life. Over the last ten years the nature of work has changed with fewer jobs for life, and more short-term or subcontracted work. Maybe you need to create your own work through self-employment if you want to get regular work.

It is very important that you answer this question 'Why bother?' and come up with an honest answer that will keep you driving on, obsessively, through good days and bad, building your business. Remember, a strong enough 'Why' will bear any 'How'.

Responsibility

Responsibility is made up of two words, 'response' and 'ability'. This implies that you have an ability to respond to any situation and it is your duty to use this ability to its fullest. If you've lost a job, found an opportunity, lost money, won the lotto, finished a relationship, whatever, you can respond. You can either use or avoid using your ***response-ability***; it's a choice you make for yourself.

You sometimes avoid using this responsibility by blaming others for the mess you're in; by playing small and fearful; by setting the bar too high to jump, so you can avoid trying; by escaping into magical thinking that something will happen without you trying; by thinking out all sorts of excuses instead of all sorts of solutions; by wishing things were different to the way they are now. If you choose to respond in any of the above ways you will end up feeling like a powerless victim. This powerless victim mentality and the feelings of self-pity that go with it will attract further problems.

Blame is the opposite to responsibility. With blame, instead of using your energy to respond and do something, you push your energy away from you in a negative way towards someone else. Even if it was their fault to start with, it'll be your fault if you waste too much time and energy indulging in blame.

Power

Is power good or bad? Do you need power? What is power? Power can be defined as: 'ability to do anything; capacity for producing an effect; strength; energy'. Given this definition, it seems that power is essential to do anything, to produce an effect. As a self-employed person you only get paid for producing effects or results, not for just turning up. You must turn on your personal power to succeed in business. Personal power is energy, health, courage, ambition, a determination to succeed in achieving your goals. Pray; visualise; be. You have all this personal power, you were born with it, so use it.

People who fail to turn on their power end up weak and powerless. This means they can blame the world (parents, FÁS, church, government, etc.) for their situation. Playing the blame game is avoiding responsibility. To the person who wasn't using his personal power and lay down in the face of adversity, there is some good advice in the Bible: 'Take up your bed and walk'.

"To thine own self be true."
- William Shakespeare

A milder version of misusing your personal power is to compare yourself to others. If you compare yourself to those with more power (money is a form of power) you can feel bad about your own lack of success. Instead, you can compare yourself now to where you will be in a year's time. Will you have made forward progress? Are you using your full power to achieve your goals? Are you being true to yourself, your dreams, your abilities?

A small, hopeless, powerless you is not the real, true you. Your real self is the courageous, successful vision of yourself so stay true to this vision.

Which Power Supply – the Positive or the Negative?

As you work towards setting up a profitable business you will notice that some things help you move forward; others hold you back. The energies attached to any real thing (person, situation, comment) are seldom neutral – they're either positive or negative. Energies cluster together with similar energies and form thinking patterns that have a huge effect on your life, and your successes or failures.

Look at these two ways of engaging with your future, and ponder the different outcomes from being positive or negative:

Positive	Negative
Good	Bad
Ambition	No goals
Optimism	Depression
Courage	Cowardice
Bright	Dark
Wealth	Poverty
Generosity	Greed
Responsibility	Blame

Your mind is like a garden, and particularly your subconscious mind is like a fertile garden. Your mind needs ongoing maintenance to get rid of the negative weeds that grow there. Negative weeds and seeds of doubt blow in on a difficult day when nothing will go right, taking root in moments of negativity. Weed them out, and sow positive thoughts and images every single day, because 'as you sow, so shall you reap'.

You tend to become what you think you should become.

Your mind divides into a conscious mind (c.10%) and a subconscious mind (c.90%). The subconscious is very fertile ground, and works 24 hours a day to make whatever it is told into a reality. It cannot tell between positive and negative, it depends on your conscious mind to have judged that. Make sure you consciously make the positive choices for your unconscious mind to obey.

In general terms you get the results you deserve. Spending too much thinking time on the dark, negative side, will create a negative outcome for your business efforts and time spent on the bright side will give a brighter outcome. The mental creation precedes the physical, so be very careful with the feelings you are creating in your mind.

If you feel you need extra work on this area, an excellent and easily-read book is 'The Power of Positive Thinking' by Norman Vincent Peale, available in most libraries and bookshops.

Committed or Just Involved?

How committed must you be in order to build a successful business? You must be **sufficiently committed to do whatever it takes** to produce the results. That's it in a nutshell – no dodges, no excuses, no half-hearted effort – a full commitment.

Sounds hard? Indeed, but you'll be glad to hear that real commitment creates its own energy, and gets you tuned into new ways of seeing things, doing things, achieving results.

In his book, 'The Scottish Himalayan Expedition', W H Murray says:

> 'Until one is committed, there is hesitancy, the chance to draw back, always ineffectiveness. Concerning all acts of initiative (and creation), there is one elementary truth, the ignorance of which kills countless ideas and splendid plans. That the moment one definitely commits oneself, then providence moves too.

All sorts of things occur to help one that would never otherwise have occurred. A whole stream of events issues from the decision, raising in one's favour all manner of unforeseen incidents and meetings and material assistance, which no man could have dreamed would have come his way.

I have learned a deep respect for one of Goethe's couplets:

> 'Whatever you can do or dream you can, begin it. Boldness has genius, power and magic in it.'

Show your commitment by investing in yourself (training, appearance, business image, stationery, transport, equipment). If you don't believe in yourself, why would you expect potential customers to?

As you proceed with building the business you will suffer many setbacks. This is par for the course as setbacks are inevitable, they are guaranteed. They are there to test your commitment, to see what you're made of. If you are really committed you will work through them; if not, they will be an opportunity to quit.

As the old wisdom goes 'if a problem doesn't break you it will make you stronger'. Overcoming setbacks and solving problems is a big part of your job, as well as an ongoing opportunity to strengthen your commitment.

Abundance or Just Survival?

Ideally you would live with an abundance of health, wealth, and happiness. Do you see abundance as your natural right, provided you work towards it? In the context of business an abundance of money and profit is where the action is. Mere survival at breakeven point is not good enough. A philosophy of abundance implies profit. Remember that business is a two-edged sword – it can be for your betterment (through profit) or to your detriment (through losses) depending on your attitude.

Do people make a choice between abundance and lacking? Yes. Would they consciously choose the poorer option? Most wouldn't, but some would. For others, it is a subconscious choice. If you have been taught to live on scarce means by a poor wage, or a period of unemployment, and you have accepted this as unavoidable, then the lesson of scarcity has been well learned.

Don't quit easily. Do whatever you must do to stay in the game, and a few lucky breaks will most likely come your way.

Examine your attitudes to wealth. Are you prepared to work towards it? Your underlying philosophy must be one of abundance. You must feel that you deserve it as much as the next person, and eliminate any negative attitudes you have towards it. This will lead to a wealthier, more comfortable life. An abundant and fulfilling life is our spiritual right, but is not offered to us automatically without effort – it is up to us to achieve it.

Change

Stupidity has been defined as repeating the same things and expecting to get different results. Starting a business will involve a lot of change to your attitudes, your values, your lifestyle. Change can be frightening, but it can also be enlightening.

Where you are today is where your thoughts have brought you. These thoughts will have been partly your own original thoughts, and partly someone else's thoughts that you have bought into. Some of these external thoughts will have come from school teachers, church men, politicians, revolutionaries, union representatives, musicians, parents ... there's a long list of people who may have been hell-bent on grabbing a piece of your mind. Some of this thinking was right, and some of it was wrong; some of it was right 20 years ago but in a much changed world is no longer right.

Emotional intelligence requires that we move on to relevant, new thinking, and drop old, damaging thoughts and attitudes. Our habits, our old ways and our old attitudes are burnt into our brains through years of practice, so we need to be quite determined if we want to shift them. As times change we need to update our thinking. As Charles Darwin observed, "It is neither the strongest nor the most intelligent of the species that survive; it is the ones that are most adaptable to change.' Embrace the changes that face you, because you have no choice!

People treat you the way you show them how to treat you.

You are constantly changing. You are not the same person that you were even one year ago. Looking back on life is sometimes like looking at a film, it could have happened to a different person – and it actually did; you were different back then! Say 'hello' to the new you, full of business!

Fear

Fear is the main thing that stops us from getting things done. If we are honest with ourselves we would have achieved a lot more in life if it wasn't for fear. We can usually try to justify not having done things on the basis of caution. However, when is caution the 'caution of a coward', and when is it shrewd, calculated business judgement? Fear stands for **F**alse **E**xpectations **A**ppearing **R**eal.

The trouble is, if you don't risk anything, you risk even more.

The main danger with taking on a new venture is that you hold back because of fear, which makes it dangerous because you then run a greater danger of failing. It's by half doing things that you create the danger, holding back your energies instead of going all out.

Can you identify with any of the following fears: the fear of not being good enough; of getting too greedy; of losing friends; of book keeping; of the taxman; of not having a regular wage; of not getting paid for work you do; of not succeeding; of losing your good name/good reputation; of the competition; of going broke; of being too successful? One of the most encouraging thoughts about danger is that most of the things we are afraid of usually don't happen. It is the fear itself that we're afraid of.

Fear is used to control, oppress and manipulate people. It causes people to do wrong things, cruel things, or nothing. The strength of your desire must overcome the strength of your fear. A little work on increasing the strength of your desire and on reducing the strength of your fear will quickly turn the tables in your favour.

Courage

To overcome fear you need courage. Courage comes from the French word for heart: coeur. It means putting your whole heart into something, not being half-hearted. It also involves spirit. A spirited person will always put up a good, courageous fight.

Until your courage is up you need to talk to people who will encourage you, and avoid those who will discourage you. It is also important to try hard to get off to a good start with your business as nothing builds courage like success.

No one can tell what they are able to do until they try. If they give it a full-hearted, courageous effort they will seldom fail. It's like going in for a tackle in sport, if you go in hard you seldom get hurt; if you go in with a weak challenge you generally come off worst.

Courage is one of the more noble of the human qualities. How much courage can you summon up, and keep up? Remember, fortune favours the brave, and he who hesitates is lost.

Confidence

Confidence is knowing that when a situation arises, you'll be able to figure out what to do – 'the job will teach you how to do it'. Confidence is achieved through doing, not through thinking.

Too much thinking will lead to 'paralysis through analysis'; in other words you'll frighten yourself and lose confidence if you don't move through to action. The more action you get through, the more your confidence builds.

Laugh and the world laughs with you, cry and you cry alone

Confidence is a key ingredient in building a business. You may have to rely on pure courage in taking on something you're not familiar with at the start, but with action your need for courage will soon be replaced by confidence.

Do you have the confidence to introduce yourself as the owner of your new business, put your name on a well designed business card and present it to someone? Do it a few times and your confidence will grow.

'So Much to Know'

That's true, but the nice thing about it is that you know most of it already. You will have picked it up through your everyday dealings with businesses, from other people, through the newspapers, everywhere. You need to sharpen up on this general knowledge by keenly observing how your type of business is conducted by the best in the game, by listening to your intuition (inner tutor) and by doing some relevant training (but don't become a course junkie). Try to learn something from every person you meet. These learning experiences will include both the technical skills relating to your trade, and the business skills relating to your business.

However well you prepare yourself, there's no substitute for doing the job. Have confidence that 'the job will teach you how to do it' if you get stuck in courageously and cleverly, and remain open to constant learning and improvement.

Successfully Failing

The dictionary defines success as 'the state of having succeeded; prosperous progress, achievement; attainment of wealth, influence, or acclaim'. If you're feeling awkward about not being successful in the past, you may need to consciously give yourself permission to succeed. Permission to have money in the bank, a nice house, a good lifestyle.

Consider the concept of 'successfully failing'. You may be successful at reaching breakeven point, but only by giving huge hours to the business, which would fail without this effort. For how long is it sustainable before something cracks? In addition to your huge effort, what price is being paid by other family members? So let's keep it simple, and define successful business as profitable business.

Emotional Business

Believe it or not, business success is an emotional thing more so than an academic thing. How else can you explain why talented people don't always succeed? The person with good common sense and the correct determination and desire to succeed will beat the talented person with a 'why bother' attitude every time. Oftentimes the most difficult step is giving yourself permission to succeed; once you do this you can apply your full effort to your goal, without holding back.

A successful person will have emotional intelligence, which is an ability to make the right decisions and do the right things in order to make their life better and fuller. The successful person will think clearly about what they want to achieve, develop confidence in their ability through doing, and do whatever it takes. The work you do on your emotional intelligence may be more important than the work you do on taxation, because a bookkeeper will do your tax returns, but you cannot hire anyone else to do your thinking. Check your emotional intelligence for business by honestly asking 'Do I deserve to be successful?' You may have to work hard on the answer.

Why would anyone hold back on their efforts? It doesn't make sense but the reality is that people do hold back on going for their goals, because even though they want to get to a better place, they are partly afraid of leaving the place they are in. The smoker may want to quit, but is afraid of the withdrawal, the drug addict or alcoholic the same way, except more severe. This semi-paralysis is referred to as push/pull conflict. Your hopes for the future are pushing you forward, and your ties to the past are pulling you back. You need to cut your ties with the past and take a leap of faith in your ability to create a better future.

A final word of caution. Many people have set themselves up for success, only to blow it all when success is at hand, 'grabbing defeat from the jaws of victory'. This tendency to self-sabotage by spending too much, arguing too much, drinking too much, working too hard causing ill health, taking shortcuts, etc. is fairly commonplace. It probably means that deep in their subconscious these people feel they don't really deserve the success they have had, and so they blow it. It is particularly evident in many politicians, sportspeople and business people; can you think of anyone like this?

Lifestyle Changes

Rely on your common sense; it is your wisdom at work.

Starting a business involves more than just a change of job – it also brings changes to your lifestyle. You may embrace these changes or you may fight against them, but know that a certain amount of lifestyle changes come with the job, and think about them in advance.

The first change will be to your working hours. Most self-employed people work more than 60 hours a week, particularly in the early years. This means you will not be able to continue with all of your current pastimes, because you will not have as much free time. Existing pastimes, e.g. coaching the local underage footballers, may need to be reduced or dropped because you may need to get out and quote for some work two evenings a week. If you open a pub or a restaurant, you can wave goodbye to free evenings and weekends.

Starting a business also involves your family, particularly your spouse or partner. Watch that the involvement isn't negative, giving out that you aren't there, but is positive, encouraging, and supportive. Support from other family members has been shown to be critical to the success of a new business, so sit down and discuss with your partner the practicalities of how this might work.

Making new contacts for work (networking) will also play an increasingly larger part in your life. Community activities, sporting activities, getting involved in trade associations all become part of your job to some extent or other. Watch how any politician does this type of work!

Your Sense of 'Self'

Your business becomes an extension of your 'self' because in your customers' eyes you are your business. Your attitude, manners, presentation, honesty, reputation, skill, reliability, etc. will all be reasons why they either do or don't do business with you. Your self-employment will bring a lot of your 'self' into it. Your self-discipline, self-care, self-confidence, self-worth, and self-motivation will all make an impact.

If that's the case then it means that you (as the driving force) have to look after yourself. Don't 'kill the goose that lays the golden egg', or there'll be no more golden eggs! Decide how many evenings you will work. Decide how many hours each week. Decide what holidays you will definitely take. Decide what hobbies you will have. Decide if you will answer the phone outside business hours or use the message minder.

The raggy colt often made a powerful horse.

Maintaining good self-confidence and being proud of what you do is very important. If we all had more self-confidence we would have achieved more. Work at developing a firm confidence in your ability to achieve your desired outcome. You need to use your natural intelligence but you don't need to be a brain box; the attitude that guides your intelligence is more important than how much intelligence you may have. An ability to size up the opportunities and organise yourself are much more important skills. Develop your self-confidence in your natural intelligence, your ability to work things out.

Have confidence in your ability: to figure things out, to work hard, to work cleverly. A kitten doesn't need to be taught how to catch a mouse, they are born with this talent; remind yourself of the special talents and ways of seeing things that you were born with. Have confidence in the hidden talents that you haven't even used yet but that will come to the surface when needed. You can't really know what these are, what you're capable of, until you try, so take that leap of faith in your own abilities.

Think well of yourself and your abilities, because you tend to get from life what you feel you deserve. Your sense of self-worth will be reflected in the prices you charge, and your resultant financial worth.

Motivation

You can't keep doing the same things and expect a different result.

Definition of motive: 'causing motion; having power to cause motion; concerned with the initiation of action.'

The gap between what a person can do and will do depends on their motivation, which is the collection of forces that moves a person to action. If you have spent a period unemployed or under-employed, it is easy to lose your motivation. Now is the time to check it out again, to ask yourself the all-important questions of 'what do I want to be?' and 'how badly do I want it?'

As a self-employed person you must be able to self-motivate. Business people are a bit like ships – they must make their way in spite of the waves, winds, storms and fogs. And like ships they only make money when they are moving!

Motivation is about movement, about getting out there and spinning the wheels until you eventually get solid ground. It is about trying. It is about asking, again and again until you succeed.

Persistence – Keep Yourself Going

'Can I really do it?' From time to time doubt creeps in, doesn't it? 'Will it work? Am I mad? Would I not be better off to put my goals aside and take the safer road and get a job, like most of my friends and relatives? Here I am, putting in all this oftentimes unseen work, taking a leap of faith in my own abilities (after all, I've never done it before), a step into the unknown, into the dark'.

As you build your business you will fall over many times. You will lose direction, lose courage, lose hope. Difficulties and challenges are inevitable. But they are really only there to see what kind of stuff you are made of. If you can get up, dust yourself off and go again until you succeed, you're made of the right stuff. Building a business will never be plain sailing, and that's where persistence comes in. It is possibly the most important quality of the lot in an aspiring business person.

Change is inevitable; embrace change!

Keep yourself going physically through good exercise and diet; intellectually by learning what you can about the business; emotionally by thinking positively; and spiritually by praying.

The importance of timing in making a breakthrough to a new reality is critical. Even if you have considered trying before but didn't, or if you tried before and didn't succeed, maybe now is the right time. Spiritualists believe that 'when someone is truly ready for a thing it puts in its appearance'.

Can anyone become self-employed? There are two answers to this question. No, if they are not prepared to do what it takes, and yes if they are. Everyone has the potential ability, but potential never buttered much bread. People are not all the same (thanks be to God or it would be a very boring world). Some people don't want the extra hassle that's on the extra mile, required for the extra rewards. And there are no shortcuts – the extra rewards don't come without the extra effort.

Effort

Effort is the exertion of body or mind in order to produce or accomplish something, and requires energy. Building a business requires a mix of cash and effort. If you're low on cash equity, then you'll need to be high on your time and effort, referred to as 'sweat equity', to make up the balance. A poorly funded start-up will require sustained effort to build it, whilst a well funded one will not have to work quite so hard.

The best example I've seen of pure, raw effort as the key ingredient of success is the Japanese transformation of their economy, from a war-ravaged, third world economy to a wealthy G7 world power today. All this despite an extremely mountainous terrain, lack of natural resources, and long distance from the wealthy international marketplace. Effort is indeed a key ingredient in success.

"He who has a strong enough why can bear almost any how."
- Friedrich Nietzsche

As a self-employed person you will have to work both hard and sharp, particularly until you are established. If it takes 80 hours a week to break even, then that's what it takes. In general, self-employed business people work at least 60 hours per week. Obviously you will be working towards reducing this, with your first aim being to break even in 40 hours a week. With increases in your efficiency and targeting better jobs, you'll then be hoping to break even in 30 hours, etc. Any extra hours will go straight to profits, which is the whole reason why you are in business.

You need to apply a lot of effort initially, and once you get up and running, maintaining the effort is easier. You do have to keep on the ball, watching out for what's going wrong and correcting it as quickly as possible. A good start is half the battle, so it's important to get stuck in right from the start, and enthusiasm will carry you a long way.

How Big is Your Thinking?

The achievements in your life and your business will be limited by the size of your thinking. It is simply impossible for your business to become bigger than your thinking. 'You cannot get ten gallons into a five gallon can', no more than you can get

€100,000 a year sales into a head that thinks about €50,000 a year.

What will happen is that you'll take it easy as soon as you get beyond the size that you consider your business should be. For many people this tends to be when they reach break even; the struggle to do so has made them tired, and they don't push for profit. If you are content to settle for breakeven, then that is where you will rest. However, in business terms abundance means profit. That is your proper resting place, and your business is only partly built until you get there.

There's very little point in working just for the sake of working – you have to be working towards something, a point in the future when you will have grown your business bigger than it is today. Base your stationery, your sales lines, everything, on this bigger version of you, where you will be in a year's time – otherwise you're playing too safe. Don't get caught up with just living from day to day. You are more than that because you are abundant. Your vision of yourself for the future must be bigger than your view of yourself at present. Think big!

Three Time Zones: Past, Present, Future

'One look ahead is better than ten looks behind' is an old Irish saying.

- Your **past** has passed. It is who you were once. You are no longer a child. You are no longer an employee, regardless of what job you held. You are no longer unemployed if you are truly working on a new business.

- Your **present** is the here and now. It is a present, like you get at Christmas time (hopefully!). It is the only place you can be, really.

- Your **future** is what you are coming to be, i.e. becoming.

Of these three states of being, the most important are the present and the future. Nobody has yet discovered a way of changing the past, which is why it's being relegated to third position (although many people insist on living in the past). Don't let your past get in front of you, because it will definitely block your way forward.

Of the remaining two states, the present is the most important, but today's future is tomorrow's present, which makes it a very close second. Because they are so close we tend to move between the two, sometimes even getting a little ahead of ourselves.

In terms of business, there's a transition period, when you're crossing over from one state to another. You are becoming a business person or you are a business person – which is it? To convince yourself (and others) there comes a point at which you have to change from becoming to being a business person. This crossing over is a big step, moving from the security of your comfort zone into the unknown, and it takes a lot of courage.

As you move to the future you will have to take chances, so how will you feel as you grow into this new reality? Inexperienced, yes; insecure, yes; and creative, courageous, and convincing, yes, yes, yes. But you cannot go forward if you're always looking backwards, so live in the present, with knowledge gained from the past and goals for the future, and you and your business will blossom.

Fulfilment

Does thinking clearly mean that you see your right to fulfilment? Did you ever ask yourself 'Do I have a right to fulfilment'? What does the word mean anyway? The dictionary definition is 'to accomplish; to carry into effect; to develop and realise the potential of'.

Look at the word and break it up into the two separate words from which it is derived; full and fill. We have a right to have all our needs met, but if we do not accept this right (and the responsibilities that go with it) we may tolerate shortage in our lives. This can easily happen as negative experience builds on negative experience, and we may be slow to move away from it on the basis that 'the devil you know is better than the devil you don't know'.

What do you feel you deserve from life? How healthy is your self-worth? Is it full, positive and wholesome, or pessimistic and tainted with negativity? Do you deserve to be financially fulfilled? If you feel you don't deserve fulfilment, you will have difficulty even reaching break even point, never mind abundant profit.

You project your self-image so that people see you the way you see yourself.

It is only natural that we progress forward towards fulfilment – otherwise we move backwards towards emptiness. Progression is a natural law. This means that all living things try to progress themselves (from a baby to an adult, a student to a scholar, a sapling to a tree, a cub to a grown animal). No living thing can stand still for long – it is either moving forward and improving itself or it is in decline.

Pace Yourself Properly

It is important that you pace yourself properly. We all have the pace that is right for us, which some may say is too fast and others may say is too slow. It is important to establish what your correct pace is, the pace which you can sustain indefinitely, avoiding both burn-out and under-achievement. It will usually involve a minimum of 40 productive hours per week, and a maximum of 65 (five full days plus a half day Saturday).

Be careful you don't exceed this upper limit, because the strain on your health and family life will begin to tell. If you are very busy the temptation is to extend these hours but don't, except in exceptional circumstances. Do as much as you can today, and let the rest of it wait. You are not a machine, and as the saying goes 'even the best horse cannot run forever'.

And to end, a bit of philosophy!

"Twenty years from now you will be more disappointed by the things you didn't do than by the ones you did do. So throw off the bowlines. Sail away from the safe harbour. Catch the trade winds in your sails. Explore. Dream. Discover."

- Mark Twain

Exercise

Make a Success List

We have all enjoyed successes and suffered failures in our lives to date. We are often more aware of our failures than our successes, so let's take stock of our personal successes, and regularly remind ourselves of these in order to maintain a positive outlook.

1.	
2.	
3.	
4.	
5.	
6.	
7.	
8.	

Notes

Chapter 3   Marketing – Research, Product, Place

What is Marketing?

Marketing is defined as '**the satisfaction of customer needs and wants at a profit.**' The key approach that sets it apart from other business practices (e.g. production) is the ability to see things through the customer's eyes, thus getting to know their needs and their wants. The most successful businesses are those who really understand their customers' needs and wants. Once they understand these, all future decisions are based on satisfying them.

The first key word in the above definition is **satisfaction**. If you don't provide satisfaction to your customers, they won't buy from you again and won't recommend you to others. You need to build up a satisfied client base who'll give you repeat work and referrals (they recommend you to their friends, family, colleagues, etc.). If customers are dissatisfied they'll actively discourage others from dealing with you. Bad news travels fast, and research shows that whilst satisfied customers will tell an average of four people about their good experience, dissatisfied customers will tell at least ten.

You can tell the people you'll meet in the house from the dog you meet at the gate.

The next main word in the definition is the **customer**. 'The Customer is King', because you want them to spend their money with you rather than your competition. The customer is the key to your business, for without them you have no business.

Customer **needs** and **wants** are the next words in the definition. There's a big difference between them, and people spend most money on their wants. People's needs are basic enough – food, clothing and shelter. Wants are more about people's discretionary spending – cars, holidays, televisions, cameras, fashion, designer brands, etc. An increasing number of businesses cater for people's wants, which makes it all the more important that you present your business properly or they may not want to deal with you.

Finally there's **profit**, the hallmark of a successful business, the lifeblood of a healthy business, and the cornerstone of good marketing.

Who is at the Market?

There are three main players at the market – the customers, your business and your competition.

Firstly, there are the **customers**. This is the most important group of players, because without them you will not succeed. You're trying to get their hard-earned money out of their pockets and into yours, and that means pleasing them. The 'satisfaction of customer needs and wants at a profit' should be your marketing mantra. There is no point going to the marketplace with things people don't want because they won't buy them, regardless of how beautiful or valuable you think they are. Your opinion as to what customers should buy doesn't matter, and 'he who pays the piper calls the tune'; so observe and listen to your customers, and pitch your product offering accordingly. Your focus should be on how you can satisfy your customers' needs and wants and how to make a profit in the process.

To ignore the competition is business suicide, because you'll have no benchmark against which to measure yourself.

Secondly, there's **your business**. The key to getting your own needs met is by meeting the needs of your customers, and one of their main needs is to deal with a reputable person. Your reputation is essential, and a good reputation earns you a good price, repeat work, and recommendations to friends and family.

Finally there's the **competition**. In striving to make sales you must compete hard with others who want these sales. You must at least match them, and should aim to outperform them. If they are well established, you may need to identify a group of customers that they are ignoring a little bit (not really satisfying their needs), and this might form your niche market. This niche will give you a platform to grow and expand from.

The strength of these different players changes from time to time. Sometimes the competition is weak and you can gain a large market share quickly. Sometimes it's a sellers' market, other times it's a buyers' market. The market is a dynamic place: new competitors enter the marketplace, products go out of fashion as they come to the end of their life cycle, recessions come and go, etc. Forecasting and observing these trends accurately is a vital business skill.

The Target Market

The market is a big place, and you're a small operator when you're starting off. You cannot be all things to all people because you're not big enough; you just don't have the resources. Knowing this, you must choose what 'target market' (small grouping within the larger market) you want to serve. Focusing carefully in order to service this target market means less wasted money and effort.

The average market is very diverse, with lots of different needs and abilities to pay. Although diverse, the customers in the market for any product are organised in a pyramid shape, with those most able to pay at the top of the pyramid. Likewise, the products in that market are organised in a corresponding pyramid shape to match the customers' needs and wants. The pyramid is wide at the bottom (lower priced product, selling to a large number of customers) and gets narrower at the top (higher priced product, selling to a lower number of customers).

You can't be all things to all people so focus scarce resources on a clear target market.

As you climb up this pyramid you go through three main price ranges:

1. At the bottom there are the lower priced products in the market. Prices are low because customers are cost conscious, trying to stretch their money as far as possible.
2. In the middle there's the mass market, where prices are higher, and the products and service are also of a higher standard.
3. Finally there's the premium end of the market, where cost is almost irrelevant, provided the product is the best that money can buy.

Your products must match the requirements of the target market you are focusing on. You cannot use a low-quality product to target a premium target market because they'll consider it poor quality and not buy it. Similarly it would be a waste of time aiming a premium product at the lower end of the market because they would consider it too expensive.

You should position yourself at the level on this pyramid where you can best fulfil the corresponding market needs, given your resources and abilities. Aiming to position yourself around the middle of the product pyramid is the safest strategy, especially at the start.

Competing on price alone can be difficult, so aim to develop a market niche where you can compete on a combination of unique service, flexibility and price. '**Niche Marketing**' is where you sit in just below a bigger operator and do the smaller work that he finds uneconomic or ignores (e.g. small building jobs, short-run printing, small quantity supplies, etc.).

The Building Blocks of Marketing – the Four P's

Any analysis of marketing will always look at the **Products** supplied, the **Prices** they sell for, the **Places** in which they are sold and the ways in which they are **Promoted**. These headings are referred to as the four P's and are the fundamental building blocks in developing and implementing your marketing plan.

The four P's are also referred to as the "Marketing Mix", and a comparison to the mix of ingredients in baking a cake is useful. Too much bread soda, and the cake rises too much, with very little substance to it. Too much flour, and the cake lies flat. Likewise with the marketing mix. Too much promotion without reliable production or customer service delivers a hollow message; too little promotion keeps the business flat or hidden from its customers, never rising off the ground.

Hitting the correct mix is an ongoing task, and one you'll have to constantly work on improving by trial and error, researching what's going on in the marketplace, and listening to and acting on customer feedback and suggestions.

This common-sense marketing involves adjusting the different elements of the mix on an ongoing basis, maybe adding a new product or improving an existing one, increasing the price on one item and reducing it on another, improving your place, or promoting a little more effectively.

Being the foundation stones for the marketing of your business, it is essential that you get a good understanding of the four P's. We will look at each of them in turn in this chapter and the next.

Market Research

Why bother with market research – why not just jump in and hope for the best? Because you want to minimise the number of mistakes you make, which can cost you lots of time and money!

Your business is part of a changing, dynamic environment so it is vital to keep your eyes and ears open, both when you start off and on an ongoing basis. You will need to change with the times, and keep on top of (if not ahead of) market trends and changes. Search, search and research continuously for relevant information.

A certain amount of market research is essential for every business but even more so in any undertaking with a high degree of risk. Minimise the potential down-side by investigating as thoroughly as possible in advance, and by adjusting as necessary on an ongoing basis. You may already have a good feel for your market if you have previously worked in the sector or have operated it on a part-time basis for a while, so you might have to do less formal research.

Research is defined as "a systematic investigation towards increasing the sum of knowledge".

The most efficient way of conducting research is by observing the best operators in your business sector. Study their business operations carefully, and with these insights in mind make informed decisions and tailor their moves to suit your cash resources. There is no need to re- invent the wheel. Remember the K.I.S.S. principle (Chapter 1)? Use common sense, in particular your two main senses (eyes and ears) with a street-smart approach. If you over-complicate your market research, you won't be able to continue doing it on an ongoing basis, which is essential. So whom do you need to listen to, talk to, and observe?

- **Your target market**
  More than likely there are plenty of people that you know who have used a service or product similar to the one you are going to provide. Take care not to ask just anybody, but ask people who fit into your target market (i.e. actually use your proposed products). These consumers will give you a more accurate picture than an undifferentiated group of people, who may just tell you what you want to hear for fear of offending you. Ask them what they looked for in the product or service, had they any problems, did it meet their expectations, etc. List off a few questions that you would ask a customer in a relaxed, friendly and informal way, whilst still getting the kind of information

that you need.

- **The trade**

  Review trade journals and magazines; visit trade shows/exhibitions/seminars; search the internet; investigate franchising/licencing/joint ventures. There are several related operators in each industry, and together they have all the information that you need. List who these might be, and what you might ask them. In addition to this you will need to find out about your competition – get their brochures, price lists/quotations, etc., either directly from them or through someone who has already used them. Outline your strategy for finding out this information.

There is never complete information about a future event; intuitive judgement always plays a role.

- **Your networks**

  Any of the people that you know who are not directly involved in the trade, but whose opinion you would value. They may be involved in business themselves, and be able to give you a few tips, insights or ideas on how they might approach things. This is a big part of the reason why people join clubs and organisations, in order to make this type of contact. List who these people might be, and what you might ask them.

- **The agencies/professionals**

  Enterprise officers in the various agencies are exposed to a lot of different businesses, and are in a position to advise on a lot of opportunities and pitfalls. Even if you're not going to get any financial assistance from them you can use them as sounding boards to bounce your ideas off. Likewise with accountants and solicitors, so it's no harm to run your ideas past them in order to gain their particular angle. List who these might be, and what you might ask them.

This kind of research is referred to as 'picking someone's brains'. If you're conscious of the need to do it, you'll automatically take the opportunities to do so when they present themselves casually because you'll be 'tuned in'. In addition, you may need to break the back of the task with a planned schedule of research. In order to get the most out of these opportunities without annoying people with lengthy chats, make sure you prepare the general questions in advance. 'Ask and you shall receive' should be your attitude, but respect people's time or they'll avoid you thereafter.

Organising Your Market Research

Like most things in business, doing research is not as complicated as you might think at first – there's just a need to be constantly tuned in to relevant information. Before you commit your time and money to research, you need to organise your approach. The best way to organise it is along the same lines as your marketing – the four P's. Simply create four headings on four pages, titled Product, Price, Place and Promotion. Start to fill in whatever you already know about the market under each heading. This will help identify any gaps in your market knowledge that you will need to investigate further; list these as 'topics for further research'.

To conduct a market research study the steps are as follows:

1. Outline what you know about the market already.
2. Decide what gaps there are in your information, i.e. what additional answers are you looking for, and why.
3. Write out the questions you need to ask in order to get these answers. Use a mix of open-ended questions (what, why, where, when, who, how) and specific questions. A general guideline is to limit your questions to around ten, making them good, clear and incisive.
4. List out where/from whom will you get this information as suggested in the previous paragraphs.
5. Write out a schedule for when you will do the research.
6. Conduct the study, and then sit back to digest the information. Talk it through with some people whose advice you trust, be they business colleagues, an enterprise officer, your spouse/partner, or your accountant.
7. Using your best judgement, make a clear decision on how to proceed.

The Marketing Mix:
Product, Place, Price and Promotion

The 1st P: Product

Introduction

Customers have certain expectations of a product. These expectations represent the minimum basis on which they'll buy from you, including a reasonable standard of quality, a reasonable image, and a reasonable peace of mind that you'll be able to deliver on the job.

Quality is always more important than price. Poor quality will be remembered long after price is forgotten.

The standard for new products keeps going up, and just as well! What was an 'extra' in a car five years ago is now considered standard, e.g. ABS brakes, airbags, CD player, GPS, eco-friendliness, etc. In quality terms what was acceptable five or ten years ago is generally no longer acceptable.

Really, all products consist of two main parts – the Basic Product and the Expanded Product. The basic product consists of the obvious basics, whilst the expanded product is comprised of the 'extras'. A Montblanc pen is not just a writing pen (basic) but a well-crafted gift (expanded). A Gucci handbag is not just a handbag (basic), but a piece of designer fashion (expanded).

Basic or Expanded Product

The customer sometimes wants just the 'basic' product, but often wants something extra – the expanded product. That 'extra something' may determine whether he'll buy from you or not, and what price he's prepared to pay, so you should generally try to provide an option of the expanded product to your customer.

Begin to analyse your different products and services in their two parts. For example, take a painter: the basic product consists of being able to put paint evenly on a wall, having prepared the surface properly, the kind of job any DIY enthusiast could do. The expanded product consists of the 'extras' – advice on colour schemes, suitability of paint, ability with different finishes – the type of service you'd expect from a qualified tradesman.

A carpenter that fits a new cupboard has done the basic job, but if he leaves the place in a mess, he has not bothered with the expanded product. A car is not just a form of transport (basic); its expanded product includes its shape, colour, safety features, in-car entertainment, economy and reliability. This concept of an expanded product has developed a lot since the initial attitude of Henry Ford who once said about the Ford Prefect, 'you can have any colour you want as long as it's black'!

In our everyday lives we all know the difference between the basic product and the expanded product. A basic model of car will have a lower specification to the XL version. A basic suit will have a different style and material to a branded suit. Both product levels have their place, but ideally will be able to offer the customer a choice (unlike Henry Ford)!

The Product Surround

Your product surround is the physical environment (e.g. premises and packaging) and values (e.g. reliability and reputation) with which you surround your product. Literally it 'surrounds' your product, presenting it in its best light and reassuring your customers that their needs will be met.

The customer is king.

One of the customer's needs when employing you is to have peace of mind. The 'values' that create this peace of mind at no extra cost are: friendliness, good manners, decency, reliability, honesty, accurate quotations, good time-keeping, good image, brand recognition, good advice, good quality, after-sales service, timely delivery, confidentiality, and the provision of references if required.

The 'physical environment' includes a good design and layout for your premises, attractive packaging and presentation, tidiness, and uniforms. You also need to show physical evidence of your commitment to your business – e.g. by investing in a good van or car, business cards, premises, equipment, etc. so that the customer knows you will be there for the long haul.

Product Groups

You need to develop several income streams by providing a balanced mix of complementary product groups or services, which together make a nicely rounded business. The main reasons for developing multiple product groups are:

1. To communicate clearly with your customer in a way they understand
2. To attract extra customers through providing a better selection and range of products and services
3. Diversification. As the different products move through their life cycles or seasonal changes, you won't be too badly affected as demand for one or two product groups reduces.

Customers buy based on value, not price. You can easily add customer value with a friendly, helpful attitude; good, solid advice when consulted; and a quick, reliable service.

Have a look at any successful business and you'll quickly see multiple product groups, and the way the business has grown over time by adding additional product groups. Take a typical petrol station: its principal product group ten years ago was fuel. But if that remained its only product it would have gone out of business. Various income streams have been added: solid fuel and gas; a car wash; a convenience shop selling groceries; take-away food; an off-licence, and so on. There are multiple product groups, with the whole business being changed into a retail outlet, and re-packaged as a 'service station'.

Likewise with a garden centre. Whilst many of them started as nurseries a few years ago, the progressive ones initially added customer-friendly displays (gravel pathways, with plants raised off the ground and attractively labelled). Since then they will have added product groups such as a shop with tools and chemicals; hard-landscaping supplies; ponds and fountains; patios and patio furniture; a flower shop; a coffee shop; and finally even a Christmas shop, to improve cash-flow during the quiet season.

A word of caution however: you need to achieve a balance

between adding income streams and spreading yourself too thinly, thereby not being able to fulfil the demand properly. Also, make sure that the different income streams are complementary to each other; if they're not you risk becoming a 'Jack of all trades, master of none'. This approach would also confuse your customers; give them a clear message as they'll be forming their opinions quickly. If you do have a completely unrelated business idea, then form another business and run it completely separately.

Product Benefits

"In the factory we make cosmetics, but in the drug store we sell hope."
- Charles Revson

The quotation on the left implies that the cosmetic is really just the delivery mechanism for the real product, which is potential beauty and hope. In advertising copy you are better to emphasise the customer benefits than the dry technical details. A fatal mistake you could make is to assume that the customer can see these benefits – but he knows neither you nor your products. Make sure that you are clear about the benefits of using your business in the first place, otherwise you won't be able to sell these to the customer. As the sales phrase goes, 'sell the sizzle, not the sausage'. We will look at this topic in greater detail in chapter 5, *Sales*.

Product Quality

Quality is a loosely used term but is best defined as 'fitness for the purpose intended'. There are several different levels of quality for every product, and it's up to you to figure out what quality specification suits your target market. A higher specification product (e.g. a drill) at a higher price would be better suited to the job for a tradesman, whilst a lower specification would suit if your target market is the D.I.Y. enthusiast.

The key is appropriate quality. A garden shed needs to be of sufficient quality to store garden tools, a mower, bicycles, etc. out of the weather and last about fifteen years (not a lifetime), and the price needs to reflect that. A garden office, housing office equipment, needs a higher specification regarding dampness, heating, security, etc.

The quality on offer must be appropriate for the purpose

intended, and match the price affordable, otherwise you've a mismatch between your offering and the customer's requirements, which makes for bad marketing and bad business.

The Product Life Cycle

What does the 'product life cycle' mean? Like any living thing, a product is growing, maturing, or dying. The product life cycle implies that every product goes through:

1. A period of development (high costs, low revenue and low profit).
2. A period of growth (rapidly rising sales and profits).
3. A period of maturity (highest sales but declining profit margin as competitors come in and prices tend to fall).
4. A period of decline (consumers shift to new products, competition intensifies, sales and profits drop).

Most of the products that occupy our homes today weren't even invented 20 years ago, e.g. CD/DVD players, microwave ovens, digital camcorders, laptop computers, etc. It is nearly impossible to get the old music records and turn-tables, and some stores no longer stock video players. Small shops are fast disappearing ahead of the 24-hour supermarkets, and new types of work are appearing, like home cleaning, gardening for people with lawnmowers, and laundrette services for people with washing machines – but no time to use them!

Failure to recognise that your products will change or be replaced over time could be disastrous. Given the existence of the product life cycle, most businesses develop a 'product mix' or 'product portfolio'. Quite simply, this means they will have a range of related products at different stages within the product life cycle, in an attempt to avoid the situation where they only have old declining products and nothing to follow them. Take care that most of your products aren't in the mature and declining stages of the product life cycle.

Adding New Products

The search for new products/income streams should happen on an ongoing basis, otherwise you'll become yesterday's hero very quickly as your existing products become obsolete over time. The time to conduct this new product search and evaluation is not when sales start to decline and you come under pressure. In your search you can review trade journals and magazines; visit trade shows and exhibitions (particularly abroad); attend seminars; search the internet; and investigate franchising/licencing/joint venture opportunities.

There is no need to re-invent the wheel; just study your competition and you'll find out all you need to know about the market.

The process of new product selection goes from recognising the need to add new products right through to final selection. You will be using your best judgement to establish whether or not it is feasible from three angles: market, financial, and technical.

First check that it meets the needs/wants of your target market (try using a focus group). The related key finance question is whether you can sell enough of it at a profit? To whom? How big is this market? What price will these buyers be prepared to pay? Will you need to carry much stock? How will you deliver/distribute? Finally assess its technical feasibility – have you the resources (time and money) and the capability to carry it? Can you produce it yourself, or are you better off to buy it in and become an agent? Can you install it and provide after-sales service?

A well-balanced, diversified business is made up of a number of complementary but distinct product groups (a product group is a group of similar products/services). Customers want to know what you or your product can do for them (W.I.I.F.M.). Presenting your business offering in easily understandable groups makes it easier for the customer to say 'yes'. These groups are then highlighted in separate bullet points on a business card.

What Product Groups will your business supply?

e.g. **Launderette**: Wash & dry, ironing, repairs/alterations, dry cleaning agency

  Gardener: Mowing lawns, laying lawns, planting shrubs & trees, hard landscaping

(A)	(B)
(C)	(D)

Two levels of product development:

1. The 'Basic' Product

Describe the minimum standard a customer will accept for each of the above product groups.

(A)	(B)
(C)	(D)

2. The 'Expanded' Product

Describe the different extras you will add to each product group in order to exceed your customers' expectations.

(A)	(B)
(C)	(D)

<table>
<tr><td>

The 2nd P:

</td><td>

Place

</td></tr>
</table>

Introduction

We can define the marketing 'Place' as the place where your product meets your customer. This can be your workshop, your retail outlet or office, your website, the customer's premises or a neutral venue. Regardless of where you meet, your customers will form vital first impressions about you and your business, based on how your place is presented. Your 'place' is literally the physical expression of your business, because you created it, and it's a key indicator to your customer of what you're about. It provides evidence of your commitment to your business and of your credibility.

Your customer base is your key business asset.

Whenever you go into a premises for the first time you'll notice a lot of things about it, and when asked about it the question will often be 'What sort of a place is it?' It's that simple – it's one of the first P's people ask about, because it's obvious, tangible, real. In response to their question you'll give your initial impression: 'It's a fine place' or 'it's OK', or 'I wasn't that impressed', and you'll back that opinion up with numerous details. Was it clean, bright, well laid out, spacious, well stocked, well equipped, well designed, well decorated, well built? Was the outside attractive?

Many highly profitable businesses operate without a physical 'bricks and mortar' place for their customers; for example subcontractors in construction, insurance agents, interior designers, photographers, and countless others. Thus 'place' in terms of marketing is not limited to your premises but may include some of the following: your website, your transport, the geographical area you cover, and your distribution channel (e.g. shops or agents you may sell through). Let's look more closely at a few of them, and think about which you can best use as your place.

Premises

The attention you give your premises will be assumed by the customer to be the same attention you apply to their work. In the customer's mind it's highly unlikely that an untidy place can turn out tidy work.

A tidy, well-organised and well-maintained place helps business from two perspectives. Firstly, it's easier to work in and secondly, it creates a favourable customer impression. We have often seen multi-million pound investments in a hotel let down by the state of the toilets. We cannot help but think that the kitchen, which is out of sight, suffers from a similarly slap-dash attitude.

Retailers use window dressing with attractive displays and seasonal themes, a good shop layout, lighting and décor to form the right impressions, and get the customer in the mood to spend money.

The Virtual Place

The technology of the internet has seen internet-adaptable business literally shut-up-shop and move to the Virtual Place, interacting directly with the consumer by means of an online shop front. The travel industry, in particular, has made big progress in this regard, an example being ryanair.com, quickly followed by aerlingus.com. In addition to moving place, they now also sell a much broader range of products than just flights (e.g. car hire, accommodation, etc.). The banks are doing likewise with internet banking becoming the norm, and organisations such as the Revenue Commissioners are conducting a lot of their business online.

You may not need a website immediately if your 'place' is local and people can call in, but increasingly customers use the internet to research their purchasing decision so it is advisable to have one if it is relevant to your target market.

The Geographical Place

The geographical place is the area in which you will operate your business. A lot of people limit their main area of operation to one hour's travel time. It goes without saying that a nationwide business has longer travel times. Because travel costs both time and money, try to generate the bulk of your work as close to your home base as possible (e.g. within one hour). However, if the work is not available locally, searching for and following the work wherever it is available becomes part of the job.

Carefully defining your 'place' can have a huge impact on your business. Look no further than Ryanair and Aer Lingus to see evidence of this, with Ryanair concentrating on a smaller marketplace (Europe) but being much more profitable as a result.

Transport

If the nature of your business is primarily mobile and people rarely if ever call to your home base, the impressions of place will be formed by your transport. A clean, well sign-written van, neatly shelved (possibly towing a tidy trailer) will help inspire more customer confidence than a higgledy-piggledy, dirty machine, resulting in more work for you at better prices.

It's easy to scoff at this aspect of place, but it's a lot of the reason people will spend tens of thousands on transport – to make an impression. A financial adviser will use a BMW or a Mercedes to assure customers he knows how to make money for himself – and how to advise his clients to do likewise. On the other hand, a tradesman pulling up in a new Mercedes to give a quote might give an impression of being over-priced, so an appropriate image is what you should aim to create.

If you're in the transport business as a taxi company or a bus firm, then your transport becomes the primary place of business. Likewise with Ryanair, in terms of place their premises don't matter as much to their customers as their transport (airplanes) and their website. Similarly, the courier company Interlink insist on their agents having white Mercedes vans, for customer impression as well as reliability and uniformity of image.

Channels to Market

Larger producers who need to move a lot of product throughout a large area need to take a different approach to the issue of place. Some of them will have a 'factory shop' on site, but in general they need to move their product through 'distribution channels' or sales outlets that have closer contact with the market.

Choosing 'distribution channels' that fit the image of the product is critical. The Cross biro company produce an exclusive writing instrument targeted at the gift market, and their channel to market is exclusive gift shops. It would damage their product image of exclusivity, and consequently their brand name, if their pens were to be sold in service stations. Likewise, Waterford Glass and Rolex watches will only associate their products with up-market shops. Even though market exposure would be greater and there would be a strong possibility of higher sales, the product would lose its exclusivity and the price it commands would fall if it were available through inappropriate 'places'.

Most dissatisfied customers will do business with you again if you sort out their complaint on the spot.

Home Base or Retail Place?

Many people who start a mobile or home-based business think that having an office or a retail outlet will provide a strong sense of place, and show that they have arrived. This is not necessarily the best approach because setting up a shop or an office is a totally different business proposition, bringing much higher overhead costs.

You cannot be in two places at the same time, so hiring somebody to staff your premises on either a full- or part-time basis will cost wages in addition to the rent and associated overheads. If you try to staff it yourself it will cut in on your existing working and earning time. It's an additional cost, so make sure it's going to pay its way. It might not help you increase sales by very much, but it will definitely cost you a lot of money to set up, and a lot of time to keep open.

Location

"There are only three words that matter when it comes to property – location, location, location."

Donald Trump

This statement by one of the world's most famous property developers highlights the fact that the place in which a business is located is of critical importance. Because more people will pass by

---

the door of a centrally located property, the opportunities to do business are increased.

It's not only the location that matters but also the attractiveness of the place. Town centre enhancement is high on the agenda of most traders' associations, and at national level the 'Tidy Towns' initiative underlines the importance people put on an attractive place. We have all heard various places described in a complimentary manner as 'lovely', or in a derogatory fashion as a 'dump'.

Galway city has been chosen as a location by many talented people who re-located there, because of the quality of life available. Kilkenny city is another example of a community that prides itself on the attractiveness of its streets and open spaces.

The traders' associations in most towns are quite happy to make a large investment each year in Christmas lights. With shoppers so mobile nowadays, these towns are competing with other towns within an hour-and-a-half's drive, and so must make the place look good for Christmas. Otherwise their potential customers will take their business elsewhere, where they and their children can better enjoy the festive atmosphere.

Your Customer Base

A critical measurement of the strength of your business is the size of your customer base, not the size of your investment in equipment, buildings, transport, etc. How do you build a solid customer base? Satisfied customer by satisfied customer, that's how. They won't all come back, but a lot of them will if you treat them professionally.

As an exercise, figure out the average spend per customer sale and how many individual sales you need to make total sales of €50,000 per year. If you only get one sale per customer you will need a lot of customers each year. Wouldn't it be much easier if you could get each customer to make repeat purchases, e.g. five per year? You would then only need one fifth of the number of customers. Customers are the key to your business, and both referrals and repeat purchases from a satisfied customer base are essential to the sustainability and profitability of your business.

In Conclusion

The issues relating to 'place' which your business faces really boil down to deciding the size of the area you are going to cover, and the different aspects of 'place' you stress when meeting customers. Each different aspect of 'place' brings an opportunity to impress your customer, so be aware of which aspects help win business and which lose you business.

(A) What geographical area do you cover at present?

_____

(B) How could your operational area be profitably extended?

_____

(C) How could you sell through agents/distributors or establish a franchise?

_____

(D) What transport do you use? What additions (e.g. trailer/replacements) do you plan?

_____

(E) Describe your physical 'place', i.e. office/workshop/shop/studio.

_____

(F) Do you have a 'virtual place', i.e. a website? What are its key features?

_____

List 10 improvements you could make to your **place**:

1.	2.
3.	4.
5.	6.
7.	8.
9.	10.

Chapter 4   Marketing – Price and Promotion

The 3rd P:	Price

Introduction

A product or service is worth what a buyer will pay for it and what your competition will let you charge.

Pricing decisions can be amongst the most difficult business decisions to make, because there is no simple formula for working out a price. The price chosen is usually based on the best judgement of the business person, informed by a combination of their costs, the going prices in the market, and their confidence and sales ability. Because of their complexity, pricing decisions are often taken quickly, and are not tested or reviewed; they become 'sticky'. Given that they have a bigger effect on profit than most other decisions, it is very important to consider them carefully.

Linking Price and Profit Maximisation

Your real job as an astute business person is to maximise your profits, and a key element in profit maximisation is price maximisation. Some people have a 'moral' problem with this approach, considering it maybe a little greedy – but where's the morality in working long hours just to make ends meet, denying yourself and your family the time and money you left behind? Should you work for €150 a day if you can get €200?

In the end the markets dictates price. Here are some pointers:

1. If you're over-priced people will tell you, and haggle with you for a better deal if they want you, so leave room in your pricing for a 'discount'.
2. If you're under-priced people will accept their good luck. A good guide to pricing is that if you're getting every job without any price negotiation, you're probably too cheap.
3. People associate price with quality. If you're too cheap people assume you're poor quality.

If you get a good price you have the time to give a better service instead of rushing jobs, and you can invest in better facilities and equipment.

The Basics of Pricing

A common problem with many start-up businesses is under-pricing. This low-price strategy is partly in the hope that customers will go for the lowest price, and partly due to a lack of confidence to go for the higher price.

Before looking at a 'scientific' approach to pricing let's look at the basics of pricing:

1. **Confidence**

   Good pricing is based largely on confidence and your sense of self-worth. The key to optimum pricing is confidence, and it's a lot easier to be confident when you're busy, so keep busy (even if you're not, act as if you are!). The key to being busy is doing good work, and letting that be known to your target market through good promotion. Good promotion leads to more demand, which leads to more confidence, which leads to better prices – a virtuous cycle. It takes confidence to sell at a good price – after all, anybody can give products away. A clear reflection of your self-worth is to be seen in your pricing, as a low sense of self-worth will result in low pricing. Of course it's easy to go to the other extreme also – overcharging. This will lose you business, but of the two extremes, it's likely to be the least costly to you!

2. **Value**

   Customers don't go for the lowest price but for the best value. Think back to your core product and product surround – the product surround has the biggest influence on the price the customer will pay. Think about your products in terms of value rather than price, and expand the product surround. This is a much better approach than just being 'cheap' – better to be 'good value'. A poor quality job is remembered long after the price is forgotten, because the bad job is there to remind the customer day after day. As a result most customers take the attitude of 'buy good quality, buy once; buy poor quality, buy twice'.

Pricing affects your bottom line quicker than the other marketing P's.

3. Impact

The trouble with poor pricing is actually double-trouble: it makes a poor impact on your bank account, and it also makes a poor impression on your customers, because they associate low prices with low quality.

Pricing Approaches

In deciding on a price you have to balance two separate figures. On the one hand you have the cost of the product (your minimum price); and on the other you have the top price your customer will pay (your maximum price). Your price should fall somewhere between these two extremes. The better your marketing mix, the closer you can go to the maximum price; if part of your marketing mix is weak, you will end up near (or below) your minimum price.

There are three broad approaches to setting a price. Let's look at them in turn.

1. The marketing approach

The simplest and most straightforward pricing strategy is to adopt the going prices in the market. It takes very basic market research to get price-lists or quotations either directly or through friends. That's your starting point, and while you're at it observe and absorb all that the market leader in your business is doing correctly; copy it, adapting it to your particular situation, and you can't go far wrong.

Pricing is a very inexact science, so it has to be constantly reviewed.

By accepting the market prices of your competitors as the standard, you are adopting a marketing approach with the focus on the competition and the customer. From an accountancy viewpoint you can then work backwards to determine at what turnover levels you start to make a profit. Pricing decisions are often too heavily biased towards costs whilst ignoring other elements of the marketing mix, i.e. Product, Place, and Promotion.

In your efforts to gain the maximum price the market will bear you can use differentiation (differences created by developing a better product surround) to get the best price. If your product is different then it doesn't allow for direct comparison with your competitors. Emphasise your 'added-value', the extra benefits you are giving. 'It might be a little dearer, but it's worth it' is the type of customer reaction you want to create.

A large determinant of your pricing is the position you aim for on the market pyramid, where prices increase in line with quality and exclusivity. Aiming to position yourself around the middle of the product pyramid is the safest strategy, especially when you get established. You may have to start nearer the bottom and work your way up to your targeted position as you grow in skill and experience, but watch you don't get caught at the bottom, as it usually means more work for less money. Be aware that prices become 'sticky' for two reasons – firstly, your customers expect a certain price level, and secondly, you train yourself to expect the same.

You don't get the price you deserve, you get the price you negotiate. In the final analysis a price is a negotiated agreement.

If you aim for the middle of the pyramid you will be selling to people with middle-class incomes. Do you know what this level of income is? Otherwise how do you hope to target it? Do you know what the average industrial wage is? Do you know what the average teacher's/nurse's/Garda's wage is? If not, it's time to get out there and find out! Research!

Don't forget inflation and deflation in your pricing calculations; because inflation erodes the buying power of the money in your customer's pocket whilst deflation allows it to go further. In an inflationary environment it's important to move prices upwards in line with it, but likewise in a deflationary environment it's important to be downwardly flexible, particularly if your competition are.

2. The 'cost-plus' pricing approach

Using this approach, the cost of manufacturing or providing a service determines the basis for pricing. It is known as the 'cost-plus' method, i.e. the cost of production plus a margin for profit. Whilst it is simple enough to work out it really only gives you your minimum price, and to sell below this would be to sell at a loss.

Working out your costs involves looking at both your direct costs and your indirect costs.

(a) The **direct costs** are the ones you can pin down directly to the product/job in question. Their calculation is fairly straightforward – add up the costs of the various materials that go into the product, and the cost of labour.

(b) The **indirect costs** are all the other costs of being in business, and you incur these whether or not you are busy. These include your overheads (electricity bills, insurance, phone, rent and rates, transport, professional fees, etc.).

In order to price individual jobs you need to total the direct costs, plus allocate a proportion of the indirect costs to each job. For example, if you're hauling sand and gravel, the indirect cost per load is the total indirect cost per week divided by the number of loads per week. If you're servicing cars, then it's the total indirect cost divided by the number of services per week, etc. Sometimes, however, it makes more sense to work out the indirect cost allocation on an hourly basis by dividing total indirect costs by 40 hours per week, and applying this figure to your time estimate for each job.

Some people know the price of everything and the value of nothing.

Indirect cost allocations can cause you to overprice jobs if your activity level is low. For instance, if you're only getting 20 hours work per week, and you divide your overheads by twenty instead of forty hours, your indirect cost allocation is double what it should be. This underlines the need to get up to full speed as quickly as possible because indirect costs are there regardless of how slack business is. In general it's best to use forty hours as your standard, producing standard costs. Finally, you add a margin for profit which is the reason you are in business.

3. The economics approach
Economics is the study of how people make the best use of scarce resources. It presents a number of factors of relevance to your pricing.

Supply and demand
The economist's approach to pricing is based on observing the two sides of the market – the supply side (sellers) and the demand side (buyers). In general, if supply is greater than demand the price will go down; if demand is greater than supply, then prices will go up.

It follows, then, that a key to increasing your price is to increase the demand for your products and services. This increased demand allows you to pick and choose the types of jobs you take on – the most pleasant and most profitable. So how do you increase demand? Firstly, by developing a good reputation or brand-name for yourself, and secondly, by promoting that name to the market. We will look at promotion in further detail in the next section.

Other pricing pointers based on the law of supply and demand include avoiding areas of oversupply, watching out for old products nearing the end of their life cycle where demand is falling, and assessing new opportunities where demand is growing.

Elasticity of Demand

If you raise or lower your prices, this will generally have an effect on demand. The extent to which a change in price leads to a change in the quantity demanded is called the elasticity of demand. Elasticity depends on two main factors: how important it is to consumers, and whether or not there are many close substitutes. If it is essential, e.g. petrol, then regardless of price people will need to buy it. If it is non-

The economy has slowed down, but it hasn't come to a standstill. People will still get work done if the price is right.

essential, e.g. holidays abroad or meals out, then it will be quite responsive. It is worth considering how elastic demand is for your products, and what steps you can you take to handle a reduction in demand.

The total profit you make during a year depends on selling the most products at the best prices. A lowering of price does not necessarily mean more sales, nor does an increase in price necessarily mean less sales, so also consider how 'elastic' or responsive demand for your work will be to a change in your price before you change it.

A horse that finishes the race by a short head is worth twice as much.

Economies of Scale

In general, a busier operation can spread the cost of their overheads across a lot of units of production, which reduces the cost per unit. In addition they can negotiate better prices for the supplies they need.

The bigger operations will have the larger economies of scale – so will they always beat you on price or service? Not necessarily, because they may also suffer from 'the law of diminishing returns'. In other words, after a certain size they will have to take on extra management staff and extra administration costs that you won't have, as you can both manage and produce. More importantly, they will have to convince their sometimes unmotivated staff about the need to put the customer first, so you have a definite advantage right there.

The Cost of Bad Pricing

Pricing is a vital aspect of marketing, because the cornerstone of marketing is profit. Give yourself a few minutes to think about these two questions:

1. How much money have you left behind in the last year because of bad pricing?
2. How much money could you leave behind over the course of the next year with bad pricing?

An obvious consequence of poor pricing is the need to work longer hours to compensate. The dangers of this are obvious. Firstly, very long hours will burn you out over the years. Worse again, employing someone else to work with you at the wrong price will leave you at the risk of running up fairly substantial losses. You would certainly be better off to work only on the better paying jobs, turn away the badly priced and awkward ones, and operate on your own for a while. Leave the bad jobs for the competition.

The Four Components of a Price

Probably the biggest mistake you can make in pricing is to leave things out. When you price up a job you have four main components: labour, overheads, materials and profit. In recessionary times you have to intelligently reduce all of these, with profit usually getting the hardest hit, but don't leave it out – always try to make some.

Firstly there are **overheads**. When charging for overheads it's important that you know from your profit and loss account how much your annual overheads are. Divide this by 46 working weeks, and by 5 for a daily overhead rate, or 35 for an hourly rate. You should know and remember this figure for all future pricing.

A pound saved is as good as two earned.

When charging for **labour**, don't leave anything out. There's the direct working time on the job, plus the organisational time spent on general administration, getting supplies, quotations, sales, debt collection; there's down-time due to bad weather, breakdowns, having no work ready; and there's an allowance for holiday time (21 days plus 9 bank holidays = six weeks). All of this 'organisational time' will account for about 10 hours per week, so if you're working a total of 45 hours per week that leaves 'earning time' of 35 hrs per week. If you need total sales (excluding materials) of €1,000 per week (€46,000 per year), then you must cost each job at €1,000/35 = €28.57 per hour to cover labour and overheads. This gives you the basis for your pricing, but obviously don't tell your client this, give them an overall price for the job.

Profit is next. On principle never leave it out, although it may only be small in recessionary times. Even if it's only a fiver on a day's work, never leave it out.

Finally there are **materials**. Obviously this varies with each job so whilst a standard hourly rate can be charged, materials need to be calculated separately on a job-by-job basis. 'A pound saved is as good as two earned' goes the saying, so firstly, price around regularly for all major cost items, don't give costly loyalty to anyone not giving you best value. Secondly, do a keen quantity survey for time and money on every job; always compare actual use with budgeted use; and adjust future quotes to reflect price changes.

Pricing Guidelines

As we have seen, pricing is a very inexact science, as dependent on the judgement of the business person as on any simple formula. Getting the best price is an ongoing quest in a dynamic marketplace, with recession, new competitors, price wars, new products etc. to be contended with on an ongoing basis. Let's finish with a few practical guidelines that might help you to improve your pricing skills.

1. Be careful in assessing the amount of time required to fully complete a job, because time over-runs cost money, reducing your return.
2. Be sure that there are no hidden difficulties, which are time and money wasters.
3. Know what your overheads are per hour, and add your direct labour costs, material costs and some profit when pricing a job.
4. Be aware of the competition's prices – you could be way over (uncompetitive) or you could be way under (giving money away).

5. After the job is done, ask what other prices were quoted.
6. Remember, any fool can drop prices (compete on price) instead of emphasising the other aspects of the job.
7. Don't assume that everybody has the time to price around.
8. Don't assume people go for the cheapest price (they don't).
9. Allow for haggling and discounting – it makes the client feel better.
10. Don't allow for easy comparisons (no two jobs/craftsmen are the same).
11. Always add on a margin for unforeseen costs and difficulties.
12. Allow a percentage for wastage!
13. Be a shrewd buyer (a pound saved is as good as two earned).
14. Know your input prices (i.e. be cost conscious) and your input quantities.

Exercise
Job Costing

Describe a typical job: _____

(1) Calculate time required: What tasks are involved? Hours required for each task?

Job tasks	Hours required
Total hours required	

(2) Calculate materials required: What materials are required? Price of materials?

Materials required (material type X quantity X price)	Cost of materials
Total cost of materials	

(3) Calculate job cost:

A	Overheads	Hours	X	Hourly overhead rate	Overhead total
B	Labour	Hours	X	Hourly labour rate	Labour total
C	Profit	Hours	X	Hourly profit rate	Profit total
D	Materials (as calculated above)				Materials total
E	TOTAL BEFORE VAT				
F	VAT				
G	TOTAL INCLUDING VAT				

The 4th P: Promotion

Introduction

Promotion is a key ingredient in the marketing mix and can have a big impact on your sales if done properly. By definition a new business is new and unknown; if people don't know you're there, what hope have you?

To promote is defined as to 'put yourself forward', and in marketing your business you need to decide on three aspects of promotion:

1. **What do I promote?**
   You will put forward the image and the reputation you develop for yourself. What trading name do you use? Is it memorable? Can you develop recognition for it amongst your potential customers? Does the graphic style on your stationery and website look well? In developing your brand name your reputation is a key component, and adds value to the prices you can charge (e.g. *Nike* trainers versus an unbranded pair of similar quality).

2. **To whom do I promote?**
   To your target customers. You cannot be all things to all men, so you must identify a niche in the market where what you offer best fits what they want or need.

3. **What message do I want to promote?**
   You will promote a message that addresses the needs and wants of your target customers, making them more inclined to buy. Clearly answer the customer's unstated question 'what's in it for me?' Promote your values, your capabilities, your reliability and the benefits the customer will gain by dealing with you, the product quality and value, after-sales service – in short, whatever message shows your customer that you're the right person to do business with.

"Generally, men judge by the eye rather than the hand, for all men can see a thing, but few come close enough to touch it. All men will see what you seem to be; only a few will know what you are."
- Machiavelli

Watch that you don't over-promise and under-deliver or you will annoy customers, and get no repeats or referrals. Better to temper your message by under-promising and over-delivering – that way your work speaks for itself by exceeding expectations, leaving your customers pleasantly satisfied.

The Main Purpose of Promotion

A shy priest never got a parish.

The primary purpose of promotion is to enable you to get more of 'the best jobs at the best rates'. When you get more work opportunities than you can take on, you can start to both put up your prices and be more selective, a double bonus.

Think of the different stages that your business needs to go through to become profitable. When you start off initially you will need to take almost any work you're capable of, and put in whatever hours are necessary to break even, because losing money is not an option. Getting out there to do work is the best form of promotion, as you're meeting people and promoting yourself to them by word of mouth. The next stage is when you can get more selective about the jobs, but still putting in any time that's required. An important benchmark is reached next, when you can break even in forty hours. The final stage is when you're breaking even in thirty hours or less, and any hours you work over that contribute directly to profit.

A major purpose of promotion is to get you through these different growth phases and up into profits as quickly as possible, and then to keep you up there in the profit zone. You promote in order to create an abundance of work, which puts you in a position to select the jobs you want and turn away the others. The low-paying and difficult jobs you turn away are for the competition who are not looking after their marketing mix as intelligently as you are.

One of the beauties of promotion is that you can quickly vary your level of advertising in order to increase sales, i.e. if you go through a slack period you can advertise more. However, a better strategy is to keep your business promoted on an ongoing basis using a mix of the four promotional methods outlined below.

Methods of Promotion

If you have put a substantial investment into your business, you need to get the maximum return possible. Promotion is a key way of getting your business in front of customers, and increasing your opportunities for sales. For small businesses there are four main methods of promotion:

1. **General advertising.** You advertise, generate a good number of enquiries, and close a percentage of sales. Advertising works in generating business. If it didn't there would be no advertising industry, as business just wouldn't spend money on it. Keep in mind the saying 'Even if you're on the right track, you'll get run over if you just sit there'. This implies that you must keep a forward momentum on your business in order to get new customers. Once you've decided to commit your money and time to a business, it is necessary to promote it regularly.

2. **Networking.** One of your main networks is your friends and family, and you also probably have some networks with sporting, business and community groups. They will all promote you to some extent, and indeed give you some work, provided they think well of you, but this circle is usually too small for your business to be confined to.

3. **Word of Mouth.** Customers come to you through recommendations. Create positive word of mouth by doing good work and delivering good products, never making promises you can't keep, sorting out problems as soon as they arise, and providing good back-up/after-sales service. When someone recommends you, make sure you contact

them and thank them – they'll appreciate it and continue promoting you. Word of mouth (people talking about your business) is the most powerful medium but remember it is a double-edged sword – people can talk negatively about your business as well as recommending you.

4. **Other**. Direct mail; website; e-mail newsletter; tickets to a sports event or a play; press releases in your local newspaper about newsworthy items (e.g. new staff, new products, expansion); trade fairs; speaking at seminars or on local/community radio; joining trade associations; entering your business for suitable awards; and participating in social activities.

The Cost of Promotion

Much of commercial activity is driven by the creation of an image. Don't underestimate its importance.

The amount of promotion you need to do depends on how well known you already are, and the level of sales you need. It needn't cost the earth, but be careful, because promotion can be the single biggest waste of money in a business. Here's a tip: oftentimes the less expensive the promotional campaign, the more effective it is. Talking to people enthusiastically about your business costs nothing; getting permission to put up attractive flyers on notice boards and in shop windows costs nothing; printing and handing out flyers and business cards costs very little; sign-writing a van costs little and goes everywhere with you for years.

Work through the accompanying exercise in order to decide on which methods give the best value for money. You can get an initial offer of business cards for free at www.vistaprint.com, and using a Facebook page for your business is both free and very effective. Draw up a realistic advertising schedule that you are willing to stick to. Budget for this expense the same way you budget for your telephone bill, loan repayments, etc. Twenty euro per week for 50 weeks is €1,000, which will get quite a bit of promotion done.

It costs just as much to print a bad design as it does a good one, so try to get an appropriate name, logo, and design for your business. Thinking up a good name is very important. Watch that the name isn't too specific to cater for future growth (e.g. Murphy's Sheds is a bit restrictive when they also start selling garden play equipment). Get someone with a flair for design to help with your graphics and colour schemes.

After an adequate amount of promotion the law of diminishing returns kicks in, and you get less return out of each additional euro spent. Do some promotion regularly, and stay within your budget. Whilst the cost of printing and van signage is a big up-front expense, thereafter promotion can be reduced to a regular spend, sufficient to keep your presence in the customer's mind. Low cost/no cost promotion should be an ongoing feature of your marketing.

The Cost of Not Promoting

You may be thinking that you cannot really afford to advertise. Starting a business, equipping it, making your time available to it but not bothering to promote it is a bit like investing all your money in a big car and having nothing left for the petrol to drive it. If you are thinking of avoiding the expense of promoting your business, remember it could be 'penny wise and pound foolish'. There could be a much greater cost in not advertising, so here are a few factors to consider.

"Have regard for your name, since it will remain with you for longer than a great stock of gold."
- Ecclesiasticus

Firstly, the cost in terms of lost earnings. Balance the cost of promoting your business against the cost of not having productive work to do. For example, losing one day per week (i.e. working four days instead of five); at €200 per day this will cost you €10,000 per year, which is the difference between a mere break-even business and a highly profitable one. In reality, can you afford not to promote?

Secondly, the cost in terms of poor earnings because you don't have an abundance of jobs to choose from. Working for €150 a day instead of a target of €200 means a shortfall of €250 a

---

week, which will cost you €12,500 per year.

A key strategy to get your prices up is getting more work than you can do, allowing you to drop the badly paid jobs. This is a clear example of the 'mix' or interaction between Price and Promotion. If you've very little work on, you'll end up doing poorly priced jobs, just in order to get the bills paid. The whole concept of abundance would be in tatters at that stage, so from the very start create a promotions plan, and allocate a definite budget to it. Treat this cost the same as you would any other cost, for example fuel for your car or van.

Image

The creation of a favourable image forms a large part of any developed economy. Just think about the 'image' shops in most towns – hairdressers, beauty salons, photography and video services, graphic designers, tanning shops, advertising, clothes shops, cosmetics, sports shops, gymnasia, all together make up a large amount of economic activity. Furthermore, people are prepared to heavily mortgage themselves for life to buy the big house that projects the right image, and to suffer expensive car repayments in pursuit of the same goal.

A large amount of effort is dedicated to image-making, and the lengths to which people will go in order to project an elevated social status is quite amazing. Regardless of the importance that we personally attach to the matter, we can take it as given that image is very important to many other people, namely our customers. It's for their 'needs and wants' that we must develop a suitable image, not for our own self-aggrandisement. Create the type of image for your business that your target customer expects, neither too flash nor too dowdy.

Most businesses create an image in order to assure customers about their service – the chef with hat and apron, the bar staff with the printed top, the airline cabin staff with the uniform. Whether it's a nurse, Garda or traffic warden, the uniform creates an image of professionalism. The drain and sewer-rod people have a traditionally dirty job, but Dyno-Rod with their bright clean boiler suits stand out for their clean image.

You can easily create an image for your business simply by adopting the best dress code for the trade you work in (e.g. a boiler suit), keeping it clean, and getting your business name and logo printed on it. Personal cleanliness and tidiness is vitally important, as dirty hair and an unshaven face turn people off. You can become a walking advertisement, projecting a good image. It's that simple, yet loads of people don't bother. Being attached to their old image or being afraid to project a professional business image will cost them money.

Why bother with marketing? In order to get the best jobs at the best price.

Good design on your stationery creates the right image, and in terms of contact details include a phone number (landline), fax (cheap to buy and good for sending quotations, reminders of bills, etc.), e-mail (accounts are free!), a mobile number, and your website address if you have one. An address is also part of the expected information as people want the security of knowing where you can be reached, to know you are traceable if things go wrong. Create promotional materials that will not outdate quickly as your business moves forward and grows – in other words don't play small and safe, talk your business up a bit, future-proof it. It's all part of building a credible, professional image.

More people will see the image your business projects than will see you; more people will see you than will see your transport; more people will see your transport than will see your office/home base – so keep the proper presentation of these elements in this order. This is also the least expensive order in which to present your business properly (a good website costs far less than an expensive office).

If you under-rate people's desire to project a good image, and their willingness to pay you in order to acquire your good image, then your understanding of the importance of image is lacking. Whilst the message you promote will vary from time to time, you are always promoting an image, so take care to ensure it's a good one.

Commissioning a Design

When working with a graphic designer, think about the look you want (logo, colours, typeface, etc.) and bring examples of other brochures, adverts, photographs and images that you like. If using photography, get a professional to take the pictures. Be consistent across all your printing (van, stationery, website). Keep it simple and clear because less clutter makes more impact, and fewer colours are cheaper to print.

Why bother with this detail? Because the quality of your advertising says as much about you as the quality of your premises, yet it will be seen by more people and will cost a lot less to put in place. You can often tell the service you'll get from a business by the quality of its marketing materials. Your marketing makes your first impression, and presents your business to your customer.

Advertising Tips

1. Consider the graphic you choose – is it attractive? Don't clutter the advert or website with too much detail.

2. If the headline doesn't grab a reader's attention, they will not read any further, so aim to stand out on a crowded page.

3. Don't try to say too much in an advert – keep the message short and relevant to the customer's needs/wants.

4. Make a list of the low cost/no cost promotional activities, and use them regularly.

5. Show your proposed advert to a number of people before placing it.

6. Cut a deal with newspapers for an extended period of advertising.

7. Keep your colour scheme, typefaces and graphics consistent on all ads and stationery, and on your van signage.

8. Use a number of small promotions rather than one big splash. 'One swallow never made a summer'.

9. Watch for misspellings, as they say a lot about your eye for detail – get your copy checked (graphic designers are not proofreaders).

10. Do a short run of prints (20-30) on a computer printer first; you will spot any necessary changes before doing a larger run.

11. Create a credible image with as many as possible of the following: landline, mobile, ▓ e-mail, address.

12. Once you print material, use it.

13. Take and keep good quality photos of your work for use in your brochure, website, advert, poster, etc.

14. Keep your promotions up to date (e.g. website/promotional material).

15. Get quotes or testimonials from satisfied customers to use in your promotional material.

What methods of promotion are you going to use? Tick your choices, cost them, and schedule a date for when you will do them.

Types of advertising	Yes	No	What month	€
Signposts/Shop fronts				
T-shirts/hats/work overalls				
Flyers				
Stickers/biros/key rings				
Golden pages				
Portfolio of work				
Printed quotation/invoice books				
Brochures				
Mail shots				
Business cards				
Letterheads/compliments slips				
Classified newspaper ads				
Radio ads				
Word of mouth				
Van signage				
Sponsorship – jerseys, prizes, etc.				
Website/Facebook				
Other				
Total cost				

Notes

Chapter 5   Sales

What is Selling?

'To sell' can be defined as 'to convince someone of the value of something'. Selling is really about helping people make up their minds. Whilst we may not think of ourselves as sales people, we are in fact selling all the time – convincing partners of the wisdom of certain projects, children of the value of school, friends of the fun of a night out, etc.

A sale is a transfer of enthusiasm from the seller to the buyer.

Selling is a critical function in any business. If you have no sales, you'll have no business, simple as that. A good sales technique is necessary even in good times (a sellers' market) in order for a business to get the best jobs, but it's absolutely essential in bad times (a buyers' market) in order to continue to make profits.

Selling goes hand in hand with marketing. Good marketing prepares the ground for success in sales. People will even approach you to do work for them if your marketing is very good, reducing the amount of sales work required. But marketing is not sales – you still have to complete the sale at your best price (profit maximisation is still your real job). Because you cannot easily delegate the sales function (unlike your accountancy or tax returns) unless you can afford a sales rep or sales agents, it is important to get as well-prepared as possible for any opportunities to sell.

Can I Sell?

Everybody sells all the time, including you. Sales people are born, including you. As a child, if you wanted something you kept asking and asking until you got it, and you still sell ideas every day (not with the same straightforward persistence, but more subtly). Unless you have worked in sales you may doubt your ability to sell. 'But I'm not a sales rep,' you'll say, 'I don't like selling,' and 'I don't have the gift of the gab'. In response to these objections it is important to make a few points.

In the past you may not have been a sales rep for anyone else, but you are now your own sales rep – it's a key part of being self-employed. You don't need to be full time on the road, selling enough product to keep a factory in production. However, what you must be able to do is make enough sales to keep yourself going.

Know also that 'the gift of the gab' can turn off as many people as it might impress. People want to be involved in the sales process; people want to buy rather than be sold to. This means your sales work is about giving them good reasons to buy, rather than actually 'selling', because people won't buy what they don't want. This is particularly true when making a large purchase which requires a lot of consideration. Genuinely consulting people about what they need is a lot more effective than 'gabbing on'.

No sales means no business.

But there is still some worry for a lot of people about selling. It means they have to move out of their comfort zone and ask people for something – the go-ahead with the job at the right price. It can cause fear because they fear rejection. If you remain detached and professional you won't take this rejection personally – it's just that this customer doesn't want what you're selling, not that they are rejecting you as a person.

In order to sell you must believe in what you are selling. You must genuinely believe that your customer is better off because of buying your product or service, so you both win. Otherwise you may have difficulty not alone in selling, but with business in general. If you're doing a good job then this person is lucky to have met you, because you will fulfil their needs or wants. If you've got a good price for your work, then you will have fulfilled your own need also. 'The satisfaction of customer needs and wants at a profit' is the definition of marketing, and sales belong in the marketing mix under the 'promotion' heading.

Selling Yourself

People will buy more from you when they 'buy' you, and they'll buy you if you help them to like themselves better. How might you do this? One of the best books written on this topic is 'How to Win Friends and Influence People' by Dale Carnegie.

He recommends that you:
- Become genuinely interested in other people.
- Smile.
- Remember that a person's name is to that person the sweetest and most important sound in any language.
- Be a good listener. Encourage others to talk about themselves.
- Talk in terms of the other person's interests.
- Make the other person feel important – and do it sincerely.

You may or may not agree with the approach recommended by Dale Carnegie, but you cannot argue with the fact that good personal relations with others makes for good business. Old fashioned good manners and genuine friendliness never lose their attractiveness.

Why do People Buy?

Why do people buy things? There are two main reasons:

(1) To remove a problem (a need), e.g. basic food, basic clothing, basic shelter, security, etc.

(2) To help them feel good about themselves (a want).

But which is the more typical reason? Is it because people need things or because they want them that they buy? Our needs are very basic – food, clothing, and shelter. Our wants – now that's a different thing, because they are practically unlimited. A person may need transport, but who needs a €100,000 car? A family may 'need' entertainment, but who needs a T.V. in every bedroom? Whether it's entertainment, food, clothes, cars, houses, even the giving of charity, the reason most people want to partake is in order to feel good about themselves.

People buy emotionally, and justify their purchases with logic later on, so you should first awaken their desire and then follow with logic. Be careful not to mismatch your sales effort by persuading customers with logic when you should be appealing to their emotions! Aside from the product itself, people must also buy another important thing – you! All other things being equal, people prefer to buy from people that they like, so you'll have more success in sales if people like you.

Prepare Yourself to Sell

First impressions count. You never get a second chance to make a first impression.

Many people are wary of sales people, they're afraid they'll be 'sold a pup'. Their first 'needs' are trust, credibility and integrity and you must establish these from the very start. In addition you must prepare yourself properly for the sales process, and to follow are a few pointers.

- **The way you think**

In order to succeed at anything you need to approach it with the right attitude, and this is particularly true of sales. The right attitude is a positive expectation, so expect to make a profitable sale. You don't necessarily need to have all the skills, but you must have the right attitude. Remember also that we project our self-image, and people tend to see us the way we see ourselves, so make sure you believe in yourself and your product.

If you aim to have fun with sales you'll love it, and you'll succeed. Selling is fun! Haggling over the price is fun! Getting a chance to size up and convince your customer is fun! Go for fun, appeal to emotions – people much prefer light-heartedness and humour to boring, downbeat nonsense. Think positively and happily. Don't think negatively because you can't afford to as a self-employed sales person.

- **The way you look**

To be successful you must look successful, and you don't get a second chance to make a first impression, so get it right first time. How you look on the outside is a clear give-away as to how you feel on the inside. We all have our own preferences for the way we dress, and the rule of thumb is to dress appropriately. A business suit to a business meeting, a pair of boots and hard hat to a site meeting, etc.

- **The way you act**

First and foremost and without negotiation, always be on time. If you're not on time for a sales meeting, the assumption is that you won't be on time with the work.

Act confidently. Confidence is a vital ingredient, and you should have a confidence-boosting affirmation ready to boost yourself. Have a successful mental image to bring to mind, and walk confidently into any sales situation, offering a hand shake (a good firm hand shake is always acknowledged).

Be enthusiastic, because enthusiasm is contagious, and there's no defence against it. Speaking enthusiastically (which is the way a kid walking into a room with news would speak) is very convincing. In this regard a sale has also been described as 'a transfer of enthusiasm from the seller to the buyer', so be sure to have some enthusiasm to transfer!

- **Know your product**

It is vital to know all about your own product. Whilst seemingly stating the obvious, many people don't know enough about what they are selling. Be clear about your core product and your product surround. In addition, you will need to list out the various features and benefits of your product. How can you hope to sell these features and their benefits to the customer if you don't know what they are in the first place, and if you personally are not totally sold on them?

- **Know your goal**

Before you leave the comfort of your home in the evening, or leave a job during the working day in order to give someone a quote, then you'd need to be clear on why you did it. You did it to make a profitable sale, not an honourable exit. That is your goal.

If you fail to make a profitable sale, your secondary objective may be to agree to place an order subject to a better quotation, a demonstration, a board meeting or some further information. That keeps the door open, but it's still not your goal. Redouble your effort to close the sale on the second visit, and if you don't it may be time to cut your losses.

The 5 Steps to the Sale

Having done the preparation as outlined, there comes a time to make the actual sale. Can you follow a system that you can repeat every time? Yes, you can!

Remember our definition of marketing (Chapter 3), 'the satisfaction of customer needs and wants at a profit'? which also applies to its first cousin, sales. Let's start by putting ourselves into the customer's shoes. The customer sees things through their eyes, and their motivation will be 'What's in it for me?' Your success in sales depends on your ability to tune into their wavelength.

Customer thinking will go like this	So we present our sale like this	
1. I want to know who I'm dealing with	**Step 1**	**I**ntroduction
2. I want my needs met	**Step 2**	**N**eeds
3. How will your product benefit me?	**Step 3**	**B**enefits
4. What are the snags? Should I?	**Step 4**	**I**ndecision
5. OK, I'll buy!	**Step 5**	**S**ale

Any attempt to complete a sale without going through these five steps is unlikely to end in an order, because the customer has to feel secure on each step before they'll move to the next. Think about it, why should they buy from you if they don't know who you are or get a good feeling about you? If they feel you don't meet their needs? If you haven't been able to translate what you do into benefits for them? If you can't allay their fears and help them make up their mind?

Realise one very important thing: if you don't know what you're going to say and do until you're in front of a customer, it's too late. Practice your sales routine under each of the INBIS headings that follow. Make them yours; customise them to your style until confident sales becomes your second nature. Then you'll complete more sales at higher prices.

Step 1: Introduction

Believe it or not, it can be difficult enough to introduce yourself.

Your main goal when meeting a customer is to have them like you and trust you, so try to remove their 'sales fear' and allow them to relax. Customers generally have a fear of being sold to, and we need to replace that with confidence that they are dealing with the right person. Because the first impression can ruin everything so easily, it's best if you have a routine to follow.

First and foremost, smile. A smile radiates warmth, and is an important sales skill. Practice it.

Look them in the eye. If a customer is sizing you up and you look past them or avoid eye contact, they'll assume you're shifty and won't trust you.

People need to buy "you" before they will buy from you.

Have a regular way of introducing yourself, e.g. "Hello, Gay Byrne from BBC", and have a business card to hand over. If you feel a handshake is appropriate, then let it be a warm, firm one.

Build a bit of friendliness with some general chit-chat at first, but without too much hesitation get down to business and show them what you propose. Remember your manners. Your body language expresses your enthusiasm and conviction, so keep it positive! A few compliments never go astray unless you overdo it, which will go against you. If you have been referred by someone then mention it, as it will reduce your customer's uncertainty. They will want to get a feel for your personality, and establish whether you are pleasant, businesslike, honest, and trustworthy.

You may be asked about your business, so have a quick description of what type of work you do, how much experience you have, etc. 'If you cannot say what you do in one or two sentences, then you don't know what you're doing' goes the saying, so have a confident reply prepared in advance.

In terms of your product, if you cannot grab someone's attention, you haven't a hope of selling to them. There are two main techniques: the **sales aid technique** using brochures, photographs or samples, and the **reference technique**, referring to somebody else in a similar situation or someone known to and respected by the customer. Both can be very effective.

Finish it up with a switchover remark, like 'OK then, let's get down to business. What do you have in mind? How can I help you?'

Step 2: Needs

The best salesmen never take for granted their ability to understand the needs of their customers, and never assume that two customers are alike.

One-way selling (i.e. you do all the talking) will miss the customer's needs every time. Find out what it is that they really want. A big mistake in sales is not spending enough time getting information.

Everyone is tuned into "What's in it for me?" Identifying what's in it for each customer gives your sales a great boost.

Start by asking open-ended questions – questions that don't have a simple yes or no answer. With these the customer will end up giving you much more information, indicating broad areas they are interested in. 'I keep six honest serving men – What, Why, How, Where, Who, When?' You should have a good number of these questions prepared on a worksheet in advance.

Having established the broad areas of interest in your product you narrow this down with further questions in order to pinpoint exactly what they want. Once you know what they want, you can tailor your presentation – a tailor cuts a suit to fit, but he won't cut the suit until he's got the measurements first. If the customer has short legs and wide shoulders, there's no point making a suit with long legs and narrow shoulders.

The best selling is 'consultative' selling, where you consult and advise a person based on their needs. Like everything else in marketing, your sales consultation must be customer focused. Remember, you have one mouth and two ears – and they should be used in that proportion. Listen to what is being said and what isn't. A good listener can learn just as much from what isn't being said as they can from what is. Don't just listen, but hear. Really hear what is being said and why it is being said. Who's doing the buying? What's the budget? Are they serious?

When added to your observations, the answers to your questions (the customer's needs) are the signposts you'll use in choosing what **benefits** to emphasise in the next step. The opposite approach to asking questions is to push your opinion down the customer's neck. But remember – 'If I say it they can doubt me; if they say it, it's true.' As a general rule of sales, it's better to ask than to tell.

Step 3: Features and Benefits

What exactly are features and benefits? A feature is and does something (e.g. ABS brakes prevent a car from skidding), whilst a benefit is a gain the customer will receive as a result of this feature (greatly reduced chance of seriously injuring themselves).

People don't just buy a product, they buy its benefits. People don't buy a cosmetic; they buy its main benefit – beauty. People don't buy insurance, they buy its main benefit – peace of mind. They don't buy a toy, they buy its main benefit – happiness for their children. You must spell out the benefits rather than assuming they are obvious. They may be obvious to you because it's your business, but don't assume the customer knows.

Translating product features into customer benefits is a key part of the sale.

Think through this aspect of your sales routine by working through the translation of the features of your products (logical) into benefits (emotional), and you'll have given your sales ability a great boost. This translation, whereby you make it easy for the customer to see exactly how they will benefit from the best features of your product or service, is a key aspect of sales.

To know what benefits to put forward you must know what the customer's needs are, so don't move onto this stage until you've found out their needs in the previous step, and if you need to take a step back and ask further questions, then do so. For instance, with the example of the ABS brakes, you'd have found out that this customer puts a big emphasis on safety (what general qualities are you looking for in your new car?) before you'd rattle on about ABS or airbags, reinforced cages or crumple zones. Had they answered 'speed and performance' you'd emphasise acceleration, top speed, torque, alloy wheels, spoilers, and put safety further down the list.

Only emphasise the appropriate benefits, i.e. tell customers enough about the product or service to sell it – not every last thing. Don't try to show off all you know; you're trying to make a sale, not win a medal. People like to be spoken to, not at, as happens if you rattle on too much, and particularly if you use technical jargon (people in I.T. or alternative health, beware!).

The secret is to match the features to the customer's needs, and translate these into benefits for quick understanding. Awaken their desire by showing them how the features of the product or service will benefit their individual needs.

Regularly check that the customer understands you – as well as confirming that you are communicating properly, it gets them involved in a two-way process, and gets them saying 'yes'!

Step 4: Handle Indecision/ Objections

Customer indecision is anything that halts the progress of the sale. Because the customer is afraid of making a mistake, they will avoid making a decision until they're sure. They will ask a few questions and raise a few issues in order to satisfy their doubts. If you can handle these successfully, then you'll get the sale in the next step. If you cannot satisfy their queries and reduce their doubts, then they won't buy.

When presenting the benefits in the previous step, you would have been pretty much in control of what was a very one-way communication process. Now the customer gets a chance to put you on the spot, and makes you cater to their needs once again – their need for satisfactory answers.

Any customer worries of this nature must be put to rest if possible, or at least reduced enough for them to justify the purchase, particularly if there is a large amount of money involved. Objections must be dealt with fully and immediately, otherwise the buyer may feel you don't know your business well enough – not a basis for confidence. In order to be able to deal with these doubts, you need to prepare yourself in advance.

To prepare properly you need to:

1. **Anticipate indecision issues**. Think about what might cause the customer some concern – obvious things like quality, after-sales service, spare parts, price, not knowing the brand name, etc. There is a prompt list of typical issues in the companion workbook, which you can apply to your own products and services.

2. **Prepare convincing answers**. If you have already thought out the answers in advance, then you can give a confident reply which will set the customer's mind at ease. If you start stalling or bluffing, maybe even panicking because you haven't done your homework, the customer will get even more worried and you'll lose the sale.

3. **Listen carefully to the customer's concerns**. As with all human relations, show respect – do not interrupt them, let them talk themselves out. Do not contradict, as nobody yet won an argument with a customer, so allow them to save face.

4. **Deliver your answer with confidence and grace**. Stay calm, collected and professional. Do not take these issues personally

because it's a matter of a customer dealing with their fears. Get them onside by saying; 'I see what you mean/I hear what you're saying but . . .' and deliver your prepared response.

Step 5: Close the Sale

The sale is never completed until you get an order. You will seldom get the order until you ask for it. 'Ask and thou shall receive' says the Bible; it was true two thousand years ago, and it is still true today.

There comes a right time to ask for the order. Like most things in life timing is everything, and you'll have to trust your instincts on when to ask. Obviously you won't ask as you are introducing yourself, as you are finding out about the customer's needs, whilst you are outlining the benefits, or when you are helping them with their indecision. But when all of these steps have been taken, it becomes time to ask for the sale.

The time to complete the sale is when the buying signals are present. Customers will usually show you they are ready by giving you signals instead of telling you so. There are two types of signals: verbal and non-verbal. With verbal signals the customer may ask more detailed questions, talk about things that would happen if they owned your product, talk more enthusiastically, say 'yes' more often, or simply start making agreeable sounds. Wanting to see a feature demonstrated again is one of the strongest buying signs, e.g. 'will you go over that one more time?' With non-verbal signals a smile can be an important buying sign. Their eyes may light up, they may start nodding. If you are selling to a couple they may show some affection for each other.

There is no such thing as a missed opportunity; even if you miss it, the competition won't.

The best way to complete a sale is to get permission to take the order/write up the quotation. You can ask for the go-ahead in a number of ways: 'Will I write it up so? Will we go ahead so? Are you happy enough to go ahead?' It's important that you get a few closing lines that suit your style, and then practice them until they trip off your tongue quite naturally. Be very careful not to change your manner and tense up when completing the sale. Treat it as the natural conclusion to your sales process.

Some obstacles to completing the sale include: lack of confidence that the product is the best one for the customer; fear that the customer will say 'no'; or being unable to handle the customer's indecision and objections.

Once you've asked a closing question, shut up. The first person to speak loses. Keep the pressure on the client to either buy or not; get them to make a decision.

To conclude, don't try to close too soon or talk yourself out of it. Don't strike until the iron is hot, but remember it doesn't stay hot for too long!

Other Issues to Consider

In addition to the sales process as outlined, various other sales-related issues need to be kept in mind:

- **Completing from the beginning**
Completing the sale starts right from the beginning. Completing or 'closing' the sale is not so much a separate step as the result of all the previous steps that were taken. If these were done properly then the completion of the sale is the easy bit.

- **Selling is consultation**
The person that is selling in consultation with a buyer's needs takes a different approach to the 'hard sell' merchant. A consultative seller consults, advises, motivates and encourages customers to buy what they need or want. The 'hard seller' manipulates, trying to 'trick' or force the customer to buy. It's important to be a good listener and learn what it is that your customer really wants.

- **Unique sales points**
No two products, people, companies or services are the same. It's up to you to identify the differences that are unique to both you and your product. These differences are your unique sales points. They are your unique features, from which your customer will gain unique benefits.

- **Don't knock your competition**

When someone else mentions your competition, don't knock them. It's a sign of bad manners, and will set your customer against you. Acknowledge them and pass them off without showing any concern whatsoever. If you are concerned with the competition, this will project to the customer, and make them feel uncomfortable doing business with you.

- **Glass half full or half empty**

Always be positive. Always state what you can do, not what you can't. For example, don't say 'I can't make it until next week', instead say, 'I can make it next week if that's OK'.

People buy emotionally and justify with logic later on.

- **'Difficult' people**

You're not trying to make friends, you're trying to make sales. Some of your customers will be bores and bullies, be objectionable in outlook or behaviour, or have opinions and values different to yours. So what? Just maintain detached, professional boundaries.

Always be prepared to let your customer have the last word. You don't want to take away his self-esteem, just his order.

- **Reading people**

There are numerous types of people, and it's up to you to read them, figuring out what type they are.

Here are some typical types:
1. **The Silent Type**: Ask them questions. Ask for their opinion. It's up to you to draw them out – this is your job. Eventually they will tell you all you need to know.

2. **The Opinionated Type**: Avoid challenging them – remember you are there to sell, not to get involved in a battle of wits. Bear in mind that 'the customer is always right', and try to get them talking positively about your product.

3. **The Indecisive Type**: Don't waste too much time on them – they may only be trying to gather information, or pick your brains. Give them two visits at most.

●   **Body language**

People can say one thing and mean another, but their body language says it all. It is always right, and harder to manipulate than speech. Look out for signals such as hand movements, face movements and body movements. If someone crosses their arms, what does that mean? If someone crosses their legs away from you, what does that mean?

Watch your boundaries and never move into someone's personal space - that will build pressure between you and your customer.

Watch for signs that you are moving too slowly or boring your customer. You can recognise this by looking for these signs: finger tapping, foot waggling, shifting posture. If you notice any of these signs then leave the subject, adjust your pace and address that subject later in the conversation if necessary.

Always try to get on the same side as the customer. Use a sales portfolio as a means of displaying your product, but also as a means of distracting your customer (i.e. taking their focus off you) so that you can read them better. This is what mind readers do with tarot cards and crystal balls, so take a leaf out of their book.

●   **If I drop my price, I'll get the sale?**

People don't buy price – they buy value. As you remember from the marketing section on price, 'price and quality are inextricably linked in the customer's mind'. A reliable delivery with a dependable back-up service is usually more important than price, so don't sell yourself short on price if your quality is good.

"Contrary to the cliché, genuinely nice guys most often finish first or very near it."
- Malcolm Forbes

- **Setting an appointment**

If you are trying to make an appointment, be sure to offer the customer a specific either/or choice, e.g. 'Which would suit you best, Tuesday at 3 or Thursday at 4?'. It gives them less of a chance to say 'sorry, no – that time doesn't suit'.

- **Try to present to all decision-makers**

Try to get both decision-makers to your presentation, or you'll oftentimes have to do it twice. If you are selling into a home, get the husband and wife/couple together or the other may over-rule the decision. Likewise with an industrial buyer, if possible get the relevant manager as well as the buyer.

- **Won't sales happen anyway?**

A common mistake people make in the business world is that they believe their product or service is something totally different, and so good that it will sell itself. This may happen to a limited degree in good times (a sellers' market), but certainly not in tight times.

Somebody must take charge of the selling function – it has to be you! This is particularly important when you have staff, but right from the start if you want to build a business you must keep a sharp lookout for sales opportunities. They will present themselves in various different places. It may be at a football match, a wedding, a funeral, whilst you're doing a job – it will come up in conversation as to what you do, so always have a business card to hand.

- **Rejection**

Don't take rejection personally. It's not you that's being rejected, merely your commercial offering. Not everybody wants it, end of story, so move on until you find someone that does.

Sales is really a numbers game. All other things being equal, the bigger the number of sales presentations the bigger the number of sales, and the bigger the number of rejections.

All else being equal, the business person with the better sales skills will build by far the better business.

Rejection goes deep into our memories. One of the first words you learned as a child was 'no'. We still feel bad when we hear it.

- **Price**

When pricing, always allow for a certain amount of haggle-room, but don't compromise on your needs. 'Put it on to take it off', like candles on a birthday cake, only there for decoration. Most shrewd buyers will not buy unless you give them a discount, so play the game.

- **Private clients versus industrial buyers**

Selling to a private client is slightly different to selling to an industrial buyer. Because the private client has full authority you can often complete the sale with one visit. Selling to a commercial client, on the other hand, is a longer process and a single call will rarely produce the order.

In Conclusion

Sales are an essential part of every business, and your aim is to sell the optimum amount of product at the best price. Done properly, in a consultative manner with the customer's needs at heart, it is an honourable undertaking. That way both you and your customers have your needs met.

Exercise

Features and Benefits

Don't sell **FEATURES** – a feature is part of the product, e.g. a service trolley has wheels.

Sell **BENEFITS** – a benefit is a gain the customer will get as a result of this feature, e.g. the service trolley is easily moved.

List all the features of a product or business service you provide, and opposite each feature, list the benefits to the customer.

Features "Another feature is ……………."	Benefits "And the real benefit to you is …………."

Chapter 6   Finance

Introduction

Because business is about money, if you have a negative attitude to money this will cause huge problems, both for yourself and those that have to deal with you. Money is just a medium of exchange, and a store of value. If you have a problem with the word, start to think of it as just a form of energy that enables you to get things done. If you remove your negative emotional reaction to the word, you'll manage it much better.

A quotation from the book *Think and Grow Rich* by Napoleon Hill goes as follows: 'More gold has been mined from the thoughts of men than has ever been mined from the earth'. It means that wealth begins with a state of mind. Wealth comes to those who become conscious of wealth, and you cannot grow rich if your thoughts are steeped in poverty, want, failure, and defeat.

Money creates a huge range of emotional reactions in people.

Our consciousness is like a magnet, attracting things similar to it. Therefore a wealth consciousness observes and attracts wealth; a poverty consciousness observes and attracts poverty. This is not a complicated concept, and is summed up in the old saying "birds of a feather flock together".

Money cannot come to you without you wanting it to, so this seems to be the starting point of wealth accumulation – the desire to have it. If you are low on money to invest in your business it can be difficult, but you must ask yourself why do you find yourself in this situation? The obvious explanation is because of your expenses, etc., but everybody has those; so if you dig a little deeper, what's the real reason? Do you have a problem with abundance, preferring the challenge of financial struggle? Do you financially overstretch yourself with unaffordable nights out, car repayments, wasteful spending, holidays, etc., to guarantee this struggle, or do you just not bother to earn enough money in the first place?

Working Capital

'It takes money to make money' goes the saying, and for the most part it's true. Apart from the money required for investment in your business, the money required to just keep working while waiting to get paid is known as working capital. Being able to hold onto sufficient working capital to operate efficiently and without undue financial pressure is a very valuable business skill. Realising that your working capital requirement increases with every stage of growth (e.g. increased sales, extra employees, etc.) is key to you making adequate provision.

Maintaining adequate working capital reserves means positioning yourself correctly so that you sit on a comfortable cash cushion, not in a restrictive cash strait-jacket. Which position you find yourself in has nothing to do with your trading circumstances, and everything to do with your ability to properly position yourself for business success.

Ideally you will maintain sufficient working capital to keep you going for three months, but two months is acceptable. One month's working capital is much too tight, and will result in regular financial shortages and pressures, particularly during holidays and slow payment periods.

Borrowing

Neither a borrower nor a lender be.
Shakespeare

Borrowing is a powerful tool and, like any power tool, it can bring benefits if used wisely; however, if used incorrectly it will do a lot of damage. The first disadvantage of borrowing is that the privilege of using someone else's money has a cost, in the form of an interest rate. The second disadvantage is that it has to be paid back, and if you cannot repay there can be serious consequences. Thus, before you borrow there are some issues to consider.

1. Do you really need it?
The major consideration in borrowing is whether you need the item or whether you just want it. If you really need it, it will be kept busy, and so should pay for itself; if you just want it, it could

end up being a very expensive ornament. A certain amount of equipment is necessary to operate efficiently in every business, but it doesn't all need to be top-of-the range, new equipment. As business improves you can expand both the range and specification on your equipment, as you earn the right to own it rather than foolishly borrow for it.

2. Will you be richer as a result?

This is a fundamental question. If you're going to be poorer as a result, then it makes no sense to borrow. However, if the item will pay for itself within a reasonable period of time by saving on hire, increasing the number of jobs you can get through in the year, or allowing you to take on new types of work, then it may make sense to borrow for it. Always calculate how much money you think the equipment will make or save you each month in deciding whether it will make you richer or poorer.

3. Can you afford to?

What's your ability to repay each month? It's OK to stretch yourself slightly, but avoid over-stretching.

You can adjust the level of your repayment in several ways:
- By varying the term of the loan/lease (the term is the number of months or years over which the loan is repayable)
- By contributing a portion of your savings to the purchase of the item required, thereby reducing the amount borrowed to what you can afford
- By negotiating a keen interest rate.

If, after careful consideration, you decide you need to borrow then settle for a repayment that will not overstretch you. If you find yourself in unforeseen trouble at a later stage, talk to your lender and reschedule repayments if necessary; don't ignore them or they'll assume you are trying to cheat them.

4. Current or capital?

There is a major difference between borrowing for capital and current expenditure. Capital expenditure goes on items of lasting use in the business, items like equipment, fixtures, property, etc. which generally increase your wealth, whilst current expenditure refers to day-to-day expenses, and once used up there is nothing left to show for them. Thus clever borrowing for necessary capital expenditure can usually be justified, whilst borrowing for current expenditure raises serious questions.

5. Cheap or expensive money?

Money is a product which banks sell at a price, namely the interest rate (plus a negotiable acceptance fee in most cases). Shopping around and negotiating the keenest rate possible can save you quite a bit over the term of a loan. Most Partnership Companies now offer a facility for low interest loans, usually in conjunction with a local bank or credit union – check with your local enterprise officer for details. Also, First Step helps business start-ups with access to loans at a reasonable rate. See www.first-step.ie for an application form.

6. Have you established a savings discipline?

The amount you save each month is an indication of the amount you cano repay each month. If you haven't been able to save money, what makes you think you will be able to repay money? Granted, a shrewd purchase of additional equipment should generate enough cash to pay for itself, but even the credit union will want to see a savings record before they will advance a loan. This is for two reasons: (a) it reduces their risk and (b) it shows that you understand the importance of money and possess the self-discipline to save it.

7. Have you established a credit rating?

If you have never borrowed and successfully repaid, a potential lender doesn't have any indication as to your behaviour with a

Forgetting a debt doesn't pay it.

loan. Although prudent, not having borrowed may go against you. Remember, borrowing is a business 'instrument' or 'tool', and just like any tool it is important you can demonstrate you know how to use it.

8. How do you build your borrowing ability?

By borrowing small amounts over a short term you will develop your borrowing skills. If you need €10,000 to equip your business, this can be borrowed in stages. Prioritise individual items of equipment and borrow for these, completing your repayments as quickly as possible. It may be a little slower but it's steadier and less risky, and will withstand any temporary business difficulties a lot better. Thus you will grow in confidence with this business tool.

9. How much should you borrow?

Use your common sense – don't over-borrow, but don't stand still for want of a small borrowing used intelligently. It is inadvisable to go to the full extent of your repayment capacity, as this doesn't allow for any setbacks that might arise due to bad debts, ill-health, or economic slowdowns. If you had all the cash you required for your business from day one, you would end up spending much of it without sufficient consideration. The slower approach forces you to prioritise your needs.

10. Should you borrow or use your savings?

Many people will say that savings shouldn't be used as they are hard to get together, and wouldn't exist in the first place if they were parted with too easily. Better to keep them in reserve to make a repayment if necessary, and make the business pay its own way each month for equipment that it is using. Certainly with low interest rates, borrowing (i.e. using someone else's money to grow the business) can make a lot of sense. It is a matter of judgement, so use whatever mix of the two you feel most comfortable with.

Leasing

Cash is king.

Leasing is a mix between borrowing for and hiring a capital item, e.g. a car or a piece of equipment. With a full-purchase lease the 'title' or ownership of the goods remains with the leasing company (the lessor) until the final payment is made, whereupon the title transfers to the person/company who has taken the lease (the lessee). A lease can usually be taken on new or relatively new equipment over a period ranging from twelve to sixty months. It is usually advisable to keep the lease as short as is comfortably possible, thereby having a residual value left in the equipment (e.g. if a van can be paid off on a three year lease and will last for eight years). The lease is therefore a mix of both an expense and an investment.

Buying Money

If you are leasing, it is very important to shop around for both the lease and the equipment. A garage sells both cars and finance, taking a margin on both. The garage agrees a lower rate with the finance company than they sign up the client at, getting the difference between the two rates for themselves. Therefore it is important that you go directly to several leasing companies asking them to beat the rate you have got. Many people just sign up for what they're offered and pay the higher rate without even questioning it. This lack of financial negotiation costs them dearly as the salesman puts the highest rate possible on their loan agreement.

Likewise with any borrowing, be it a mortgage or a credit card – it pays very well to shop around.

Refinancing Your Borrowings

The old truism that 'a lot of little holes will sink a ship' states the obvious, particularly with borrowings where several short-term repayments can mount up to quite a bit. We live in a credit culture where it is too easy to buy unnecessary luxuries on credit, the 'buy now and pay later' syndrome. As a result, many people find that their repayments on small and often unnecessary borrowings often exceed their essential borrowings, for example a mortgage.

If you find yourself over-exposed on repayments, the question arises whether you should 'tough it out' and get them repaid as quickly as possible, or consolidate into a medium-term loan or mortgage extension. The danger is that if the lesson of over-borrowing isn't properly learnt the same situation will develop again over the following few years, with the same solution required. If you borrow, make yourself pay for it as planned, knowing that a hard lesson isn't quickly forgotten.

Borrow or Save?

Having carefully evaluated the borrowing issues as outlined earlier, the argument can be made that borrowing for a piece of equipment (or property) that you need (and can afford) is quite similar to saving for it, with two differences – the risk and the timing.

For instance, if a gardener decided to buy a second-hand mini-digger (costing €10,000) rather than keep hiring one – should he save up for it, or should he borrow the money? His savings plan might be €4,000 a year for three years totalling €12,000 (allowing €2,000 for inflation in the price). His borrowing plan might also be €4,000 a year for three years, repaying €12,000 (allowing €2,000 for interest). Pretty much the same thing! However there is risk attached to borrowing, and he needs to balance the risk of not being able to repay the loan against the opportunity cost of missed earnings through not having the equipment.

If you buy what you don't need, you may have to sell what you do need.

This principle also applies to general business investment in equipment and property. Most successful business people had to borrow at a low rate, and through wise investment in their business get a return at a much higher rate.

Overdrafts

An overdraft is a borrowing facility available on a current account for when you run out of cash in the short term. It serves the same purpose as a reserve fuel tank in a motorcycle, buying you some time to get your finances sorted out. Ideally it is used only in the short term, i.e. a few weeks. The problem arises when you start to rely on it, and don't clear it off – then it becomes a medium-term borrowing, and is no longer available to retreat to when you find yourself tight for cash. If this situation develops you will have yourself incorrectly positioned, living in overdraft.

It is a much more comfortable position to be €2,000 in credit than €2,000 in overdraft. When positioning yourself financially, bear in mind that a major reason businesses get into trouble is because they haven't themselves properly financed from the start, or have failed to manage their financial position. Living in overdraft is one such position and should be avoided as it leaves no fallback position if cash gets tight.

How will the Bank Assess your Proposal?

Before you can make a convincing approach to any third party for funds to invest in your business, you will first need to 'put your own money where your mouth is'. They will ask the obvious question, 'Why should we invest our money if you won't invest your own?' A possible answer is 'I don't have any money' which begs the question 'why not?'

Bank managers are trained in assessing loan risk, and in the current economic climate they are very cautious. Their evaluation of any loan proposal will proceed through the following steps.

a. **You, the promoter**. Bank managers will always try to read from your enthusiasm, attitude, preparation and experience whether or not you'll make the proposal happen. This is their most important assessment.

b. **Your business**. Some businesses are more lucrative than others. The banks will be slow to fund a sector that is oversupplied, regardless of how well they perceive you.

c. **Your security**. The amount of security/collateral available makes the loan high or low risk. All else going wrong, it's their fall-back position, and will be called in if you fail to meet your repayments.

Because borrowing and saving are so similar, the skills that are needed to save money are the same skills that are required to repay it. Thus, even the most customer-friendly lending institution in the country – the Credit Union – requires that you have understood and applied this basic principle. Before they advance a first loan they will want to see a savings record, and will initially advance twice the amount saved. Financial institutions are not charitable institutions, but hard-headed maximisers of profit. Remember, nobody owes you a loan, and nobody owes you a living.

Presenting Your Case

It is important that you always approach any lender or grant agency with a strong proposal, made up of two elements – a clearly thought-out plan that shows how the business will make money, and evidence of your own investment.

A well thought-out plan backed up with good research increases the chances of a positive outcome. You will generally only get one bite of the cherry, so don't go half prepared. Get assistance with your business plan from an enterprise officer or accountant, but the bulk of it should be your own thinking. Add to this your personal power, i.e. your self-belief, your confidence, your appearance – which all speak volumes and can contradict or complement what you say.

There is no such thing as a free lunch.

A vital second component is your cash input, 'putting your money where your mouth is'. You must cobble together as much start-up cash as you can, using all your determination and creative abilities. What can you sell? What part-time jobs can you get? What expenses can you cut out (cigarettes, alcohol, unnecessary shopping)? What favours can you call in? What low investment jobs can you do quickly to earn money? Give yourself a deadline to put as much cash together as possible, and work tirelessly towards that.

When outlining your investment in your business make sure to put a fair value on all the equipment, tools, training costs, etc., that you have put into your business over the years. Your past investments of time and money increase your credibility.

Low-cost Business Loans

A final word on loans. As already stated, most Partnership Companies have established a low-interest loan fund to support viable businesses which cannot get a loan from the banks or credit unions.

In addition, 'First Step' at www.first-step.ie is a great source of microfinance, providing loans up to €25,000. If you have drawn a blank with the regular banks they're worth checking out. They won't fund bad business propositions, but may help someone with a good proposal who hasn't got the credit record required by the banks. Talk to your local enterprise officer for details.

Savings

You can look at savings in two ways: firstly, they will literally save you from going broke in the short term when your business hits the inevitable rough patches. Secondly, they are the key to accumulating wealth in the medium to long term, for direct reinvestment, or for leverage to raise a borrowing several times greater. The reason it is necessary to make a choice to save is because of the universal truth of Parkinson's Law: 'Expenses rise to meet the income available'. In other words, unless you direct some cash towards savings, expenses will gobble it all up.

Expenses rise to meet the income available.

Like most things in life it's a question of attitude, and the emotion you attach to saving. If the emotion is one of pain and sacrifice, of having to do without, then you'll probably not succeed in carrying this burden for long. However, if the attitude is one of freedom from financial pressure, and getting money to work for you rather than you always having to work for it, then you'll insist on doing it.

A good attitude to start with and get the ball rolling in your favour is 'A tenth of all I earn is mine to keep'. Don't mind giving away nine-tenths of your earnings to the supermarket, the landlord or mortgage company, the garage and service station, the publican, whoever; but why would you give it all away? As you get better at saving you can increase this fraction to two-tenths, or whatever you can comfortably afford; but at a minimum feel that you deserve to hold onto at least a tenth of your own money – otherwise it isn't really your money at all, you are just an economic slave.

No System = No Savings

Savings are an invaluable asset and creating them is all about setting up a system. For example, many people keep a big jar on a shelf for loose change, and the amount gathered in small amounts adds up to quite a bit when it's counted up at Christmas or holiday time. This saving couldn't happen if the system wasn't set up in the first place.

The same principle applies to larger savings. If you don't organise a dependable system that works automatically each week, then you'll end up with no savings. A suggested system is:

1. Open a savings account in a different bank/credit union.
2. Direct a monthly standing order from your business account; alternatively, earmark some source of your earnings (e.g. Saturday earnings or a particular type of work) for this account.
3. Only withdraw from this account if you absolutely need cash. Remind yourself not to make it a habit!

Bear in mind that developing any new good habit will stretch you a bit at the start, but you'll soon get used to it and do it automatically. After the first thousand saved it becomes a source of pleasure. It's a bit like physical exercise, hurting you initially until your muscles get fit, but then becoming enjoyable if you keep it up.

Debt Collection

When it comes to work, getting paid is the single most important part of any job. The job is never finished until the money is collected. Someone else is holding onto what is now your money once the work has been completed. Some people believe in holding on to it as long as possible, maybe never paying you if you let them away with it. Remember 'people will treat you the way you show them how to treat you', so from the very start show reluctant debtors that you are strong on debt-collection, and they will treat you with financial respect; show them you are a soft touch and you will be treated as such.

Prevention is better than cure, so clarify payment details on a written quotation, check credit worthiness in advance (can they pay you? will they pay you?) and arrange payment by instalments on a big job (weekly if possible). When payment is due on completion make sure to invoice promptly; put simply, if you do not ask to be paid on time there's a good chance you will not be.

A tenth of all I earn is mine to keep.

When you do encounter a slow payer, don't ignore them. Remember that eaten bread is soon forgotten, so it's easier to collect a week after you've finished than a month later. Persist in following your money – it shows you intend to collect if you keep calling. Make sure to be civil, because if you fall out you've very little chance of collecting. Chase outstanding debts weekly, concentrating on the largest and oldest. Legal action should be a last resort, but don't hesitate to use it if all else fails.

In trying to evade paying you there are some typical dodges to watch for, like a client finding fault with your work, playing an adult version of hide and seek with both themselves and their cheque book, or being the nice guy who's just hit a spot of hard luck. If you feel you're being messed about, give notice that you have to stop work/stop supplying, and don't restart until you are paid. This should be quickly followed up with a letter giving seven days notice that you intend to hand the matter over to your solicitor. Don't falter at this stage in the interest of saving the relationship, because it is over anyway. Don't restart until you are prepared, and let it be on your terms – cash on delivery.

Payback/ Return on Investment Scenarios

It is important to work out what benefit an investment in equipment will bring to a business before making the purchase. Take the following example of an industrial floor sander:

A new business specialising in laying timber floors was hiring a sander in the initial stages until the owner felt comfortable about the future of the business. He then had to decide whether or not to buy a machine for €3,500, which was a substantial additional investment at that stage of the business. The expected working life of the machine, if properly maintained, was 10 years.

His weekly costs at that stage were as follows:

Hire: Average 1.5 hires per week @ €30 per hire	€45.00
Petrol, wear & tear on transport, collecting and returning sander	€5.00
Time: One hour per run @ €10 per hour	€30.00
Total cost per week	€80.00

The payback period is calculated by dividing the total cost of the equipment by the amount it is currently costing each week to hire;
Payback period = €3,500 / €80 = 43.75 weeks

The business was able to avail of assistance of €500 towards the purchase of the machine, thereby reducing the payback even further to €3,000/€80 = 37.5 weeks.

In other words, the machine was fully paid for without any additional weekly cost in a period of thirty-seven and a half weeks, merely by organising the same cost differently. Thereafter the business was up by €80 per week for the following nine years, assuming it stayed at the same level of trading. If trading levels increased then the saving would be even greater, and this was likely as the owner was more secure and optimistic about being able to take on further work, thereby maximising his return on investment.

Grants

'There's no such thing as a free meal' goes the saying, and it is particularly true when it comes to grants. The notion of something for nothing can be irresistible, but there is quite a lot of work involved in securing a grant. There are also quite a few conditions attached, making it less attractive than it may first seem. Whether or not you'd be better off putting the same time and money into seeking extra clients from whom you might earn similar money and get repeat business is a judgement call you must make. Unless the grant is substantial and clearly the best return on your time, you may be best to avoid it as a distraction from your ongoing work of building a satisfied customer base.

Grant-seeking can take your focus off your real business of making profits.

It may sound like a contradiction in terms, but grants can be very bad for your business because they can make it soft. Most successful businesses did not have these 'gifts' when they were starting off, making them stand on their own two feet from the very start. Any investment had to be made from profits, not from hand-outs, so the thinking had to be stronger and healthier. Having said that, if grant supports are invested wisely then the business can make progress faster.

Getting a grant takes work, and the grant agencies are obliged to make applicants jump through quite a few regulatory hoops before they can pay out. Also bear in mind that quite a lot of applicants are turned down, so watch that your confidence isn't damaged by a refusal.

Grant Agencies

There is a wide range of specialised grant agencies out there, with each agency catering for clients in its own sector. For specialised grants you will need to check out the relevant state agency for your sector at www.basis.ie (a Government website that provides businesses with a single access point to all Government information and services). Before you get your hopes up, know that despite the many different agencies, it is the exception rather than the rule for a new business start-up to get a grant, so if you do get a grant consider yourself one of the lucky ones.

The general agencies include County Enterprise Boards (www.enterpriseboards.ie), LEADER (www.pobail.ie), and the Department of Social Protection (www.welfare.ie)

Note: Contact these agencies for details of their individual schemes and qualifying criteria, as each case is unique.

General Guide to LEADER & CEB Grants

There are some similarities between these two agencies, both in terms of what they can fund and the type of funding available, so they will both be dealt with under the same heading. Note that the following provides general guidelines only. Make an appointment with your local LEADER company or County Enterprise Board to arrange an evaluation of your particular project.

The purpose of grants is to broaden and expand the economic base of the country, so projects in those sectors of the economy that are already oversupplied cannot be funded, e.g. construction, retail, taxis, etc. For those sectors that can be funded, projects have to display innovation (i.e. new and different products/practices), whilst not causing the loss of other local jobs through displacement.

Types of Grants

County Enterprise Boards (CEBs) and LEADER companies provide cash assistance in the form of capital grants (part of which is repayable), employment grants, and feasibility study grants. In addition they provide management training, grants towards specialised training, marketing grants, and mentoring services, amongst others.

Capital grants are up to a maximum of 50% of the cost of eligible fixed assets (plant, equipment, some buildings), to a maximum of €75,000. Equipment must be new, tax clearance must be in place, several quotations must be secured, and you must show evidence of sufficient funds available to purchase the assets in full. Grant payment is made after you have acquired the assets, as a refund.

Employment grants towards the cost of labour are up to a maximum of €7,500 per job (including yours as the promoter), or €75,000 for ten employees. You cannot apply for both employment and capital funding, nor can you receive funding from both agencies.

Feasibility grants may be provided to assess the feasibility of the project from a technical, marketing and financial standpoint. Maximum funding available is €6,350 (Border Midland Western region) and €5,100 in the rest of the country.

The business plan template required for the CEBs is available as a download at www.enterpriseboards.ie.

Guidelines for Submissions

1. Business plan.
2. Budgeted accounts for the last two years in the case of an existing enterprise.
3. Projected profit and loss account/cash flow statement, and balance sheet for the first year of the enterprise.
4. Letter of confirmation from lending institution, verifying loan/overdraft approvals – if borrowing/overdraft is required to support the enterprise.
5. Planning permission – the premises in which the project is carried out must have formal planning permission.
6. Tax clearance – no grants will be paid without a tax clearance certificate.
7. Grant aid cannot be provided retrospectively.
8. A grant cannot be considered approved until confirmed in writing.

Department of Social Protection

The Enterprise Allowance (self-employed) is a great financial support to anyone starting a business. If you have recently become unemployed, you may get immediate access to a one-year Enterprise Allowance if you qualify for Job Seeker's Benefit. Payment will be for a maximum of one year, whilst starting your business, and finishes when your Job Seeker's Benefit entitlement ceases. Note that you only receive 12 month's support in total between the Job Seeker's Benefit and the Enterprise Allowance, so the later you start on the Enterprise Allowance, the less time you will have on it.

Total equity = cash equity + sweat equity. Make up for any lack of cash equity with plenty of sweat equity.

If you've been unemployed or in receipt of qualifying benefits (e.g. on a Community Employment scheme) for more than one year you may qualify for a two-year Enterprise Allowance, provided you have an underlying entitlement to Job Seeker's Allowance. If you qualify you can get the equivalent of your social welfare payment at the rate of 100% in year 1, and 75% in year 2. In addition, you may qualify for secondary benefits.

The Department of Social Protection also has a technical assistance fund up to a maximum of €1,000 per business which you can avail of for certain business start-up expenses (you are required to partly fund these costs).

They require three pieces of paperwork – a simple business plan, evidence of tax registration (form TR1) and a completed application form. Over the past number of years they have proven to be very supportive of their clients. If you qualify it adds up to a substantial financial support over the period and a real opportunity to move ahead. Contact your local enterprise officer for details; also check out their website at www.welfare.ie.

Be careful to consider how you will use the funding to develop your business. This allowance is not a subsidy to be wasted on a loss making business, but an opportunity to build your business for the future.

MABS

The Money Advice and Budgeting Service (MABS), at www.mabs.ie, provides excellent assistance in dealing with debt, which unfortunately is a situation many self-employed people have to deal with if their business starts to struggle. They provide help with assessing the situation, doing up a budget, dealing with debtors, and general money management. As with every problem, the sooner it is dealt with the better so don't delay in making use of their services if you need to.

WESTBIC

WESTBIC is the official EU Business and Innovation Centre in the Border, Midland and Western region of Ireland, providing tailored support to innovative enterprise through the initial stages, from concept to commercialisation. Established in 1987, WESTBIC is a specialist provider of supports to indigenous industry. See www.westbic.ie for more information.

Enterprise Ireland

Enterprise Ireland is the government agency responsible for the development and promotion of the indigenous business sector. Their mission is to accelerate the development of world-class Irish companies to achieve strong positions in global markets, resulting in increased national and regional prosperity. See www.enterprise-ireland.ie for more information.

Additional Information

The website of the National Consumer Agency is another useful resource worth having a look at. See www.itsyourmoney.ie.

If you would like to check out your own credit status, you can do so on www.icb.ie, the website of the Irish Credit Bureau.

Names	Lender	
	Borrower	
Addresses	Lender	
	Borrower	
Amount of loan	€	
Interest rate, calculation		
Term (no. of months)		
Purpose		
Security		
Monthly repayment amount	€	
Repayment method		
Recording/receipts		
Details		
Signed by lender		Date
Signed by borrower		Date
Signed by witness		Date

Notes

Chapter 7   Accounting

Introduction to Accounting

To see if you are making any money, the golden rule in business is to take in more money than you let out, and to maximise the distance between the two as you develop the business. That's fairly simple to understand, but begs the question 'how do you know how much money is coming in and going out?' Again the answer is simple – by counting it! That's what accounting is about.

"That which we persist in doing becomes easier – not that the nature of the task has changed, but our ability to do it has increased."
- Emerson

But why bother? If you keep an eye on the cash balance in your bank account isn't that enough? Indeed, understanding how your cash flows, and maintaining a positive cash balance are critical business skills – but of little use in terms of managing costs. Unnecessarily high costs (e.g. on phone, transport, drawings/wages, etc.) can hide away amidst a strong cash-flow, but to control costs you've got to know them individually. Reducing costs is one of the three keys to profitability, so whilst good cash-flow skills are needed for survival, good accounting skills are needed to maximise profitability.

Remember also that maintaining accounts is a legal requirement that goes with being self-employed.

Is Accounting Difficult?

The average child of ten can keep an account of their money; they can also explain who gave it to them and what they spent it on. Practically all adults can also, provided it makes sense to them. Like any aspect of business it is important that you get started at a basic level, and 'the job will teach you how to do it' as you get practice at it.

Other than keeping a written record of what money is moving in and out, and keeping the evidence (the bills, receipts, chequebook stubs, etc.), there are no major rules about how to keep your accounts. You also have the back-up of your accountant, so you cannot fail! Because the job is usually done in

---

partnership with your accountant, it makes sense to organise yourself along the lines recommended by him/her.

Three Approaches to Bookkeeping – an Overview

Accountancy is really a process of grouping and summarising categories of cost and income so that you can see them and understand them more clearly. For example, how much did your phone cost you last year? The information on an itemised bill would be too detailed to answer this particular question, so a summary would be clearer – got by adding twelve monthly bills together. With a jig-saw the individual pieces are meaningless in themselves until they are put together to form the total picture; likewise individual bills are important components, but to see the full picture you need to see the totals.

Depending on the totals you want, there are different approaches you can take; the following are three.

1. By Group

Remember the KISS principle – "Keep It Simple, Stupid"

If you group your bills together under the relevant heading (car costs, wage costs, material costs) and add them up, then you have a basic set of expense accounts. If you do the same thing with each type of sale, you will have a basic set of sales accounts. Put the two together in the format given in the profit and loss account (see Chapter 8), and you have an actual profit and loss account for your business.

The clear advantage of this approach to bookkeeping is clarity and simplicity – you can clearly see the cost of each area and it's simple to maintain. The disadvantage is that you may not see the full picture until the end of the year, when money out (cost of sales and overheads) is subtracted from money in (sales), resulting in either a profit or a loss on your accounts. The way to counteract this delay in getting the information is to do up profit and loss accounts on a quarterly basis, thus combining the benefits of simplicity with timely information, allowing you to make any necessary changes to your business quickly.

2. By Month

In order to keep a closer eye on what's coming and going on the money front each month, you need to count up all ins and outs each month.

The simplest way of doing this is to summarise all on a double page, with the left-hand page listing any amounts of money in, and the right-hand page listing money out. Total both at the end of the month, and compare the two – you're either up money or down money on the month's business. If you're up (with bills paid) then happy days; if you're down, then figure out why, and quickly change the situation for the following month.

For a basic set of monthly accounts you only need four columns on each page, one each for:

1. The date you got paid/paid a bill
2. The details – what you got paid for/who you paid
3. A reference – which invoice was paid/what cheque number
4. The amount that was received/paid.

These are the same four headings you are required to fill in on a chequebook stub (money out) or lodgement slip (money in), so they're simple to maintain. In actual fact you're only copying the same information from these stubs onto a book in order to get a summary; the only new information involved is the summary total at the bottom, which is the main reason for the exercise.

A key to keeping any set of books is to 'Keep It Simple, Stupid'. The simplest system available is a chequebook account with a bank – all money out is recorded on a cheque stub, and all money in is recorded on a lodgement stub. This is the way practically all businesses account for their cash movements, because it couldn't be any simpler. If you move away from this system by paying some bills by cash, and not lodging some money from sales, you complicate things by creating a second system of cash movements – thus doubling your accounting problems.

A further aspect of keeping it simple is to operate on a cash basis – i.e., only write an entry into your books when payment is received and lodged (lodgement slip) or made (cheque). This saves complications with credit received or debts owed – keep a file of these separately, and only remove them from the file when paid.

3. Analysis

"Where did all my money go?" is a key question you must be able to answer.

Combining both of the above methods into one will create a third system which will answer the key questions 'where did the money come from?' and 'where did all the money go?'. The four-column system used above (date, details, reference, amount) is extended by a further five 'analysis' columns on each page, and the various amounts are entered a second time in the relevant column. This analysis should concentrate on grouping your main costs, e.g. labour (drawings/wages/subcontractors), transport (repayments/fuel/maintenance), office/workshop (electricity/telephone/office supplies/materials/goods for resale), other (all other costs, e.g. advertising, legal).

The benefit of this type of analysis is in allowing quick comparisons from one month to another between groups of cost and income. This enables analysis of growth/reductions in costs and income, and the taking of further remedial or supportive action as necessary.

Getting Organised and Keeping Accounts

Given the overview above, you now choose which system to use. Regardless of the system chosen, much of the organisation involved is the same so most (but not all) of the tips in this section will apply. In order to keep your accounts with the minimum of work, it is important to organise yourself with a SYSTEM that will Save Your Self Time, Energy, and Money. A system will work every time if you use it properly, but will break down if you start interfering with it.

Your first decision in organising an accounting system is deciding whether or not to channel all your cash movements through a current account (chequebook/online banking). It makes for easy accounting, and on that basis it will be the system described here.

As we describe the workings of an accounting system, the items you need to get are summarised with bullet points after each section.

It is your choice on whether to keep a paper-based system or to use your PC and a programme such as Excel or a specialist accounting package.

Start by opening a separate bank account for the business; keep a record of all 'cash in' going through your lodgement book, and all 'cash out' going through your chequebook, direct debits or cash withdrawals. Note: never remove a cheque or lodgement slip from the book until you've written up the stub.
To do this you'll need:

- A separate current bank account solely for your business
- A lodgement book
- A chequebook.

It is vital that the amount of lodgements tallies with your sales.

You must still keep your records as evidence, i.e. the purchase invoices you pay (out) and the sales invoices you get paid for (in). Those invoices arriving by post (e.g. telephone, electricity) can be recorded on the 'cash out' and then put directly into a ring binder, and those you collect on the road can be kept in a wallet/the cubbyhole until you get home (don't lose them!). Mark one binder 'Invoices in – 20XX', and the other 'Invoices out – 20XX'. Get two new binders each year.

For invoicing clients you'll need a duplicate book, with your business name printed on top (pre-printed or get a business stamp), or type your invoices in Word or Excel. As you go from month to month, use a divider to keep invoices for each month separate from each other.
To do this you'll need:

- Two separate ring binders
- A two-hole punch

- A duplicate book for your sales invoices
- If your duplicate book is not pre-printed you'll need a business stamp
- Folder dividers.

Make sure not to mix up the invoices/bills paid with those unpaid! Keep unpaid bills at the front of the ring binder, filing them under their proper subject/monthly divider only when they're paid. By keeping them at the front they serve as a reminder of what you owe at all times. Similarly, do not remove duplicate sales invoices from your book until paid – they remind you of what you're owed at all times.

To do this you'll need:
- Two sets of 10 dividers.

It is inappropriate to pay 'petty cash' (small cash) amounts by cheque. Anything below €20 may not merit a cheque, so pay it out of your own personal funds, i.e. cash from your pocket. Paying these little bills (e.g. drill bits, photocopying, stamps, etc.) all adds up, so staple these small receipts onto an A4 page, total them at month's end, and write a business cheque to your personal account for the amount. As with any other bill, write the cheque number and date of payment on the top of the sheet, and file it away as paid.

To do this you'll need:
- A stapler.

Remember, only pay to the amount of the actual receipts – lost receipts, like lost money, are lost and gone forever.

Having written up your cheque and lodgement stubs as you use them, you need to summarise both into a monthly total. Rather than use a blank page, it is easier if you use one that is ruled with 'Analysis' columns (known as an analysis book). Open a double page, and title the left-hand side 'Cash in', and the right-hand side 'Cash out', putting the month in question on the top of the page, and some of the headings already suggested on the top of each column.

On the 'Cash out' side record your cheque payments (stubs), bank charges, standing orders, and direct debits. On the 'Cash in' side record all the cash received and lodged (lodge all cash and cheques).

To do this you'll need:

- A nine-column analysis book.

If you use a till, keep your daily till rolls, and any cash receipts for amounts paid out from the till. Staple both into an ordinary hard-backed copybook, allowing a page for each day.

To do this you'll need:

- A hard-backed notebook/diary.

Total both sides of your analysis book each month, which gives you a monthly summary of what money was taken in and paid out by your business for the month. Order your bank statements to finish at the end of the month, and include any direct debits, interest, charges, etc. which didn't go through your chequebook. You cannot finalise your monthly totals until you get this statement, which means you cannot finish monthly totals until the first week of the following month. Alternatively, if you use online banking your statement is available immediately. Compare both totals, and at the bottom of the page calculate whether you are up or down money for the month.

To do this you'll need:

- Your bank statements
- A calculator.

This monthly balance will give you a clear picture of how your business has done in cash terms during the month. Also look at the total amount you owe (unpaid bills) and are owed (unpaid invoices out), and compare the two. Finally, look at the cash balance on your bank account. These four bits of financial information give a good indication of the state of your business.

Accounting for your money is probably the most important bit of work you will do each month. Like any work, you have to set aside time for it. Pencil in the afternoon of the first Friday of every month for this task, and after the first two months meet with your accountant or accounting mentor to check over what you've done. After that it will be plain sailing as you apply your new system, and keeping it done each month prevents it from building up into a major (and less valuable) task at any stage.

To this you'll need:

- An accountancy afternoon per month in your diary (first Friday)
- An appointment with your accountant (twice yearly).

You can't control your costs if you don't know what they are, and they are a key to profitability. If you can't measure them you can't manage them, so count them carefully with a view to reducing them.

Go to a new double page at the back of your book, and title it 'Annual Summary'. Using the same column headings for cash in and cash out, at the end of each month transfer the monthly totals onto these pages, which will give you a yearly total after twelve months. These are your trading figures for the year, and with very little work they become your profit and loss account.

Finally, your sales as outlined in your accounts should correspond with the amount of money lodged in your bank. Cross-check your actual bank statements with your accountancy records, and reconcile any discrepancies – ask your accountant for assistance if you have any difficulty.

In conclusion: *A simple accountancy strategy.*

1. You concentrate on making money
2. Set up a simple system to trap your accounting information
3. Summarise this information into monthly totals for cash in and out; total these to form yearly totals
4. Let your accountant complete your tax return, and inform you of your tax liability in plenty of time to put it aside.

Online banking is invaluable in keeping control of your money.

At the end of the day, the only way to become good at keeping your accounts is by doing them, with the guidance of your bookkeeper or accountant. After the first two months you will know what is needed and thereafter you will only need your accountant occasionally. Keeping your books is your responsibility. Always make sure you are in charge and know what is going on. It's your business and your livelihood; it's just another job for your accountant.

Employing an Accountant

You are not required by law to use an accountant. As a sole trader you can submit your own tax returns. As a limited company you can seek an audit exemption if you meet certain criteria (see www.cro.ie for details). Whether you are a sole trader or you form a limited liability company, engaging an accountant is advisable.

The main jobs for an accountant are:
1. Prepare tax returns – the work and the stress are dealt with by someone who knows what they are doing.
2. Provide tax advice – your accountant should more than pay for themselves with good advice. Make sure to ask how you might minimise your tax bill every year.
3. Prepare certified accounts – you will need independently prepared certified accounts in support of any application for a bank loan. As your business grows you will need access to finance other than your own. Be aware that as lenders get more cautious they are also likely to look for a tax clearance certificate and/or a revenue receipt for tax paid in the previous year.
4. Provide general business advice – a good accountant can give very good business advice, so your choice of accountant is an important decision for your business.

The more work they have to do for you the more they will charge, so complete the basic bookkeeping yourself and use the accountant for their professional expertise. Always negotiate a price with your accountant in advance. An accountant wouldn't let you into their house to work without first discussing the range of work to be done, and negotiating a good rate with you, so why would you not do the same?

Management Accounting

Management accounting is not complicated, it's based more on common sense than technical training. It is simply an analysis of 'where did all the money go?' and 'where did the money come from?'

Equally important is keeping an account of your time. Time is money in business, and needs to be budgeted just as carefully as money, so keep a time record (on a time-sheet or a diary) for your work. Comparing time invested with cash returned will enable you to refocus on areas showing the best return.

Understanding your financial position is your responsibility, not your accountant's.

Most businesses do some degree of management accounting. For instance a hotel will have a different till for the coffee dock, the bar, the conference centre, the guestrooms, the nightclub, etc. If they didn't they would have difficulty knowing the profitability of each separate area.

Financial Accounting

Preparing the 'Financial Statements' (end-of-year accounts) is principally the job of your accountant. They are the standard measurements developed over time to describe the financial situation of your business, and are used by bank managers, the tax office, and any third parties. Their preparation is a technical job, so a qualification in accountancy is generally needed.

The financial statements consist of the trading, profit and loss account and the balance sheet, and are statements (expressed in figures) about the business.

The trading account is simple, consisting of 'sales minus cost of sales equals gross profit'. Sales are your total sales for the year; cost of sales is just the cost of the materials or products you are reselling (e.g. drink supplies in a pub); and gross profit is what's left over before you pay the overhead bills.

The profit and loss account tells you how you have done during the year in terms of making or losing money. It consists of gross profit minus overheads equals net profit/loss. Overheads are the ongoing costs of being in business (e.g. rent, phone, etc.) and the net profit or loss is the final amount of money either made or lost on the year's trading.

The balance sheet is a sheet listing the financial balances for your assets (items of value), liabilities (money owed), and owner's equity (the remaining value for you as owner) at that date.

Counting Money – Cash or Accruals Basis?

The accruals basis includes income due under agreements regardless of whether it has been actually received or not. It includes expenses incurred regardless of whether they have been actually paid or not. It includes an estimate of the cost of consuming fixed assets during the period (depreciation). The cash basis only includes money actually received or paid in the period – i.e. no debtors, creditors, etc.

It is important that you adopt one position or the other. Be careful not to mix the two, e.g. use the accruals approach when counting what's owed to the business, and the cash approach when counting what the business owes.

From a small business point of view the best approach is the cash basis, with a separate balance for the money owed to the business (debtors) versus the money owed by the business (creditors). There are two main reasons – safety and simplicity.

In the final analysis, you cannot argue with the figures.

Firstly, the cash approach is the safest. If you don't build up any major bills with suppliers, paying for most things on a cash basis, you will avoid a lot of potential risk. Even if things go quiet for a few months, you will survive. The other side of the coin is that you collect your bills on a cash basis. Collect as the work is being done; you are not a bank, therefore you should avoid giving unnecessary credit.

Secondly, the cash approach is the simplest. Keeping accounts on what you owe and what you are owed can get complicated. The accruals approach is OK for larger businesses who have a computerised bookkeeping system and a dedicated bookkeeper to maintain it – but it takes time, and taking time without a need to is wasting time. The simplest method, in terms of work and in terms of accounting, is to keep your business on a cash basis as far as possible.

Having said that, there will always be a few outstanding bills in and out, and if both are kept as low as possible they won't be that important, and will usually cancel each other out.

Maintaining Working Capital

Working capital is the capital (cash) your business needs to keep working until you get paid. Maintaining enough working capital is essential to survival, and essential to being able to seize opportunities in the second. Working capital maintenance is based on good management of its constituent parts – cash-flow, debtors, creditors and stock. We'll look at each one in turn:

Cashflow
- Cash is king. Profitable businesses fail because of cash shortages.
- If giving credit, cash inflows and outflows will not coincide, causing cash shortages whilst awaiting payment.
- Set realistic forecasts for both sales and cash collection; compare actual to forecast at month end, and take action on cashflow.
- Arrange a short-term overdraft well in advance for seasonal surges in demand.
- The shorter your working capital cycle (i.e. from stock purchase to payment of invoice), the faster cash will be realised.
- Improve cash flow by reducing or suspending capital expenditure; do not mismatch short-term financing with long-term investment.
- If in a very tight cash position, only pay essential bills until more cash flows in; avoid returning to that position
- Surplus cash should be deposited at maximum interest rates.

Debtors

- Avoid giving credit if possible; offer early payment discount.
- Get bank and trade references to check credit worthiness.
- Set credit limits; send regular statements.
- Maintain accurate accounts for goods paid and payments received.
- Keep an aged debtors listing; insist on being paid on time.
- Effective credit control will ensure debts are settled quickly, and will help to avoid losing customers because of debt problems.

Creditors

- Avoid taking maximum credit except as a fall-back position.
- Can represent a short-term interest-free loan, helping cash flow, but taking time to manage carefully.
- Suppliers may withdraw credit facility, especially if payment is late or credit limits are exceeded.
- If not taking credit, arrange a clear price reduction.

Stock

- Only buy stock that you know will sell.
- Maintain good stock control procedures, avoiding damage, theft, obsolescence and expiration dates.
- Holding excessive stock costs money (rent, staff, insurance, etc.); investigate a 'just-in-time' system.
- Apply maximum and minimum stock limits; check what stock is moving well at the end of each month.
- Review the reliability of your suppliers, and use several if appropriate.
- Plan for seasonal surges in demand to avoid shortages.

Paying Yourself

For a small business starting off, you are usually the biggest expense! You are also usually the last to get paid. If cashflow is tight you can pay yourself by cheque from your business account each week, provided the cash is there. After you get established you can set up a standing order on your business account to transfer your drawings (wage) to your personal account each week.

Remember the need to maintain a good financial boundary between your personal and business affairs. Other than for your budgeted wage, do not use your business chequebook to pay any personal bills. If you do, account for these as additional drawings in the labour analysis column. Also beware of losing receipts for business expenses – if you cannot account for lost money or receipts, it's assumed to be part of your drawings i.e. you drew it out for your own needs.

It is important that you don't leave yourself out of the equation when it comes to payment. Some people struggle on, getting everyone else paid and forgetting themselves. By all means let it be your fall-back position in tight times, but don't set your drawings up this way. If the business is failing to pay you a reasonable wage for the effort you are putting into it, there's a problem, and talk it through with your accountant/business adviser.

If business is primarily about money, then counting it regularly is the key to its good health.

Benefits of Good Accounting

1. **Staying in business**. Not keeping a close eye on money in and out is one of the main reasons people go out of business. If the cash position was looked at regularly they would have known in time that their costs were too high, or their sales too low. Having seen trouble coming they could have avoided it.

2. **Peace of mind**. Having a good record of what's coming in and going out of your business will give you peace of mind, knowing that you are maintaining profitability and in control of your costs, and that you can hand it all over to your accountant to complete your tax return.

3. **Maximising profit and opportunity**. Good accounting will result in optimum pricing, and cost reductions. You can only comfortably grab opportunities if you know whether or not you can afford to.

Computerised Accounts

If you are computer literate, there are numerous bookkeeping packages available, ranging from simple spreadsheets (usually Excel based) to special accounting packages. Once the initial set up is done, such packages will do a lot of the hard work for you, and will add a sense of professionalism to your business. Accounting packages can do everything from generating quotes and invoices to calculating your VAT payments, your PAYE and PRSI, and preparing payslips for your employees.

Time is money – account for both.

Before you make your purchase, it would be useful to check what package your accountant uses so that both systems are compatible; many accountants use Sage. Another useful way of deciding which package to buy is to ask other small businesses which one they use or which one they'd recommend. Packages aimed at sole traders or start-up businesses cost in the region of €150; free 30-day trials are available with most packages.

Some examples:
- Advent: www.advent.ie
- Big Red Book: www.bigredbook.com
- Quickbooks: www.quickbooks.ie
- Sage: www.sage.ie
- Sort My Books: www.sortmybooks.ie
- Tas: www.tassoftware.ie

Evening Courses

There are several good evening courses in computerised bookkeeping so it could be a good use of your time to attend one. The County Enterprise Board (www.enterpriseboards.ie), your local VEC (www.ivea.ie), Institute of Technology (www.ioti.ie) or FÁS (www.fas.ie) office will have more information.

Record of monies received

MONEY IN		MONTH			ANALYSIS				
Date	Details	Ref	Total €	VAT					
	TOTALS for month								

Record of monies paid out

| MONEY OUT | | MONTH .... | | | ANALYSIS | | | | |
Date	Details	Ref	Total €	VAT	Labour	Transport	Office	Materials	Other
	TOTALS for month								

Notes

Chapter 8   Profit and Loss Account

Introduction

A profit and loss account is a one page summary, usually for a year, of the money taken into a business (sales) and paid out of the business (cost of sales and overheads), and the balance arising (either a profit or a loss).

Regardless of whether it is a multi-national corporation employing thousands or a small, part-time business, its profit and loss account will summarise these key figures. The profits or losses it shows are the basis on which your tax liability is calculated. It is important that you become familiar with its layout and the kind of information it contains, because this knowledge will serve you throughout your business career.

Turnover for vanity, profit for sanity.

An actual profit and loss account can be produced after the first year of trading, and will give an account of cash in (sales, grants, disposals, etc.), cash out (cost of sales, overheads, etc.) and the balance between these two (a profit or a loss). It's based directly on your actual accounts and forces you to focus on how big your profit is, not on the illusion of how big your business seems to be.

Forecasting

With a forecasted or projected profit and loss account you project the amount of your expected sales, overheads, and remaining profit or loss. Based on your vision for the future of your business you can create a forecast of the cash movements in and out of the business for the year ahead. It is particularly important for a small business to get a decent forecast, otherwise it has no targets to aim at. As a result it risks failure, and will almost certainly not be as profitable as it might.

A forecasted profit and loss account is a standard planning tool used across business today, and is an essential part of every business plan. A saying that holds true in business is that 'you cannot argue with the figures'; opinions can be expressed about this and that, but accurate figures make issues and decision-making clearer. The accuracy of forecasted figures is only as good as the research and the judgements of their creator, but they cannot be purely guesswork.

Your overheads figure should be within 5% to 10% accuracy, because you must know how much your costs will be before you take them on – otherwise you are gambling, not taking a calculated risk. Your sales figures are more speculative, especially if it's a brand new venture. As a result you will know how much you must sell in order to meet your costs (your break-even point). Start with calculating your costs and calculate your required sales afterwards.

Make sure you consider your forecasted profit and loss account, as it's a lot less expensive to make your mistakes on paper. You then have a 'benchmark' or set of targets against which you can chart your progress each month.

Vision

The vision and determination of the owner has a major bearing on the profitability of the business. Profit is the lifeblood of business, an absolute necessity. Without clear profit the business becomes stagnant, with no spare cash to reinvest in equipment, property, savings, and general expansion. It becomes a struggling business.

Profit is the lifeblood of business.

Some people are inclined to stop taking in cash when they reach their break-even point. Why do they not continue on until they hit a higher target of clear profit? The reason could be that people will struggle on until they get their bills paid and enough drawings to keep themselves going, and will settle for this. They do not have a clear profit goal in mind. They tend to forget that the main reason to start a business in the first place is to make extra profit.

On the other hand, some owners simply will not stop searching for improvements and additional income streams until they achieve profitability. They think creatively about sales, with several product options and sales strategies, and keep going until they drive their business into the profit zone. Much of this desire to reach profits can be seen in the thoroughness and detail with which they prepare their projected profit and loss account.

The Three Keys to Profit

1. **Costs**. It will be next to impossible to make profits if you don't know what your costs are likely to be. It's just not possible to know if sales of €1,000 per week are enough if you don't know whether your costs are going to be €200, €300, €400, or €500. A rough idea is not good enough, so work thoroughly, getting quotations and experienced opinions where possible.

2. **Prices**. You need to have a clear pricing policy for your products and services. Modelling your pricing on the competition is always a good starting point as it gives you an indication of what customers are prepared to pay. It's only by trying a few different price levels, and comparing these to both your competitors' prices and your overhead costs, that you'll be able to discover your optimum pricing levels.

3. **Sales**. It is essential to have some sales targets for your business each year, otherwise it will be very difficult to motivate yourself, and very difficult to measure how you are doing. Look at your business in its different product groups/income streams as outlined in marketing, and then quantify the amount of sales you hope to get from each product group. There are two steps in doing this: set sales volume in units (e.g. lawns mowed, meals served, appointments made, etc.) and then multiply this number of units by the sales value of each unit. Take average jobs at average prices for your units where jobs vary a lot.

Working the Keys to Profit

Knowing the keys to profit is one thing, but working them is another. In general you need two of the three keys to profit to be operating properly in order to make profit; if only one works, it's not enough.

1. Reduce costs

Example: The effect of **reduced costs** on your bottom line (net profit)

	Case I	Case II - 20%	Case III - 30%
Sales	€40,000	€40,000	€40,000
Cost of sales	- €8,000	- €6,400	- €5,600
Gross profit	€32,000	€33,600	€34,400
Overheads	- €10,000	- €8,000	- €7,000
Net profit	€22,000	€25,600	€27,400

If you can operate your business on a very low cost base it will survive indefinitely. Many businesses that boomed during the Celtic Tiger years got used to operating on a high cost base and may not survive in tougher times. Always minimise unnecessary costs (e.g. high transport/phone bills) by examining them in detail on a regular basis.

'A pound saved is as good as two earned' goes the old saying, because it costs money to make money. It is crucial that you keep a close eye on costs, as a lot of little holes will sink a ship. The established aid to achieving cost control and reduction is to work out an accurate budget before starting, and then to insist that costs stay within the budgeted figure. Parkinson's Law of 'expenditure rises to meet the income available' comes to mind, and helps us understand that the only way to control costs is to put a limit on them. Every medium and large company works to a budget as an essential aid in maximising profitability, and it is important that you do so too.

A word of advice: drawings are usually the biggest cost for any new business, so it's important to minimise this cost. This means looking at your own expenses also, and reducing these as far as possible.

2. Increase prices

Example: The effect of a **price increase** on your bottom line (net profit) assuming overheads remain fixed

	Case I	Case II + 30%	Case III + 50%
Sales	€40,000	€52,000	€60,000
Cost of sales	- €8,000	- €8,000	- €8,000
Gross profit	€32,000	€44,000	€52,000
Overheads	- €10,000	- €10,000	- €10,000
Net profit	€22,000	€34,000	€42,000

Total equity is comprised of both cash equity and sweat equity.

If demand increases, prices can be increased (more work at higher prices). Increases in price are the simplest way of improving your bottom line, as neither the cost of sales nor your overheads increase as a result. However, sales volume may start to fall off with each price increase. The extent to which this happens depends partly on the level of customer satisfaction you deliver through the other elements of your marketing mix.

Given the recessionary times at present, the scope for major price increases is very limited, so this may be the least effective of your three keys to profitability.

3. Sell more stuff

Example: The effect of **sales growth** on your bottom line (net profit)

	Case I	Case II + 30%	Case III + 50%
Sales	€40,000	€52,000	€60,000
Cost of sales @ 20%	-€8,000	-€10,400	-€12,000
Gross profit	€32,000	€41,600	€48,000
Overheads	-€10,000	-€11,000	-€12,000
Net profit	€22,000	€30,600	€36,000

The direct cost of sales (supplies) will increase at the relevant percentage, whilst overheads do not generally increase substantially.

How does Sales Growth Happen?

The reality of the situation is that although you may want to get up to a targeted sales figure of €1,000 per week (€48,000 per year) it may or may not happen in the first year. So, how does it happen in years two and three?

Firstly, your sales will go up as your reputation for good work spreads. This means less downtime, or fewer days with no payment.

Secondly, your speed will go up with practice, and with each new piece of equipment purchased, so you'll be able to get through more work. This rate of increase will slow by year 3 unless you take on extra staff.

If you were to undertake a review of your business at the end of the first year you might draw the wrong conclusions, as you'd have made a premature judgement on the underlying profitability. It takes time to build a business by building a loyal customer base, building sales, and building your productive capacity.

Gross Profit and Net Profit Percentages

The profit and loss account is the basis for your tax returns, and is used for desk audits by the Revenue Commissioners. Desk audits are easy to carry out as tax returns are submitted electronically through ROS (Revenue Online Service), allowing returns to be compared to trends and patterns in the particular business or profession. They will compare exceptionally high input costs to the average for the trade. In the example below business B is obviously understating its sales, yet including all costs. This shows up immediately by doing a simple calculation of the gross profit percentage. If business A represents the average for the trade, then business B can expect a full tax audit to investigate its comparatively low profit percentages.

Profit Percentages

	A	*B*
Sales	€100,000	€100,000
Cost of sales	€60,000	€80,000
Gross profit	€40,000	€20,000
Gross profit %	40%	20%
Overheads	€4,000	€4,000
Net profit	€36,000	€16,000
Net profit %	36%	16%

Cost of Sale or Overhead?

A cost of sale normally relates to the purchase of goods for resale, e.g. the beer for a pub, the timber for a joiner, the food for a restaurant, and it varies in direct proportion to sales. Little can usually be done to influence these costs from within the business as it's the external market forces of supply and demand that decide it.

Overhead costs reflect more on the efficiency of the business, and cost much the same whether the business is busy or not.

If you are wondering about whether or not a particular cost fits into either category, don't worry too much; just make sure you include it in one or the other, and make sure not to double count it.

Break Even as Soon as Possible

A good start is half the battle.

Consider the scenario of two businesses with equal profit growth (€4,000 per year), working from two different starting points. Even though the growth in profitability is the same, the result is quite different, because business A gets into profit just one year earlier.

Business A: Breaking even in the **first** year

Year 1	Break even x 50 weeks	€0
Year 2	€80 profit x 50 weeks	+ €4,000
Year 3	€160 profit x 50 weeks	+€8,000
End result	Solid profitability	+ €12,000

Business B: Breaking even in the **second** year		
Year 1	*€80 loss X 50 weeks*	- €4,000
Year 2	Break even x 50 weeks	€0
Year 3	€80 profit x 50 weeks	+ €4,000
End result	Back to square one	€0

Of even greater impact would be a case where the owner of business B got tired of struggling, and decided to quit at the end of the third year because he figured he had made no profit overall.

Both of these scenarios underline the importance of attaining profitability as soon as possible. A good start is half the battle, so try your very best to get your business off to a good start, at least breaking even in the first year.

Cashflow or Profit and Loss Account?

A cashflow forecast shows month by month the predicted flow of cash in and out of the business, and the closing balance will show what your bank balance will look like at the end of the month. It is concerned with the timing of the flow of cash through your business bank account, not your profits or losses.

A projected profit and loss account shows the predicted profit your business is likely to make for a particular period (month, quarter, year). It is concerned with profit or loss, not the flow of cash.

Cashflow forecasts

- Identify potential cash shortfalls before they happen.
- Enable potential surplus cash to be identified and used efficiently.
- Allow you to plan that adequate cash is available for any necessary capital expenditure.

There is a thin line between a profit and a loss – make sure you end up the right side of it.

Projected profit and loss

Comparing projected with actual profit and loss identifies difficulties early and allows you to:

- Take appropriate action.
- Make realistic plans for the business.
- Project your net profit before drawings and tax.

If you maintain a good working capital balance, you can handle a stop-start cashflow. However, profit is the ultimate goal.

Conclusion

1. If your forecasts are profitable, make the figures stick; if loss-making, then think them out again and re-work them.
2. Always apply the three-step profitability formula: reduce costs; increase prices; sell more stuff.
3. Remember: 'One look ahead is better than ten looks behind', so forecast ahead to avoid ending up in serious trouble.

Know your weekly overhead figure, i.e. the amount you need to earn for the business each week before you start earning for yourself.

Completing the Exercises

If you're new to business and profit and loss accounts, you might need some assistance completing the following worksheets. Your local enterprise officer (Partnership Company or Department of Social Protection) may provide assistance, or you can attend a course on business planning and forecasting.

Exercise 1

'Budget for overheads' is a very important exercise. If you think carefully about each cost (make a note as to how you made your calculations) you should be able to forecast to within 5% accuracy. A 10% margin for error is the most that would be acceptable if your calculations are to be useful.

Think again about any costs that at first glance you might not think you'll have – for example, part-time staff. Who will cover for you if you're sick, on holidays, or falling behind on a big job and need a helping hand? Even one day a month at €100 per day adds up to €1,200 per year. Ignoring a thousand here and a thousand there quickly adds up to €5,000 or €6,000, which would be a serious understatement and could put you out of business. In general you won't foresee all the costs as there are always unexpected ones, so it is prudent to allow 5%-10% for unforeseen costs. Don't understate costs – better to properly allow for them on paper, and then beat this budget in reality. Don't over-inflate your cost either just to be on the safe side, as that's just as unrealistic and may stop you from starting altogether.

Exercise 2

Refer back to Chapter 3 on Marketing in order to help clarify your different product groups. Figure out how many units you expect to sell within each group, and at what price; then multiply units by price to get a sales value per group. Do this exercise for each month if your sales fluctuate widely; otherwise go directly to the total sales value column.

Exercise 3

Transfer subtotals from exercise 1 onto the corresponding headings on exercise 3, transfer sales total from exercise 2, complete calculations for year 1, add 20% for year 2 and a further 10% for year 3.

Exercise 1 – Budget for Overheads

	Total	Description
Employment Costs		
Part-time/casual staff wages		
Full-time staff wages		
Employer's PRSI		
Overtime, bonuses, etc.		
Total employment costs		

	Total	Description
Transport Costs		
Lease costs		
Fuel		
Insurance/tax		
Maintenance and repairs		
Deduct private use	[ ]	
Total transport costs		

	Total	Description
Production Costs		
Subcontractors' charges		
Heat, light and power		
Hire/lease equipment		
Premises rent/rates		
Incidental materials		
Total production costs		

	Total	Description
General Administration		
Advertising/promotion		
Telephone/postage		
Employee/public insurance		
Stationery/office supplies		
Professional fees		
Total general administration		

	Total	Description
Finance/Depreciation		
Interest on loans		
Bank charges/fees		
Motor depreciation		
Equipment depreciation		
Total finance/depreciation		

Calculations

Exercise 2

Forecasted Sales

Income stream		Q 1	Q 2	Q 3	Q 4	Total sales €
		Quarters 1-4				
Product Group 1	Sales units					
	Sales value €					€
Product Group 2	Sales units					
	Sales value €					€
Product Group 3	Sales units					
	Sales value €					€
Product Group 4	Sales units					
	Sales value €					€
Product Group 5	Sales units					
	Sales value €					€

Annual total. Transfer to the trading, profit and loss account	€

Exercise 3
Trading, Profit and Loss Account

	Year 1	Year 2	Year 3
Sales			
Cost of sales			
Gross profit			
Gross Profit %			
Overheads			
Employment costs			
Transport costs			
Production			
General administration			
Finance/depreciation			
Total overheads			
Net profit/(loss) **(Gross profit – total overheads)**			

Chapter 9   Outline Business Plan

Business Planning

We have already considered creation which involves three stages: Thought, Word, and Action (Chapter 1). Business planning is concerned with stage two, i.e. Word, and includes the written word, figures, and drawings. By developing a well thought-out plan you create the second stage of reality, the paper reality.

By failing to plan you are planning to fail.

The main purpose of creating this reality is to give yourself a better picture of how your business might work out. It's a bit like trying to hit any goal or target; the clearer you can see it, the better your chance of hitting it. The clearer the picture you can build of your business, the better your chances of achieving it in the final stage of creation, which is Action. A picture on its own would be one-dimensional, but once you put quantities of time and money into the equation, it becomes much more powerful. The more carefully you think out the figures, the more likely you are to achieve them.

Without this clarity it is possible to continue to break even, maybe even break through to profits, but impossible to reach the kind of profits that a well-planned approach would have given you. Not breaking through to profits is what we referred to earlier as 'successfully failing'. You have not failed, but neither have you really succeeded.

Why a Plan?

A business plan has two main purposes –
1.   Calculation
2.   Communication.

Calculation involves engaging your mind with the different quantities of time and money needed to make a profit. It gives you an opportunity to make your mistakes on paper, rather than losing money and possibly years of your time. Once you are happy with your calculations, you are then in a good position to communicate these to other people.

Communication means letting other people know about your plans. You need to have a plan prepared before you meet any investor, be they a bank, grant agency, or partner. You can supply the time, they can supply the money. The more prepared you are the better the chances of them backing you. Remember our definition of luck – 'when preparation meets opportunity'.

The potential financier will ask you questions to make sure you know what you are talking about. If you don't know (e.g. if someone else prepared your plan for you) you are in trouble, because your financier will figure it's only a paper exercise for you and that you won't be able to take it any further. It is OK to get an accountant or enterprise officer to polish up your plan, provided you've done and understood the preparatory work yourself.

Some people make a big deal about a plan, and never get through to the Action of stage three. A plan is not the end of the journey, it's only the road map, plotting your course of action. The action is the journey. So keep your plan short enough to be read quickly, yet detailed enough to be meaningful.

Know Your Plan

It is cheaper to make your mistakes on paper than in action.

A question that's often asked is whether it is more important to have a plan on paper than to have it in one's head. 'In your head to calculate; and on paper to communicate' is the usual reply. It is very important that this plan is clearly understood in your own head, and this is more important than having it well documented on paper for others, although both aspects go hand in hand. The clearer you have it on paper the more clear it is likely to be in your head, as the writing will have clarified your thoughts.

Your first draft plan will contain a good bit of guesswork, but your final plan should be well researched, with figures to back up your forecasts. Put your best foot forward and plan with courage for a bigger situation than you are presently in, so that it doesn't go out of date immediately.

Four Areas to be Planned For

All business plans have four main sections – Management, Marketing, Finance, and Production.

Management

A simple section where you outline some basic information about yourself, your experience, your qualifications, etc. and what your vision is for the years ahead. This is a crucial section as the success or failure of your business is very dependent on the people running it, be that just yourself or additional management.

Marketing

A vital part of any business plan, and that most closely read. It's best to organise your marketing plan along the lines of the four P's: Product, Price, Place and Promotion (see Chapters 3 and 4). What the reader really wants to know is how well you know your target market and whether your mix of products, price levels and promotional strategies are appropriate to them.

Finance

The business plan will require you to think about key financial aspects of your business. You need to know how much it will cost to start up. You need to know how much it costs to run your business each week. You will need to know how much money you have to take in each week to cover these costs, cover your drawings, and provide for your profits.

Production

This section is all about how you are going to get things done. You will outline what equipment you have now and what extra equipment you need; likewise with premises. The production process itself, what time it takes, what labour you need, what stock and where to get it, and any other issues relating to actually getting work produced also need to be outlined.

In Conclusion

Your plan is an expression of your vision for the future.

There is no room for uncertainly or lack of focus if a business is to be successful. Business demands clear thinking, clear plans, and clear action to produce results. The more focused your resources and efforts are, the more likely you are to be successful.

In Japan they spend on average four times longer in the planning process than their European counterparts. As a result, a small economy with no major resources of steel manages to be one of the largest car manufacturers in the world, whilst their British counterparts no longer own a single manufacturing car plant, having had over 50 of them after the second world war. A lot of this comes down to clarity of planning, and planning for zero defects was the Japanese approach. Thus you can sit into a Japanese car more than ten years old, and the radio, wipers, etc. will still be working. Not so with European or American manufactured cars until quite recently, when they had to improve their whole planning and quality assurance procedures in order to match the standards of their Japanese competitors.

In conclusion, planning and carefully thinking things through are vitally important elements of getting the job done correctly. It brings to mind the saying 'It takes less work to succeed than to fail', which is where planning to avoid unnecessary mistakes proves its worth. Putting your planning brain into gear before you put your money and time into action will save you a lot of both.

Business Plan Templates

Over the following pages the business plan template required by the Department of Social Protection to qualify for the Enterprise Allowance is presented.

If you are applying to other agencies for grant assistance, e.g. County Enterprise Board, or LEADER company, they will have their own business plan template. It will largely be similar to the template that follows but you should check to establish their preferred format. For examples of business plan templates see www.enterpriseboards.ie or www.first-step.ie

Business Plan Workbook
Contact details

Business name	
Owner's name	
PPS number	
Address	
Telephone number	
Mobile number	
Email address	
Website address	
Business description *Short description of the business you are starting*	
Proposed start date	

Management

This section looks at how you will manage your business and who else will be involved

1. Why do you want to start this business?	
2. What experience do you have of working in this type of business? *e.g. doing it, selling for it, etc.*	
3. Who will make most management decisions?	

	Task	Who'll do it?	Time required	Frequency
4. Administration: Who will perform the secretarial, bookkeeping and sales tasks in the business?	Bookkeeping			
	Sending and paying bills			
	Quotations and debt collection			
	Typing/filing/letter writing			
	Banking and tax returns			
	Ordering suppliers			
	Sales and marketing			

5. How will you ensure that you get paid for jobs done and get paid on time?	
6. What other type of work can you (or your spouse/partner) do outside of the business if your business is slow to take off?	
7. Where do you want to see your business in _**one**_ year's time?	
8. Where do you want to see your business in _**five**_ years' time?	

	Type of training	Who will do the training?		
		You	Spouse/partner	Other
9. What type of business training do you think you may need during the coming year?	Sales and marketing ☐			
	Bookkeeping ☐			
	Taxation ☐			
	Other *(Specify)* _____ ☐			

10. Business registration	Are you registered with the Revenue Commissioners (form TR1)?	Yes		No	
	Do you have a Tax Clearance Certificate (form TC1)?	Yes		No	
	Have your registered your business name with the Companies Registration Office?	Yes		No	
	Have you registered with the Revenue Commissioners as an employer?	Yes		No	
	Have you registered with the Revenue Commissioners for VAT?	Yes		No	
	Do you intend to form a limited company?	Yes		No	
	Have your registered the domain name for your website?	Yes		No	

11. What accountant will you use?	

Marketing

This section looks at your product/service; pricing, place and promotion.

1. What makes you think there is a demand for your business?	

2. If your business involves making and/or *selling products*, please list the main products and prices. (If you already have a price list please attach)	Product type	Price per unit
	1.	€
	2.	€
	3.	€
	4.	€
	5.	€
	6.	€

3. If your business involves *providing services* please list the main services and how you will charge. For each, state whether you will charge per hour, day or job.	Service type	Price	
	1.	€	Per hour/day/job
	2.	€	Per hour/day/job
	3.	€	Per hour/day/job
	4.	€	Per hour/day/job
	5.	€	Per hour/day/job

4. What geographical area will you cover with the business?	

5.	What types of customer do you expect to buy from you?	**What type of people,** e.g. professionals, housewives, students, farmers, businesses, tradesmen, etc.	
		1.	2.
		3.	4.

6.	How will you advertise your business in order to attract your customers?	Flyers ☐	Business cards ☐	Letterhead ☐
		Van signage ☐	Premises signage ☐	Event sponsorship ☐
		Local radio ☐	Newspaper ☐	Branded clothing ☐
		Invoice books ☐	Trade shows ☐	Website ☐

7.	What other ways might you promote your business?	
8.	Summarise the features and benefits of your product/service/ business?	
9.	Who are your main competitors and where do they operate?	
10.	What can you do to improve your product/service/ business to be better than your competitors?	

Finance

This section looks at money needed for the business, how much you will take in and how much you will pay out.

A. Investment and start-up costs

1. Estimate how much you have already invested in the following items.	Equipment	Transport	Workspace	Materials	Total
	€	€	€	€	€ A

2. What additional investment will be needed?	Equipment	Transport	Workspace	Materials	Total
	€	€	€	€	€ B

Total Investment in your business (A+B) =	€ C

3. Where will you get the finance you need for your investment?	Already invested (A)	Savings	Grants	Loans	Future income	Total
	€	€	€	€	€	€ C

Calculations / additional information

B. Profit & Loss: Money that will come in & go out during first year, and the profit or loss made

1. Sales	On average, how many jobs can you complete each week?	No:	A
	On average, how much will you get for each job?	€	B
	Weekly cash in = (multiply A by B)	€	C
Total annual sales	= (multiply **C** by **48** weeks)	€	D
Cost of sales	How much will you spend on supplies (% cost of sales X total sales)?	€	E
GROSS PROFIT (F)	Subtract E from D	€	F

2. Overheads	Amount per year	**Brief description** *Short note of what you are including in your figures*
Full-time/part-time wages	€	
PRSI @ average 10% of wages	€	
Van/car repayments	€	
Fuel	€	
Insurance and tax	€	
Maintenance and repairs	€	
Electricity, telephone, postage	€	
Hire or lease equipment	€	
Rent and rates	€	
Disposable items	€	*(e.g. blades, drill bits, etc.)*
Advertising	€	
Other insurances	€	
Office supplies	€	

Accountant/solicitor fees	€	
Interest and bank charges	€	
Vehicle wear and tear	€	
Equipment wear and tear	€	
TOTAL overheads (G)	€	

3. Net profit/loss	Gross profit (F)	€
	Minus total overheads (G)	€
	Net profit or loss (H)	€

Calculations / additional information

Production This section looks at premises, equipment and materials needs.

1. Describe where you will operate your business from. Will you have separate business premises or operate from home/your van etc.?	
2. How suitable are the premises and do they need any extension or modification?	

3. Which of the following licences or permits do you have to operate your business?

Planning permission ☐	Health & Safety certificate ☐	Safe Pass cert ☐
Various insurances ☐	HACCP *(Food business)* ☐	C2 Certificate ☐

Driving licences ☐   Classes _____

4. List the additional tools and equipment, transport, premises and materials you will require for start-up.

Tools and equipment	1.	2.	3.
	4.	5.	6.
	7.	8.	9.
	10.	11.	12.
	13.	14.	15.
Transport	Van/truck ☐	Car ☐	Trailer ☐
Premises	Workshop ☐	Office ☐	None ☐

	Type of materials	Supplier	Location
5. **What different materials will you require for your business, and who and where are your suppliers?**			

Have you secured trade discounts with any of the above

YES ☐   NO ☐   % Agreed _____

6. **Where will you get additional labour as needed or specialist skills as required?**	

Calculations / additional information

Notes

Chapter 10   Taxation

Introduction

Taxes are essential to the running of any state, and were first introduced by the Romans. A modern country that provides services to the public in the form of social welfare, education, transport, health, industrial development, Gardai, army, fire service, water, etc. simply must collect tax in order to pay for those services.

There are only two certainties in life – death and taxes.

Most people don't mind paying their fair share of tax provided they know that everyone else does likewise, and provided they feel it's being spent properly. The collection of taxes is the job of the Revenue Commissioners, and in recent years they cannot be faulted for their ability to collect from tax evaders at all levels in society. The proper spending of the money is down to the government and that is a separate issue!

Taxes can be broadly divided into direct taxes, e.g. income tax, corporation tax and stamp duty, and indirect taxes like VAT and excise duty. We will look at income tax, PRSI and the new Universal Social Charge (USC) for the self-employed in this chapter. In the next chapter we will examine VAT for small business owners and employers' PAYE/PRSI.

Your main job in business is to make a profit, and like many business people you can choose to leave the tax details to your accountant. However, you must know the basics before you can effectively delegate this important job.

Tax Myths

There's a lot of half-baked nonsense floating around with regard to tax, and if you believe it you'll end up in trouble. You're far better off to know nothing about tax and leave it to your accountant, than to know the wrong thing. A good place to start in getting to know what role taxation will play in your business is to tackle a few of these misleading myths.

1. **If you're clever you can avoid paying any tax.**
   Not if you need to earn a reasonable income; in the final analysis you have to show how you live, and pay for your home, car, lifestyle, etc. These things all cost money, and unless your earnings are very low (less than €4,004 per year) you will have to pay tax on them like everybody else. Be aware that even if you make a loss, you still have to pay €253 PRSI towards your pension.

2. **The self-employed get better tax allowances than employees.**
   They actually get a lower tax credit (€1,650 lower – they do not get a PAYE credit) which partly compensates for the fact that they can claim for some expenses (e.g. motor) that employees cannot. In general the tax breaks are available to higher earners, be they business or salaried people. The distinction should be between the high earners and the low earners, not between employees and the self-employed. There's many a very poor self-employed person, and many a very wealthy employee.

3. **If you're in business you'll get the VAT back.**
   Wrong. Firstly, unless you choose to register for and collect VAT, you just pay it and forget about it like everybody else. Secondly, even if you do register you don't really get your VAT back – you offset it against your VAT return every two months, and usually still have a balance to pay.

4. **I'm only 'small fry'; if I keep my head down the 'tax man' won't notice.**
   The 'tax man' will expect you to contribute as much to the public purse from your self-employment as if you were an employee, and why shouldn't he? The tax system is fairly tight at this stage with few evaders; all public sector payments (including grants) and more and more licences require up-to-date tax clearance certificates.

The Revenue Commissioners maintain tax records for every person legally in the state for the duration of their working lives, and when it comes to claiming a pension you will be glad that they did.

5. **I don't have to pay tax on my first year's income.**

   Yes you do – you just don't have to hand it over to the revenue until the second year. Not paying it during the first year means you'll have two years' tax to pay during the second year – a double hit. That's why, although not obliged to, you are advised to pay tax as near as possible to the amount due after you have completed your first tax year.

6. **If I get a good accountant he'll show me how to dodge tax.**

   Wrong! Accountants are professionals who must develop and maintain a reputation for honest dealings with the tax authorities on behalf of all their clients. They will advise you on how to legitimately avoid tax, but not how to evade tax (which is illegal).

7. **If I 'play dumb' and pretend I didn't know and have no money, they'll leave me alone.**

   Wrong. Neither stupidity nor reckless spending is a defence against not meeting your obligations. Some of the duties that go with self-employment are registering for tax, keeping your accounts, and paying your tax bill.

8. **If he wants it then it's up to the tax man to calculate and collect my tax.**

   Wrong. The system that operates is a self-assessment system, meaning it's up to you to calculate and pay your own tax liability. It would cost a fortune to have tax inspectors chasing every Tom, Dick and Harry for their tax. In order to make sure people make accurate returns, there are enough inspectors to 'audit' one in eight taxpayers each year.

An audit is a thorough check through your books (which you're obliged to keep for a minimum of six years) in order to verify the accuracy of your tax returns.

9. **If I buy loads of equipment, I can write it all off against tax in year 1.**
   Wrong. You can write a percentage of business plant and equipment off against tax – 12.5% per year over eight years to reflect wear and tear. However, if you lease the equipment you can accelerate this write-off to the period of the lease. As with other expenses, it doesn't make sense to spend €1,000 euro just to save €200 (at 20% tax) or €410 (at 41% tax). Incurring unnecessary expenses just to avoid paying tax would be like cutting off your nose to spite your face.

10. **Tax evasion is the same as tax avoidance.**
    No, although the end result is the same – i.e. you end up paying less tax – but tax evasion is illegal and tax avoidance isn't. Tax evasion is where you understate your actual earnings or inflate your expenses in order to underpay your tax. Tax avoidance, on the other hand, is where you use legitimate tax incentives, considered worthwhile by the government, in order to reduce your tax bill. The most obvious of these is a contribution to an approved pension plan, which is tax deductible up to certain limits depending on your age.

Registering for Tax

Once you decide to start your own business, you need to notify the Revenue Commissioners of this change of tax status by registering as self-employed. You can do this by filling in a Registration Form TR1 which is available from any tax office (if you are setting up a company you should use Form TR2). There is no advantage in delaying this registration, and the disadvantages include losing out on PRSI contributions, and a possible backdating of any assessment for tax. On the TR1 form you can register for any or all of the following:

- Income Tax
- Employer's PAYE/PRSI
- Value Added Tax

Most people starting off will only register for income tax if they don't plan to employ anyone and if they expect their turnover to be so low that they aren't required to register for VAT.

If you decide to employ someone you must register as an employer for PAYE/PRSI immediately you start to pay them. If you decide to set up a company, the company must register as an employer and operate PAYE/PRSI on the pay of directors (most likely yourself) even if there are no other employees.

Self-employed people assess themselves for tax (usually with the help of their accountant) which gives greater control over, and extra responsibility for, their tax affairs.

You must register for VAT if your annual turnover exceeds or is likely to exceed the following annual limits:
- €75,000 in respect of the supply of goods (e.g. joinery, coffee shop)
- €37,500 in respect of the supply of services (e.g. cleaning, gardening).

You may choose to register for VAT even if you don't reach these limits, which will be of benefit if you are supplying to the VAT registered trade, e.g. shops, as they don't mind being charged VAT because they can offset it against their bill. Once registered, you can do likewise with the VAT you've been charged (i.e. offset it against your tax bill). However, if you are supplying to non-VAT registered customers they won't want to pay VAT so you will be better off not registering until you hit the turnover threshold that requires you to.

If you have paid tax previously under PAYE you will keep the same Personal Public Service number (PPS). If you set up a company the company will be given a separate registration number, and as a director of the company you will retain your own PPS number for your personal tax.

Income Tax

Under the self-assessment system you are responsible for making your own tax returns. You pay tax on the annual profits of your business (the tax year runs from January 1st to December 31st).

If you also have a job (either full or part time) you can pay the income tax due on your business activities separately. Your income will be totalled for the purpose of determining the rate at which you pay tax. You will also pay tax on any other income you receive such as investment income, rental income, etc.

If you don't keep proper accounting records you have no defence against what Revenue might estimate you owe – so keep proper records.

As a self-employed person you will be taxed under the Pay and File Self-Assessment system. You pay your tax (money) and file your returns (the figures) before 31st October each year.

Under this system there are two separate jobs to be done:

- You must pay the preliminary tax due for the current year and any remaining balance from the previous year's assessment
- You must file the tax return (i.e. the figures) for the previous year.

Because October 31st is the final date, this means you have to guess or estimate what sales profits you'll make in the following two months of November and December, and pay any shortfall the following year. Thus the tax you pay each year is made up of an estimate for the current year (called preliminary tax) plus the exact balance left unpaid from last year.

Similarly, the reason you are filing your figures for the previous year is to allow a full tax year to finish. It is impossible to finalise figures in October because the year doesn't finish until December.

You do not have to pay preliminary tax by October 31st of your first year in business, because although you are building up a tax bill you may not have that much to pay. However, if you have been doing a lot of business it is recommended that you pay preliminary tax as near to your final liability as you can estimate. This will avoid cash flow problems the following year, when you will have to pay the bulk of two years' tax at the one time (all of year one, plus preliminary tax for year two).

October 31st is chosen as the date because the government needs to know what taxes are in before it can accurately do up the 'Budget' for its spending in the coming year, which it normally releases a few weeks later during the first week of December.

Tax Tips

Income from all sources is added together to get your total income for tax purposes.

1. **'All I earn is not mine to keep'**
   This is the most realistic attitude to taxation for the self-employed. When you were a PAYE tax payer what you earned was yours to do what you liked with, but this is one of the main changes that comes with self-employment – you don't pay your tax as you earn it. This means you must pay it later, so all you earn is not yours to keep.

2. **Set aside a percentage (approx. 10-15%) of your gross profit for your income tax bill.**
   This implies that you need to include an allowance for tax in your pricing. If you are registered for VAT you must charge it on every invoice. As you must also pay for income tax you should also charge for it on every invoice. The fact that you don't have to itemise it separately doesn't mean it doesn't exist – you still have to pay it every year (before 31st October).

3. **Keep on top of your tax payments as you go along by using Revenue's Direct Debit scheme.**
   That way it won't mount up to several thousand in October, resulting in maybe having to take out a loan to pay your bill. After your first full year of trading, get your accountant to calculate taxes due. Then set up a direct debit to pay this by the October 31st deadline.

4. **Always pay your PRSI – it's your contributory pension.**
   Always pay it to the full amount due, as this gives you a full year's contributions, whilst leaving it short gives you no 'stamps' for the year – it's an all or nothing situation. Even if you make a loss there's a minimum of €253 PRSI to be paid.

5. **Reduce your tax liability through investment in a tax-avoiding pension scheme, etc.**
   Use the services of your accountant in the first instance and your investment broker in the second to advise you on these.

6. **If you form a company and it pays tax at 12.5% it may be possible to save substantially on your tax liability.**
   This will be of little, if any, benefit in most cases until you're earning enough to hit the higher (41%) tax bracket. Any income you draw will still be taxed as normal, but for retained earnings (earnings you don't spend) it makes a difference. In particular if you are hoping to put together enough cash to buy a commercial property, it will be very hard to save for this if you are paying tax at 41%, PRSI at 4% and the Universal Social Charge (USC) at 7%. Total tax and levies = 41% + 4% + 7% = 52% at the marginal rate.

7. **Form the habit of getting your tax returns in on time.**
   This causes you less stress, gives you time to consider your tax-avoidance options, saves you interest and penalties, and doesn't annoy the tax man so he's less likely to audit you. October 31st is a deadline and not a target, so aim to have your return in before going on holidays each summer.

8. **Keep good records of your sales and expenses.**
   If you fail to keep records (copies of your sales invoices and bills) you cannot assess your tax liability – so the tax man will do it for you. Neither can you disprove his assessment if you have no records, so you'll probably end up paying a lot more than you should.

Preliminary Tax

Preliminary tax is your estimate of the income tax payable for the current year (November and December will be estimated). It includes income tax, PRSI and health contribution.

The amount of preliminary tax you must pay to avoid an interest charge is the lower of:

- 100% of your tax liability for the previous year
  or
- 90% of your final tax liability for the current year.

Your tax clearance certificate is a very valuable document, and is increasingly needed for a variety of licences and different types of work.

Once you register as a self-employed person you will receive a Notice of Preliminary Tax every September. Remember that the notice you receive from your Inspector serves mainly as a reminder to you of your obligation to calculate and pay your preliminary tax. If the preliminary tax on the Inspector's notice is too high or too low, you should substitute your own calculated preliminary tax liability. If you do not substitute your own figure, the Inspector's figure must be paid and there is no right of appeal against this amount.

If for any tax year you consider that you are not going to have a tax liability, you should enter "0" on the Preliminary Tax Payslip and return it to the Collector-General. Don't forget, however, that even if you have no income tax to pay, you may still have a liability for PRSI and the Universal Social Charge (USC). Any self-employed person earning less than €4,004 per year is exempt from the Universal Social Charge (USC), so would only pay PRSI at 4% of their total income.

Note: The minimum annual PRSI contribution is €253 (even if you make a loss) which Revenue forwards to the Department of Social Protection towards your pension.

Average Tax Rates for Self-Employed Persons

The table below shows the 2011 average tax rates for self-employed persons.

Gross income € *Net profit*	Single	Married, 1 income, 2 children	Married, 2 incomes 2 children
15,000	15.7%	6.7%	6.3%
20,000	19.3%	7.6%	9.8%
25,000	21.7%	11.8%	13.3%
30,000	23.2%	15.0%	16.0%
40,000	29.0%	19.0%	19.5%
60,000	36.6%	29.4%	23.2%
100,000	42.8%	38.4%	33.6%
120,000	44.3%	40.7%	36.6%

Source: 2011 Budget summary available on www.revenue.gov.ie

Note: Average Tax Rates 2011: Total of Income Tax, PRSI and Universal Social Charge as a proportion of gross income. This measure includes only the standard employee credit, personal income tax credit and home carer credit, where relevant. It does not include the impact of any other allowances or reliefs.

Profits and Expenses

Thinking back to your projected profit and loss account, you calculated your profits by deducting business expenses from your turnover (sales). If you are registered for VAT your profit and loss figures should exclude VAT, because VAT gets sorted out every two months and it would cause confusion and double-counting to also include it in the income tax return.

If you make a loss you can either set off the loss against other taxable income (if you or your spouse have any), or carry the loss forward to be set against future profits of your business.

You can claim for any business expenses which you have to pay in order to earn your profits. If you think about it, why would you be expected to pay income tax on a business expense that had already cost you money? Having said that, not everything you buy for the business is treated as an expense and so cannot be fully written off in the first year. For example, a piece of equipment – a part of it gets worn out during the year and you are allowed for that, but the remaining value means you are richer as a result – so it's not tax deductible.

The type of expenses you are allowed to claim for include:
- The purchase of materials/goods for resale.
- Wages, rent, rates, repairs, lighting and heating.
- Running costs of vehicles or machinery used in the business.
- Professional fees – accountancy, legal, consultancy.
- Interest paid on any monies borrowed to finance business. expenses or items of equipment.
- Lease payments on vehicles or machinery used in the business.
- Telephone, ESB, refuse charges.

In general you cannot claim for any private expenses, i.e. 'any expense, not wholly and exclusively paid for the purposes of the trade or profession'. These include any private expenditure, e.g. your own wages, food, clothing (except protective clothing), income tax, etc.

Your PRSI payment goes towards your contributory pension. It is paid to Revenue as part of your tax return and forwarded to the Department of Social Protection.

You cannot claim for any business entertainment expenditure, i.e. the provision of accommodation, food, drink, or any other form of hospitality. The cost of food whilst working is not allowed, except for business journeys outside the normal pattern.

Expenditure is regarded as 'capital' if it has been spent on buying or altering assets which are of lasting use in the business. As we have already stated you cannot deduct the cost of buying equipment or buildings (referred to as capital expenditure) in calculating your taxable profits, because you are richer as a result of owning them. However, you can claim what are known as capital allowances on these, which is an allowance for the 'wear and tear' they suffer through use. This is generally set at one eighth of the value of the equipment (12.5%) each year until it is fully 'written off' after year eight.

Where expenses relate to both business and private use, only that portion which relates to your business will be allowed. Examples of such expenditure are rent, electricity, telephone charges, etc., where the premises involved is used partly for business and partly for private purposes. These expenses need to be 'apportioned', i.e. split into the portions that are private and business, and only the business portion is allowable as a claim against tax.

A typical example is motor expenses. When you use a car or a van for both business and private purposes, a split of both the capital allowances (wear and tear) and running expenses has to be made. In order to do this accurately you need to keep a note of your business mileage. If you lease an asset for business use, you can claim a deduction for the lease payments as a business expense.

If your business is set up as a partnership, there are special rules used to calculate the assessable profits. The total profit of the partnership is calculated and is then divided between the partners in accordance with whatever profit-sharing agreement they have made. Each individual partner's tax liability will then be calculated using the same rules that apply to self-employed people working on their own.

PRSI and the Universal Social Charge (USC)

As a self-employed person you will pay PRSI at Class S (self-employed).

PRSI
PRSI is Pay Related Social Insurance, i.e. a contribution to social

insurance (e.g. your pension) based on a percentage of (i.e. related to) the amount of pay you receive. It is charged as follows:

- Minimum contribution is €253.
- 4% on all income over €5,000 per annum *all income*

Universal Social Charge (USC)

The Health Levy and Income Levy have been abolished in Budget 2011, and are replaced by a new Universal Social Charge (USC). The rates and thresholds are as follows:

- 2% from €0 to €10,036
- 4% from €10,037 to €16,016
- 7% over €16,017

There is no charge if you earn less than €4,004 per annum.

Tax Rates, Tax Bands, Tax Credits

Figuring out how to earn extra income is much more rewarding than fretting over a percent or two in extra taxation.

Tax rates: The rates at which income is taxed are 20% (standard rate) and 41% (higher rate).

Tax bands: The amount of earnings you can have at any tax rate. For instance, the standard rate band (20%) for a single person is €32,800; any earnings above this band are taxed at 41%. The bands as they apply to different personal circumstances are outlined below.

Personal circumstances	2011 €
Single/widowed without dependent children	€32,800 @ 20% Balance @ 41%
Single/widowed qualifying for one-parent tax credit	€36,800 @ 20% Balance @ 41%
Married couple, one spouse with income	€41,800 @ 20% Balance @ 41%
Married couple, both spouses with income	€41,800 rising to €65,600 @ 20% Balance @ 41%

Tax credit: The actual euro amount by which your tax bill is reduced as a 'credit' from the Revenue Commissioners (it replaces the old 'tax free allowance'). The main tax credits as they apply to different personal circumstances are outlined below.

Tax Credit	2011 €
Single person	€1,650
Married person	€3,300
PAYE credit	€1,650
One-parent family credit	€1,650

Note that if you are a single person with a family you get both the single person and the one-parent family credits. If you are self-employed you do not get the PAYE credit.

Taxation of Companies

Companies pay corporation tax. This tax is charged on the company's profits which include both income and chargeable gains.

If you set up a company, the company will be obliged to register for and operate PAYE/PRSI on your salary as a director. You will have to pay income tax on any dividends received by you. As the company may be required to deduct Dividend Withholding Tax on dividends paid, only such tax deducted will be available to you as a tax credit.

If you are trading through a company, any losses arising cannot be offset against any other personal income you might have. The losses can only be set off against any other income of the company or against future or past profits, subject to certain restrictions.

The self-assessment system also applies to companies. If your company makes less than €200,000 profit, it is treated as a 'small' company. It can then base its preliminary tax payable on 100% of

"We don't pay taxes. Only the little people pay taxes."
- Leona Helmsley, American businesswoman

the prior year's corresponding corporation tax liability and is payable on the 11th month of the accounting period (the period for which the company makes up its accounts).

If the preliminary tax is paid late or the amount paid is too low, interest will be charged at 1% per month on the balance of tax due.

There are two rates of corporation tax, as follows:
- Trading income @ 12.5%
- Non-trading income @ 25% (e.g. investment income, rental income).

Your own circumstances will dictate whether you should operate as a limited company or as a sole trader. In addition to the taxation issues you need to consider, there are various other practical and legal matters which should be taken into account when setting up a company. Have a look at Legal Issues in Chapter 12 to assist you in making the correct decision, and then seek professional advice from your accountant and solicitor.

Tax for New Start-up Companies

New start-up companies which commenced trading in 2010 were exempt from corporation tax and capital gains tax in each of the first three years, provided that their tax liability in the year did not exceed €40,000.

The scheme is being extended to include start-up companies which commence a new trade in 2011. The scheme is being modified so that the value of the relief will be linked to the amount of employer's PRSI paid by a company in an accounting period subject to a maximum of €5,000 per employee. If the amount of qualifying employers' PRSI is lower than the reduction in corporation tax liability otherwise applicable, relief will be based on the lower amount.

Keeping Books and Records

You are obliged to keep records for tax purposes. Otherwise it would be impossible to properly calculate what tax you pay. Failure to keep proper records is a revenue offence, for which you may face a heavy fine. You must keep full and accurate records of your business from the start. You need to do this whether you prepare the accounts yourself or use an accountant.

You should also bear in mind that you may need to keep accounts for reasons unconnected with tax. For example, your bank may want to see your accounts when considering an application for a business loan. In this regard they like to see accounts prepared by an independent accountant, rather than the home-grown variety prepared by you. It is important for you to remember that the figures which are contained in your accounts and your tax returns must be correct.

You must keep sufficient records to make a proper return of income for tax purposes. Transactions must be recorded in a way that will clearly show the amounts involved and the matters to which they relate. All supporting records such as invoices, bank and building society statements, cheque stubs, receipts, etc. should be retained for at least six years.

At the end of the accounting period you must have details of:

- Your business takings.
- All expenditure incurred: purchases, rent, lighting, heating, telephone, insurance, motor expenses, repairs, wages, etc.
- Any money introduced into the business, and its source.
- The amount of any cash withdrawn from the business or any cheques drawn on the business bank account, for your own or your family's private use (these items are normally referred to as drawings).
- Amounts owed to you by customers, showing the total amount owed by each debtor.
- Amounts owed by you to suppliers, showing the total amount you owe to each creditor.
- Stocks and raw materials on hand.

"The promises of yesterday are the taxes of today."
Mackenzie King

The manner in which your transactions are recorded will vary from a computerised or 'double entry' bookkeeping system to some more basic system. Regardless of what way your books and records are kept, they must be capable of showing the amount and source of:

- All income
- All purchases and other outgoings.

Simply keeping the bank statements for the business does not fulfil your requirements to keep proper books and records. Your accountant, if you have one, will advise you on a bookkeeping system suitable to your circumstances.

Generally you are not required to submit your business accounts with your income tax return. However, you must still prepare accounts, and then extract the relevant information from your accounts for entry in the 'Extracts From Accounts' pages of the Return of Income, Form 11.

The accounts you will need to prepare are:

- A trading and profit and loss account, showing details of goods sold during the period and the cost of those goods, and the various expenses of the trade during the period, the difference being the net profit/loss of the business for the period.
- A capital account showing details of opening and closing capital, net profit/loss for the period, cash introduced and drawings (not usually required for small businesses).
- A balance sheet setting out details of the business assets and liabilities at the end of the period (not normally required for small businesses).

The KISS Approach to Tax

The best attitude to tax involves accepting that you have an honourable and a legal obligation to pay your fair share towards the social services which you and your family enjoy. That said, there is a hard way and an easy way to keep on top of your tax obligations.

Because it's one of your major bills and potential downfalls, it's vital to adopt a simple, practical approach. Try the following:

1. **Estimate**. You need an advance estimate of your tax liability in order to put an 'easy-payment plan' in place. Once you've done your first tax return, this estimate suggests itself – just

   Corporation tax on company profits is 12.5%. However, any income taken out of the company is taxed at 20%/41% as appropriate.

   allow for the same amount again. For a first year estimate you or your accountant can calculate the figure based on your projected profit and loss. If you don't do this, 10% of your sales isn't a bad estimate – after business expenses and tax credits are deducted, it would be a reasonable provision to make.

2. **Budget**. By far the simplest and best way to budget for your tax bill is to arrange a monthly direct debit to the Revenue Commissioners. This helps you to keep on top of your tax bill. You could also put a direct debit into a separate bank account to save for your tax bill. Organise the appropriate amount from January each year after consulting with your accountant.

3. **Delegate**. To avoid both the work and the stress involved in doing their own tax return, most self-employed people subcontract this part of the work to their accountant.

Tax Audits

A 'tax/revenue audit' checks to see if the information submitted on your tax return is correct, i.e. it checks if your self-assessment is accurate. Tax audits apply to sole traders, partnerships and companies.

Revenue audit covers the following types of tax returns:
- Income tax, corporation tax or capital gains tax returns.
- The returns submitted for VAT, PAYE/PRSI or relevant contracts tax.

Three methods of selection are used. These are:

1. **Screening tax returns** – examining the returns made by a variety of taxpayers and reviewing their tax compliance history. The figures are then compared to trends and patterns in the particular business or profession, and evaluated against other available information.

2. **Projects on business sectors** – from time to time projects are conducted to examine tax compliance levels in particular trades or professions. The returns for a large number of taxpayers in a particular sector are screened in detail and a proportion of these are selected for audit.

3. **Random selection**. This is in addition to the first two methods. It means that all taxpayers have a possibility of being audited. Each year, a small number of businesses are selected using this method.

If a business is selected, 14 days' written notice is given. The notification letter shows:

- The name of the person who'll carry out the audit
- The date and time of the audit
- The year/(s), accounting period/(s) or VAT tax period/(s) which are to be audited.

The actual audit involves a series of steps, as follows:

- On arrival, the auditor identifies themselves to you and explains the purpose of the audit. An indication of the length of time he or she expects to spend on your premises is also given
- You are given an opportunity to disclose to the auditor any inaccuracies in your tax return
- The auditor will examine your books and records to verify that the figures have been correctly calculated and that the tax returns and/or declarations for the different taxes are correct
- If the auditor finds the returns to be largely correct, as is often the case, you will be told so as soon as this becomes clear

- If the auditor finds that adjustments are required, he or she will quantify the adjustments and the additional tax. The details of how the additional tax arises will be discussed with you and you will also be notified in writing
- At the final interview, the auditor will ask for your agreement to the total settlement figure
- Once agreed, the full amount should be paid to the auditor who will issue you with a receipt

Never go into an audit without the assistance of your accountant, and if you don't have one, then get one, as this is a situation that requires professional help. Also, don't panic too much if you do have an audit – at least after it's over you can rest assured that your tax affairs are in order!

Reference

See www.revenue.ie for a wide range of detailed publications on all topics raised in this chapter.

Chapter 11   Value Added Tax (VAT)
and
Employer's PAYE/PRSI

Value Added Tax (VAT)

What is VAT?

VAT (Value Added Tax) is a tax on consumers, which implies that the more they consume the more VAT they pay. The standard rate of VAT is 21%; the reduced rate of VAT is 13.5%. It is collected by VAT registered traders (i.e. you, if you register for VAT) on their sales invoices as part of the sales price. If these sales are to the general public, VAT is included in the price; if sales are to the trade, VAT must be itemised separately on the sales docket/invoice. This separate itemisation makes it easier for customers to see the real price to them, and makes accounting for their VAT a lot easier.

The standard rate of VAT is 21%. There is also a reduced rate of 13.5%, a zero rate and special rates for specific sectors.

VAT is a two-way street, with a trader paying it out on their purchases, and taking it in with their sales. But whilst taking it in, it is not for their own use – they are merely collecting it for the Revenue. The amount of VAT taken in on sales and paid out on purchases is totalled every two months; if the VAT taken in is greater than the VAT paid out, the difference is paid to the Revenue, and vice-versa.

Registration for VAT is simple – you simply tick the box after the question 'Do you wish to register for VAT' on the TR1 form. Never imply that you're registered for VAT by saying something like 'Price includes VAT'. In order to charge VAT or imply that it's included, you must have your VAT registration number printed on the bottom of your invoice.

To Register or Not

Once you start in business you can register for VAT at any stage if it suits you – but you are obliged to register, collect and return VAT once your turnover/sales reaches €37,500 if you are selling services, and double that at €75,000 if you are selling goods. The figure for services is €750 per week (based on 50 working weeks per year) so all but very small businesses are obliged to register.

You are also required to register if you expect to reach these limits. For instance, if you were opening a coffee shop costing €30,000 a year to lease, with projected overheads of €30,000 a year, plus the cost of supplies for resale and your own drawings, then it would be fairly obvious that you would exceed the compulsory VAT registration limit of €75,000, so you would register for VAT from day one.

On the other hand, if you didn't think you'd reach the obligatory limits and were dealing with unregistered customers, then you'd delay VAT registration, because it would mean an increase in your prices with little benefit to your pocket. Effectively, non-registration can be seen as a small tax break for a low-turnover business. Registration would also mean extra administration with bi-monthly VAT returns, and a probable loss of custom because of the price increase.

A VAT registered person normally accounts for VAT on a two-monthly basis (Jan-Feb, Mar-Apr, etc.).

If your customers are VAT registered they can offset the VAT element against their own VAT return. Thus they generally like to get a VAT invoice because they feel they are getting best value from a legitimate, well-established, VAT registered business.

Note: although you are not obliged to register for VAT until you reach the threshold, remember that some larger companies will not deal with a small business unless they are VAT registered.

The **standard rate** of VAT is 21%. This applies to all goods and services that are not exempt or are taxable at the zero or reduced rates.

The **reduced rate** of VAT is 13.5%. This applies to certain fuels, buildings and building services, repair, cleaning and maintenance services, restaurants, newspapers etc.

Exempted goods and services charge no VAT, and include financial, medical and educational activities.

It is proposed in the **National Recovery Plan 2011-2014** that the standard rate of VAT will be increased by 1% to 22% in 2013 and by a further 1% to 23% in 2014. The 13.5% rate will not be changed.

Don't assume a VAT rate. Always check out the relevant rate for your business through your local tax office or at www.revenue.ie.

Bi-Monthly VAT Returns – the VAT 3 Form

Every two months the Revenue will send you a form for the two-monthly return of VAT (known as a VAT 3 Form) if you are registered for VAT. The form is very simple, with just three boxes to be filled unless you are importing or exporting.

These entries on the VAT 3 Form are as follows:

- VAT collected on your sales for the period [Box T1].
- VAT already paid on your purchases for the period [Box T2].
- VAT due to Revenue (if the VAT collected on sales is greater than the VAT paid on your purchases) [Box T3].
- VAT due from revenue (if the VAT collected on sales is less than the VAT paid on your purchases) [Box T4].
- Goods supplied to and received from another member state of the EU [Boxes E1 and E2].

Filling in the boxes is simple, provided your accounting system traps the information in such a way that the VAT position can be clearly established.

In general this is as simple as dedicating one analysis column for VAT on both the 'cash in' and 'cash out' sides of your accounts book, filling in the itemised figure for VAT from each invoice, and totalling them every month. If you are worried as to whether or not you are doing it correctly, you can ask your accountant or consult www.revenue.ie.

The completed VAT 3 form, along with a payment for the amount due, should be sent to the VAT section of your local tax office before the 19th day following the end of the two-monthly period (e.g. Jan-Feb payment to be made before 19th March). You are required to make a VAT return even if you do not have a VAT liability for the period, i.e. the tax office wants the form returned with nil on it. Should you lose the particular form for a period you cannot just photocopy another one and fill it in, as they are all coded with a specific number. Reorder the form you need from the VAT section of your local tax office.

Paying and Claiming VAT

Registered persons can account for VAT either on the basis of sales made or on the basis of payments actually received (cash basis).

If you feel you may have difficulty keeping on top of the paperwork involved in two-monthly returns, you can arrange to pay your VAT through Revenue's direct debit scheme and make an annual return and declaration of your liability.

This method requires that you pay one twelfth of your previous year's liability by direct debit each month. Where you have recently registered for VAT you will need to estimate your likely VAT liability for the forthcoming year and pay one twelfth of this amount monthly. There is also a more flexible option for people with seasonal businesses, which allows for varying amounts to be paid each month to coincide with the seasonal nature of the business.

How do I Claim a VAT Repayment?

If the VAT paid by you exceeds the VAT charged by you, the excess will be repaid automatically by the Collector-General following the submission of the VAT 3 return. VAT repayments are paid electronically (it is no longer possible to get a cheque) directly to your bank. You can provide details of your nominated bank on the VAT 3 Form.

Whilst you are allowed to offset the VAT on purchases 'wholly and exclusively incurred' for your business (e.g. phone, electricity, diesel, office supplies, purchases of goods, etc.), no VAT deduction is allowed for the following, even if they are used for the business: food and drink, entertainment expenses, petrol or the hiring of cars.

Calculating VAT – 'Cash Receipts' or 'Invoice' Basis

There are two main methods of calculating VAT – 'cash receipts basis' or the 'invoice basis'. Most small businesses opt to use the 'cash receipts' basis when calculating liability. For larger businesses with a computerised invoicing system, VAT is normally calculated on the invoice basis because it's the most convenient – getting invoicing and VAT calculations completed at the one time. It does not matter whether payment has been received or made; it's on the invoices that the calculation is made.

Retailers or others who do not normally issue VAT invoices will usually calculate their VAT liability on the cash receipts basis. These businesses will generally quote VAT inclusive prices (i.e. the VAT element in the selling price is not shown separately).

Note: Care should be taken that a transaction which may appear to be the supply of services is nevertheless taxable as a supply of goods if the value, exclusive of tax, of the goods supplied in carrying out the work exceeds two-thirds of the total charge, exclusive of VAT.

Books and Records

You must keep your books and records in such a way that your VAT position can be clearly established. You should ensure that they are properly written up and balanced on a regular basis. In addition, you must keep all invoices, credit and debit notes, receipts, vouchers, till rolls and all other supporting documentation relevant to establish your VAT position. You must retain these VAT records for a period of six years unless your Inspector of Taxes advises you otherwise. These records must be available for inspection by an authorised Revenue Officer, if required.

Annual VAT Return

In addition to paying VAT every two months, an annual Return of Trading Details (RTD) is required. The RTD form details purchases and sales for the year, broken down by VAT rate.

VAT Invoices

Once you are registered for VAT, you are obliged to issue an invoice when you supply goods or services to another registered trader or to a person entitled to a repayment of VAT.

The invoice must contain the following details:

- Your name, address and VAT number.
- The name and address of the customer.
- The date of issue of the invoice and the date of supply of the goods or services.
- The quantity or volume of goods supplied.
- The amount charged (excluding VAT), the VAT rate, and the amount of VAT.

The invoice must be issued within 15 days of the end of the month in which the goods or services are supplied.

Employer's PAYE/PRSI

PAYE/PRSI for Employees

The following pages are intended to give an appreciation of the main issues involved with PAYE and PRSI, which you'll need in order to deal with employees' queries. It will also help if you are forming a Limited Company and becoming an employee yourself. The tax rates and tax bands, as outlined in the previous chapter on taxation for the self-employed, also apply to employees.

In reality most small employers use their accountant to maintain their PAYE/PRSI records, as it's very precise work which requires both understanding and experience. In addition the accountant uses a computerised payroll package to simplify the job, which is also required by the Revenue for anyone newly registering as an employer. A comprehensive 'Employer's Guide to PRSI' is available at www.revenue.ie.

The electronic Tax Deduction Card (TDC) is an improved system that replaces the paper TDC.

The term PAYE stands for Pay As You Earn, and means that an employee pays their tax as they earn it rather than letting it build up into a big bill at the end of the year. The PAYE system which you, as an employer, must operate collects both the income tax due and the PRSI (Pay Related Social Insurance). These are deducted before the employee gets their hands on them, so in a way they are 'out of sight, out of mind'.

Once you start to pay an employee, you have to apply the PAYE system. Apart from being illegal, there is no advantage in paying 'cash in the hand' to an employee. You cannot declare any wages you pay in this manner against your business tax bill, so they end up costing you more on your tax.

The system for calculating tax is based on tax credits and tax deduction cards as outlined in the box below. The legal obligation is on you, the employer, to ensure that the correct taxes have been deducted.

Tax Credit System and Tax Deduction Cards

Under the tax credit system, all of an employee's gross pay is taxable (other than approved pension contributions). This gross tax figure is then reduced by the amount of the employee's tax credits, giving the net figure for the tax due.

In order to know what taxes to deduct, you, as the employer, will receive a Tax Credit Certificate which will show the tax credits and standard rate cut-off point for each individual employee. The tax credits are simple to understand – as we have said (Chapter 10), they are the amount by which gross tax is reduced, depending on employee circumstances (e.g. single/married, PAYE tax credit, etc.). The standard rate cut-off point is the point at which an employee gets cut off from the standard rate of tax (20%) and starts to pay at the higher rate (41%).

The Revenue's electronic Tax Deduction Card (TDC) facility assists employers in keeping a complete employee deduction record of all employees' pay, tax and PRSI details. The electronic TDC is an improved system that replaces the paper Tax Deduction Card (TDC).

An employer need only enter the annual tax credit amount and cut-off point shown on the employee's Tax Credit Certificate into the electronic TDC to calculate an employee's weekly or monthly tax credits and cut-off point.

Your local enterprise officer or your accountant can help with the details. The Revenue Commissioners also have an online enquiry system, Revenue Technical Service (RTS), which is a useful tool for employers. Full details are available on www.revenue.ie.

Pay, Holiday Pay and Expenses

Pay and holiday pay

All payments of wages, salaries, overtime, bonuses, holiday pay, etc. are regarded as pay for tax purposes.

Expenses

Be careful how you classify expenses, as most expenses are treated as pay. Expenses which are not treated as pay must 'not only be actually incurred in the performance of the duties of the employment but must also be wholly, exclusively and necessarily so incurred.'

Subsistence payments can be paid where an employee is working temporarily away from their normal place of work. Such expenses (including accommodation and meals) may be claimed at civil service rates (if the business is a limited company rather than a partnership or sole trader), or to the amount of actual subsistence expenses which have been vouched with receipts.

It's up to each employee (not their employer) to make their own claim for tax reliefs.

Motoring expenses in the course of work (not to and from work) can also be paid at civil service rates. These rates are quite generous, and allow many director employees to draw a lower taxable wage, and supplement it with these non-taxable expenses. The schedule of civil service rates is available on www.revenue.ie.

Tax reliefs

There are a range of tax reliefs available, many of which go unclaimed every year. It's up to each individual (not their employer) to make their own claim, which can be easily done on www.revenue.ie.

Some of these include tax relief for permanent health contributions, medical insurance, medical expenses, mortgage interest relief, rent payments relief, and domestic refuse collection.

PRSI & the Universal Social Charge (USC)

In addition to deducting PAYE you are also obliged to deduct Employee PRSI (Pay Related Social Insurance) from employees on behalf of the Department of Social Protection.

You will also have to pay Employer's PRSI (10.75%) for your employees, but not for yourself if you are a proprietary director of your company (i.e. if you own more than 15%).

The PRSI contribution consists of social insurance which helps pay for social welfare benefits and pensions; a health contribution which goes to the Department of Health and Children; and a national training fund levy.

PRSI Rates

There are many different classes and sub-classes of PRSI so they can be quite difficult to understand. Add in exemptions, and the confusion is added to. For the brave, there is a 'PRSI contribution rates and user guide' available at www.welfare.ie and an online PRSI calculator at the same address.

The following is a summary for 2011:

- PRSI is charged at 4%
- It is payable on all earnings with no exemption ceiling as was the case prior to 2011
- The Health Levy and Income Levy have been abolished and replaced by a Universal Social Charge (USC), payable as follows:
    - 0% if income is less than €4,004
    - 2% on income between €0 and €10,036
    - 4% on income from €10,037 to €16,016
    - 7% on income greater than €16,016

Employees are exempt from PRSI on the first €127 per week.

Payments to the Collector-General

If you are making monthly returns, the total of the PAYE income tax and PRSI deducted should be sent to the Collector-General within two weeks of the end of the month. If your total PAYE and PRSI payments for the year are €30,000 or less, you have the option of making quarterly payments, again within two weeks of the end of the quarter.

Payment may be made at any bank, by post, or by direct debit.

Monthly payment by direct debit involves less paperwork, as monthly returns are not required. If arranging a direct debit you should make as good an estimate of your monthly liability as possible, and any overpayment or underpayment can be rectified at the end of the tax year when the form P35 is submitted.

What Duties Arise at the End of the Tax Year?

There's quite an amount of work involved in form-filling at the end of the year, which is where a computerised payroll system is invaluable, as it does it automatically and sends the information to the Revenue electronically.

The following must be done:
- Total and complete each Tax Deduction Card in use.
- Complete forms P35, P35L and P35L\T.
- Calculate any PAYE or PRSI outstanding and send it to the Collector-General.
- Give a Form P60 to each employee who is employed at the end of the tax year. You will already have given a Form P45 to those employees who left employment during the year.

Common PAYE Forms

1. P45 (a certificate given to an employee when he/she is leaving an employment).
2. P50 (employee's application to the tax office for refund during unemployment).
3. 12A (form to be completed by an employee who was not previously employed).
4. P30 (employer's monthly remittance form for PAYE and PRSI contributions).
5. P35 (employer's annual declaration of liability for PAYE and PRSI contributions).
6. P35L and P35L/T (employer's annual return of pay, tax and PRSI contributions in respect of each employee).
7. P60 (employee's certificate of pay, tax and PRSI contributions for the year).

www.ros.ie

The Revenue Online Service (ROS), www.ros.ie, is an internet-based means of conducting business with the Revenue. It also allows PAYE employees to view their revenue PAYE record.

Through ROS an employer can do the following:
- Receive employer copy Tax Credit Certificates for employees.
- Upload form P45 for employees who commence or cease employment.
- Use form P46 to notify Revenue of a new employment.
- File monthly and quarterly P30s.
- File employer's end of year return (P35).

Customer information services on ROS can be accessed to instantly view full details of payments made, returns filed and collection details covering the last seven years.

ROS also has the facility for paying and filing online, filing only, or paying only. All payments can be made by ROS debit instruction or Laser card.

Chapter 12   Legal Issues

Introduction

Law can be defined in many ways, but it usually means a body of rules, principles, and standards applied by the courts.

"Good fences make good neighbours."
- Robert Frost

There is always a need for a group of people to organise their dealings according to a set of rules. Otherwise some people would do what they liked without regard to others, resulting in trouble. The original laws in Ireland were the Brehon Laws (250 AD – 1606). These were replaced by the common law of England in 1606, which also forms the basis of the legal systems in the USA, Canada, Australia, New Zealand, India and parts of Africa. This makes them all very similar and quite easy for Irish people to understand, unlike the legal systems in France or Spain, for example, which are quite different.

Apart from this common law basis, our laws have been created through several means. One such is the Irish Constitution of 1937, which is a major source of law. We also have government-made law, European Union law, judge-made law, and various regulations by local authorities (e.g. planning regulations).

You might be surprised at how much you already know about the law. In this chapter we will look at some relevant issues as they apply to business.

Legal Structures

It is necessary to have a legal entity in order to be able to act through the legal system (i.e. the laws, the courts, etc.). The legal system does not recognise people or groups who do not have legal status. For instance, if seven or eight people form a group in order to take on a project (e.g. develop a local playground), they cannot just buy the land or hire a contractor as 'the playground group'. The law doesn't recognise such a loose grouping. The contractor (e.g. plant hire supplier) will have to make his contract with some specified, named individuals within the group. Each of these individuals will have their own personal legal entity, and provided they are over 18 and not wards of court, they will have automatic 'contractual capacity', i.e. the ability to enter contracts.

Without legal status one cannot enter into contracts (e.g. buy certain products, employ people, borrow money, etc.) nor can one bring legal proceedings in court nor be sued in court. In our playground example, the contractor would have to take a legal action against whoever directed him to undertake the work (if over 18 and of sound mind), as this person would have a legal entity recognised by the courts.

When starting a business, three main types of legal entity apply:
1. Sole trader
2. Partnership
3. Limited company.

Over the following pages we will examine them in more detail.

Sole Trader

The sole trader is the most common type of business entity in Ireland. Farmers, construction subcontractors, small shopkeepers, accountants, hairdressers, etc. almost all operate as sole traders, particularly in the early years of business when their business would generally be fairly small. As the business becomes larger and more complex, it may become more appropriate to form a limited company, but starting off as a sole trader is very common.

Never enter a business partnership without first drafting a partnership agreement. Anticipate all issues that might cause conflict and agree terms for avoiding/ dealing with them.

Being a sole trader does not mean that you are a one-person operation, but that you are trading using your own personal legal entity. This means that legally, there is no separation between your business activities and your personal activities. The legal privileges granted to you under the law of the land extend to cover your business activities, e.g. the right to own property, to enter contracts, etc. From a legal point of view there is nothing you have to do to set up in business as a sole trader, because your personal affairs and your business affairs are considered to be all the one in the eyes of the law.

It could be argued that it is too easy for a sole trader to open a business, resulting in insufficient advance planning and a high failure rate. The sole trader option is a simple way to get started, but if you are undertaking projects that have substantial risks attached you need to consider transferring to a limited liability company.

Advantages of operating as a sole trader:
- There are no legal requirements or costs in setting up – you can just start trading.
- You don't have to get an auditor to audit your books every year, nor do you have to lodge details of your accounts with the Companies Registration Office.
- You don't have to calculate PAYE every week or every month on your drawings, just calculate your annual income tax and PRSI once a year.

Disadvantages of operating as a sole trader:
- Because there is no legal separation between your personal and business activities, you are personally liable for all business losses incurred. Your personal assets can be seized by the courts.
- Because you do not pay tax on your income as you earn it, it can build up to a substantial bill each year which can make managing your cash flow difficult.
- If you need cash for a big expansion you will have to use savings or borrowings, as it's difficult to sell a share of a business that's not set up as a separate legal entity.

Partnership

A partnership merely combines the legal entities of two or more individuals, and so is very similar in legal terms to the sole trader. There is one major difference though, which is that all partners are 'jointly and separately' liable. In other words, each partner is separately liable for all of the debts of the business, and it is up to them to sort out the sharing of liability between themselves. If you think about it this makes sense, because otherwise you could always be met with an excuse that 'it's my partner's responsibility' if you went to collect money!

As with a sole trader, a partnership can be established without any legal formalities; however, it is asking for trouble to join a partnership without first drawing up a partnership agreement. For example, what happens if you and your partner start to disagree on important matters like holidays, hours of work, debts, new partners, how to settle the finances and business arrangements if one partner wishes to leave, etc.? It is very important to think these things out in advance, because some difficulty or difference of opinion is bound to arise at some stage.

A good exercise is to try to anticipate what issues might cause difficulties, and then write some terms to deal with this situation in advance. It's probably not enough for potential partners to just say 'we trust each other'. With the best will in the world, people might genuinely disagree on something and at least a partnership agreement will safeguard trust in the business relationship, and reduces the chance of serious misunderstanding. As with any business agreement or contract, it is important to put the terms agreed in writing, as the goalposts can move and people can forget. This thoroughness helps prevent good, profitable partnerships turning into acrimonious disagreements.

Advantages of operating as a partnership:
- 'Two heads are better than one', especially if they bring different abilities to the party (e.g. a salesman and a production man).
- Two cash inputs mean you may be able to take on a project that you cannot afford to on your own.
- Two work inputs means you can share the responsibilities, particularly during holiday time and if working weekends/evenings.

Disadvantages of operating as a partnership:

- Profits are split, so profits need to be much higher than if you were a sole trader.
- You are jointly and separately liable for all business debts, so if the business gets into difficulty and your partner does a runner ….. you are responsible for sorting out debts.
- Personality clashes and serious disagreements can arise, especially as circumstances change. Spouses or partners of your business partner can also sometimes put a spanner in the works.

Limited Company

The main point which distinguishes a limited company from other forms of business is that it is regarded as a separate legal entity from the people who own and run it. This means that the affairs of the company are separate to those of its owners.

The word 'limited' in this context means your liability to repay the business' debts is limited to the amount you have agreed to contribute to them. Therefore, if the business goes bankrupt your personal possessions cannot be seized to pay the company's debts, unless you've committed fraud, which will remove your protection from liability. On the other hand if the company is doing well, you don't have a right to go in and raid its bank account or dispose of its assets. The protection offered by this separate legal entity works both ways.

Forming a company can provide advantages in limiting your liability, reducing your taxes and enabling you to take a share in a bigger project.

A private company requires a minimum of two directors, who direct the affairs of the company. One of these can also serve as the company secretary, who has the added responsibility of ensuring compliance with the laws of the land in terms of making returns to the Companies Registration Office (CRO), etc. There is a reasonable amount of work in meeting these requirements, and any company not fulfilling these obligations will be struck off. A limited liability company must be run according to the rules set out in company law.

Advantages of operating as a company:

- Liabilities are limited to the assets of the company, and do not affect your private assets (provided you have not committed fraud).
- You can sell a share/shares to raise cash. With 100 shares you could potentially have 100 investors.
- Although a director, you can also be an employee of your own company, gaining employee benefits (pension, travel and subsistence expenses, etc.).
- Money left in the company will be taxed at 12.5% instead of a possible 52% if you were a sole trader with income in excess of €32,800 (41% income tax + 4% PRSI + 7% Universal Social Charge).

Disadvantages of operating as a company:

- If you're not making a profit after drawings there's no tax advantage.
- You may have to pay an auditor for an annual audit (turnover in excess of €7.3 million) and you will also need a solicitor's advice more often.
- If a bank requests a personal guarantee on company loans, then you're still liable if the company fails.
- There is a lot of additional paperwork and associated costs in running a company, e.g. CRO returns.

Sole Trader, Partnership, or Limited Company?

You have several choices when it comes to deciding a legal entity for your business. There is no one 'correct' legal entity so it is important to consider each of the three main options. Whilst they may not be of relevance to you just yet, as your business progresses or as new opportunities arise you may need to change part or all of the business to a new entity, i.e. a partnership or a limited liability company.

In trying to decide between sole trader, partnership, or limited company, think yourself through the following questions:

- **What's the risk?**
  If you're in danger of losing a substantial amount of money if things go wrong, maybe even losing your home, then a limited liability company may be the most appropriate legal structure.

  The sole trader or partnership route provide no protection if things go seriously wrong. Accidents happen, and trading circumstances change, so if the risk gets higher it might be prudent to separate the business into a limited liability company.

- **Will the business be very profitable?**
  If the answer is yes, there is a tax advantage in operating as a limited company, as profits retained within the company (after you have drawn a salary) will be taxed at the corporation tax rate of 12.5%. As soon as you hit the higher personal tax rate of 41% plus PRSI @ 4% and Universal Social Charge (USC) at 7% = 52%, you should give serious consideration to forming a company for part or all of the business.

- **Do you have investment or expansion opportunities that you cannot afford on your own?**
  Involving one or more partners with money to invest may be the answer, in preference to using savings or borrowings. A company may be a more flexible structure for involving a number of people willing to take a piece of the action through the issuing of shares. For instance, if you required a €300,000 down payment (with a €700,000 mortgage) to purchase a property for your business, this could be split several ways in a property company formed for its purchase,

with your business paying it a guaranteed rent each year. Using a company as an investment vehicle would probably suit these investors far better than getting involved in personal loans, etc.

- **Do you want to build a good pension plan?**
People also use companies in order to accelerate putting together a good pension (provided sufficient profits are available). The joint contributions from you as an employee and from your company as your employer can provide a means of getting tax relief on your maximum contributions to a pension fund. This is particularly important if you are a late starter on a pension plan, as a lot of self-employed people are, having concentrated on investing in their business in the early years.

- **Do you want to protect your business name?**
Registering your trading or business name is a legal requirement, but does not give you sole rights to the use of the name. If you are investing heavily in the branding of a good business name it may be wise to protect it from being used by others by registering it as a trade mark, which does give you sole rights to its use.

As you can see, there are a number of factors involved in choosing between sole trader, partnership or limited company. Some of them require professional advice tailored to your individual situation. However, from a taxation point of view most are irrelevant unless your business is quite profitable, so you may not need to worry unduly about becoming a company for tax purposes for the first few years.

Patents and Copyrights

Copyright and patent law exists to protect a product or work of creation from being exploited by someone else. Whilst the best way to protect your idea is to change it from an idea into a commercial reality, and work it as hard as possible to gain the major share in the marketplace before anyone else does, sometimes this is not possible. Maybe you don't have the necessary finance to run with it as fast as you might like, so a larger, better-financed competitor could beat you to it and be the first to the market with their product. It is for this type of reason that your original creations can be protected.

1. Patents

A patent is an exclusive right given by the state and enforceable in the courts. It provides a monopoly in the manufacture, sale and use of an invention for a period of sixteen years. If you have invented a product that you consider might have real commercial value, you need to consider how to protect it. There are two main ways you can do this.

Copyright is an automatic right, and is deemed to exist from the moment of creation of the "work".
- Irish Patents Office website

Firstly and most comprehensively, you can apply for a patent. If you do, you will find it a complicated and costly procedure, requiring the services of a registered patent agent. Having done all of this and registered your patent, you will find that an international competitor can still run with it because Irish patent law does not apply outside Ireland – there is no worldwide patent, and European Union patenting is still in its early stages. If you want further information on the matter look up the Irish Patents Office' website at www.patentsoffice.ie

Alternatively you may make a detailed sketch or description of your product, post it to yourself or your solicitor in a sealed, registered envelope, and do not open it, so it can be used in court as evidence of your being the inventor. Whilst not a patent, it can prevent you being barred from continuing to produce the item, and help with a subsequent patent application.

2. Copyright

Another legal protection is copyright. Copyright is the creator's (or legal owner's) rights in creative works like music, painting, writings, photographs, advertising concepts, artwork, videos, TV commercials, etc. So if you are putting together a brochure you cannot simply scan photographs or designs from another brochure or website for your own brochure or website. Likewise you cannot print new covers for your favourite book and start selling it as your own! Unlike patent protection, copyright arises automatically, e.g. on this book.

General Legal Issues

• Keeping records

Keeping records is one of the main differences between being an employee and being self-employed. As an employee it is advisable to keep financial records; as a self-employed (sole trader or in a partnership) person you are legally obliged to keep financial records in order to establish your tax liability for both VAT and income tax. You must retain these records for a minimum of six years, but preferably longer. If you have a tax audit, you must be able to produce the evidence to back up your tax returns.

Engaging in legal action should be a last resort in resolving a conflict. The only guaranteed winners are the lawyers.

As a limited company, you are required to submit an annual return (a B1 form) and a set of abridged accounts to the CRO. If your company turnover is greater than €7.3 million or if you have more than 50 employees, you are also required to have an annual audit. You are also required to keep records of board meetings and transactions in your company's shares.

• Forming a company

Forming a company is a relatively straightforward process, and can be done with the assistance of your accountant or solicitor, usually for a fee of c. €700, inclusive of stamp duty. Because you are creating a new entity, the reporting requirements are higher, and if you don't report properly the company will be struck off the register. Check out the full details on the Companies Registration Office website at www.cro.ie.

• Income tax/corporation tax on profits/PAYE

If you are a sole trader or in a partnership you pay income tax at year end (before 31st October). If you form a limited company, corporation tax is due on the profits your company makes, and your wages are subject to income tax each month, the same as for any other employee. Wages must be paid under the PAYE (Pay As You Earn) system, with monthly or three-monthly returns as agreed with the Revenue Commissioners.

When you employ someone you must inform your local tax office. You will then receive a tax certificate for each employee which shows how much you need to deduct from their wages. These deductions are made and returned to the Revenue every month/three months, and you must also send an annual summary (P35) to the Revenue Commissioners, giving full details of pay and tax deducted in respect of all employees for the year.

Each employee should also receive details of pay and tax deducted by you from him/her (a payslip) with every pay packet, and an annual summary for the year (P60).

- **Pay Related Social Insurance (PRSI)**

The main benefit of PRSI for the self-employed is that it provides you with a contributory state pension on retirement. It is charged at 4% of all income, if your income exceeds €5,000 per year.

If you employ another person (part time or full time) you, as the employer, must also pay employer's PRSI (10.75%) in addition to deducting income tax and PRSI from their wages. If you are a proprietary director, i.e. if you own more then 15% of the company, you do not pay employer's PRSI for yourself, you only pay it for your employees. More details are outlined in Chapter 11.

How Does the Legal System Operate?

- **The legal profession**

The legal system is operated by the legal profession through the courts. The legal profession is made up of solicitors, barristers and judges.

A solicitor is the first port of call for the public, with numerous solicitors throughout the country. Their services include giving advice on legal matters, doing routine legal work (e.g. forming companies), and preparing cases for trial in the courts. They will normally represent their clients in the lower courts, up to the point where the special talents of a barrister are required.

Barristers are specialists in the effective presentation of a case in court. Depending on their success and experience they are divided into junior and senior counsel. You cannot consult a barrister directly, but must go through a solicitor. On important points of law the solicitor may require a counsel's opinion. If a difficult court case is expected, the solicitor will gather the evidence, and the barrister will present and argue the case.

A judge is required to hear a case, determine the relevant issues, and make a just decision according to the law. He/she is a neutral decision-maker. Judges are appointed by the government of the day as vacancies occur.

- **The courts**

The courts are organised like a pyramid or hierarchy, with the district courts at the bottom (there are over 200 district court areas). Next up is the circuit court (there are eight circuits), followed by the high court (one or three judges, depending on the case), with a final appeal possible to the supreme court (a chief justice and four judges).

Other courts for specific purposes include the Special Criminal Court, The European Court of Justice, and the Court of Human Rights, but these seldom directly involve the general public.

The Law of Contract

Put simply, a contract is an agreement which is legally binding. Almost all business transactions are based on the law of contract, e.g. the sale of goods or the hiring of employees. In general people are free to make whatever agreements they wish, subject to some restrictions, for example if something is contrary to the public interest.

The state also imposes certain legislation in favour of the weaker party to the agreement, e.g. with regard to employment contracts, protecting employees against ruthless employers. Likewise consumers are protected from ruthless manufacturers (or tradesmen/service providers) by the Sale of Goods and Supply of Services Act 1980.

"Patent Pending" is a term often used on products to alert competitors that an application has been made to protect the invention.
- Irish Patents Office website

Most of us enter into contracts every day without realising they are legally valid contracts, e.g. every time you buy something. If your goods are faulty, then you become aware of the contract, and will usually insist on a replacement or your money back.

The notion that an agreement has no legal significance unless it is in writing is incorrect. Some agreements must be in writing, e.g. regarding land, but most are made without any such formality. The difficulty with such contracts can be proving exactly what was said, so from a business point of view you should get into the practice of giving quotations for work before you start – specifying the basics of design, extra features, material to be used, finishes, payment details, etc. As always, specify the exact details on items about which there is potential for disagreement, and you'll learn with experience what to watch out for. Prevention is better than cure, so clear communication is a good basis for any contract.

It should be fairly clear from the above that you don't need a solicitor to make a contract, but you may need one to enforce it if things go wrong.

In legal terms, there must be three elements to create a valid contract:

1. An **agreement**, involving a definite 'offer' by one side, and an 'acceptance' of this offer by the other (e.g. offering a price which is accepted).
2. There must be an **intention** to create legal relations, i.e. the parties must intend to be legally bound by the agreement.
3. There must be **consideration**, i.e. an agreement struck to supply something on the one hand, and to pay for it on the other. Clear consideration would be the offering and acceptance of a deposit (except with land, which requires an exchange of contracts).

Labour Law

Labour law issues are dealt with more fully in Chapter 14 on Employment, but here are a few basic points to consider.

*   **Contract of employment**

You are obliged to give every employee a written contract of employment within a month of taking up his or her employment. Check out the Department of Enterprise, Trade and Innovation website at www.deti.ie

*   **Discrimination at work**

Ensure that any job advertisement issued does not offend against anti-discrimination legislation.

A concise guide to labour law is available at www.deti.ie

*   **Health and safety**

Remember that everybody is entitled to go home from work as healthy as they came in, so don't put anyone's health at risk. Be sure you draft a health and safety statement, as outlined in Chapter 13. Check the Health and Safety Authority website at www.hsa.ie.

*   **Dismissing an employee**

Be very careful if you have to let someone go from your employment. Consult your solicitor and follow the legal procedures to the letter of the law. Summary dismissal (i.e.

'You're fired!') should be the last resort. Unfair dismissal cases are increasingly common and very expensive.

Business Names

What's in a name? Quite a lot if it's a successful brand name. A good name can be a very valuable business asset. Make sure you don't start using a name (either consciously or by mistake) that is the property of some other business, so check it out in advance at www.cro.ie, and get your solicitor's advice. If you are stopped from using a name after a period, the cost and disruption to your business of a name-change will be quite substantial.

We will look at five different categories of name as they apply to business:

1. Your own name

If you trade under your own name for the purposes of your business (e.g. Kelly Curtains) there is no need to register this as it is already registered (on your birth cert!). A bit like using your personal legal entity for your business, it the simplest way of naming your business. It has the advantages of simplicity and benefitting from your recognition as a person. The main disadvantages are, firstly, if you wish to sell on the business at some stage in the future it may need a change of name and consequent loss of its brand recognition, and secondly, it may not have widespread marketing appeal outside of your circle of colleagues and acquaintances.

2. Internet names/addresses

Email is a vital means of contact for business today. You can register an email address for free at sites such as www.eircom.net or www.gmail.com (the email function for Google).

If you have a website for your business, it is better that your email address is linked to your website rather than an eircom or gmail address. Choosing the name for your internet site is important and it should be as closely linked to your business name as possible. For example, if your business name is Kelly Curtains, then you should try to have your internet site as www.kellycurtains.ie. Alternatives are a .com address or a .org address. The best for business is .ie or .com. Anyone can register a .com address but to register a .ie address, you will need to have your business name already registered with the CRO (www.cro.ie) and submit the certificate of business name registration.

3. Business/trade names

If you decide to create a name for business purposes (e.g. Home Grown) you are required by law to register it. If you try to lodge a cheque made out to this name, the bank will not cash it for you unless they have a copy of the name registration on file. Before deciding on a name and spending money on stationery etc. you need to check out if you can use it by checking at www.cro.ie. An explanatory leaflet 'Business Names – Explanatory Notice BN1' is available from the Companies Registration Office, Parnell Square, Dublin 1. Telephone 01-804 5200.

If you do use a trading name you are required to print your trading name, your own name and your permanent business address on all business letterheads, invoices, receipts, etc. You are also required to display your certificate of name registration at your place of work. Registration costs €20 online and €40 offline.

Registering your business name does not protect it from being used by someone else, so why would you bother? Because it is a legal requirement to ensure traceability of business operations, and prevent fraud. If you have come up with what you consider to be a really good name, your best option to protect it may be to register a company, with it as the company name.

4. Company names

Unlike a trading name, you own exclusive rights to a company name. The rules and regulations regarding the formation of a company are explained in the leaflet 'Company Names Check – Leaflet No.2', which is available from the Companies Registration Office. As with a trading name, you will also need to make sure that there will be no objection to the name you choose. Obviously if it is already registered it would be blocked, but even if the name you want to use is similar to an already registered name it could also be rejected by the CRO. Do a name check for both business and company names at www.cro.ie.

5. Trademarks

Trademarks come at the top of the pile in terms of name registration and exclusivity. A trademark is a mark (generally a word or symbol) used to distinguish the goods or services of one particular business from those of its competitors. Coca-Cola, Guinness and Weetabix are trademarks that spring to mind. However, don't rush out to spend valuable money on a trademark registration during your first few months in business – the business may not even be in existence a year later unless you focus all available resources on building it up during the early stages.

Business Premises

In general a business needs a base from which to operate, be that a space at the house (even if only the kitchen table on occasions) or a commercial property (workshop, factory, office, storage or retail unit).To use such a property you will have to have a legal right to use it, either through ownership or through a lease. Before you commit yourself to either leasing or buying a property, you should talk to your solicitor. Check in particular for planning permission and compliance with all regulations that govern the use of the premises for trade.

Remember that a building designated as residential cannot be used for business proposed without approved change of use from the local council. There are some exceptions to this rule, for example if you operate an office from your home that does not have public callers. These rules are to be considered even if you are trading from home, where for instance you may need planning permission to convert old out-buildings. If you proceed, keep nuisance to a minimum, and don't fall out with your neighbours. If you can claim to be using the premises for the purposes of business (even on a part-time basis) for in excess of six years, you stand a good chance of getting retention of this use from your local planning authority.

If you are considering buying a property, ownership is usually in the form of a 'freehold' interest. Some properties in old town centres and cities may also have a ground rent attached, which may never be collected but may need to be bought out if you wish to buy the property. Your solicitor will advise you as to the title; the seller's auctioneer is not in a position to.

For most new businesses that need a commercial premises, an option for the first few years is to lease. The lease contract will cover the extent of the property, the parties to the agreement, the commencement and duration of the tenancy, the rent, the use which can be made of the property, liability for rates, electricity, repairs and insurance.

Most new tenants need to install fixtures and fittings to suit their business, and many will install free-standing shelving etc. in order to minimise damage on their removal, as the landlord is entitled to reasonable compensation for damage caused by their removal. As a result many tenants leave fixtures behind at the end of the lease.

A tenant who quits (other than by surrender or because of non-payment of rent) is entitled to be paid compensation by the landlord for every improvement made which adds to the letting value of the property. The amount of compensation may be agreed, or determined by the court. In general the landlord is entitled to an improvement notice in advance of improvements.

The tenant has a right to a new tenancy where the property was continuously occupied for five years, provided the tenancy agreement was not breached. The tenancy agreement may allow the landlord or the tenant to end the tenancy at an earlier date, or as they both agree at any stage.

If you do decide it is economically feasible to lease a premises, make sure you are familiar with all the details of your lease.

Marketing and the Law

People are very aware of their consumer rights, an outline of which are available at www.consumerassociation.ie

Again favouring the weaker party in the deal, the law regulates the ways in which business deals with consumers.

Firstly, it protects consumers by imposing obligations on business people to meet certain standards. Any weighing and measuring devices (e.g. a petrol pump or a weighing scale) must be approved, and can be checked for accuracy by the Gardai. Various food hygiene regulations are in place to protect the customer, and enforced by health inspectors who have the authority to close down a premises they consider unfit.

The usual way these standards are imposed is through the issuing of licences, and non-compliance results in the withdrawal of the licence. On a separate point, this licencing system is now also being used by the Revenue Commissioners to enforce tax compliance, and the renewal of many licences (e.g. pub or taxi) now requires presentation of an up-to-date tax clearance certificate.

It is also an offence to publish an advertisement or a price which is likely to mislead the public. The policing of these areas is the job of the Director of Consumer Affairs.

The second main area of relevance in marketing law is that of product liability. Firstly, there are implied conditions (i.e. they can be assumed). For instance, that the person selling actually has a right to sell, i.e. they own the goods. If the goods are sold based on a sample, there are implied conditions that the bulk corresponds with the sample in quality. It is also implied that the goods are fit for the purpose for which they are bought (e.g. outdoor furniture isn't glued together with glue only fit for internal use).

Another aspect of product liability that arises is that of negligence. Negligence is neglecting to do something which a 'reasonable man' would have done, and where damage is caused to the party to whom a legal duty of care is owed (e.g. a plumber who fails to properly test his work, resulting in an explosion or leak which does serious damage). It is up to the person taking the case (the plaintiff/complainer) to prove his case. A defendant (the person defending himself in the case) may be liable for breach in his duty of care if he fails to provide adequate warnings or directions (e.g. a builder who fails to put up notices warning people to wear hard hats, or a shop that fails to put out a 'wet floor' sign).

Consumer Rights

The following is an extract from the Consumers' Association website www.consumerassociation.ie.

Under the Sale of Goods and Supply of Services Act (1980), anything you buy from a retailer must be:
- Of merchantable quality.
- Fit for its normal purpose, and reasonably durable.
- As described, whether the description is part of the advertising or wrapping, on a label, or something said by the salesperson.

When you buy goods from a retailer, you make a contract with him. He agrees to provide certain goods to you for a certain price. If your purchase turns out to be faulty, the retailer, not the manufacturer, is responsible to you and must sort out your complaint. You are entitled to a refund, a replacement or a repair.

You do not have to take a credit note if your complaint is covered by the Sale of Goods Act. You can insist on a refund, a replacement or a repair.

If you have a genuine complaint about faulty goods, you can ignore shop notices such as 'No Refunds' or 'No Exchanges'. Such notices cannot take away any of your statutory rights under the Sale of Goods Act.

You have no rights under the Sale of Goods Act if you simply change your mind about wanting the goods. You also have no rights if faults are due to misuse of the product after purchase, or if faults should have been seen on examination or were pointed out at the time of purchase.

The person who purchased the goods holds the rights under the Act. If you receive the goods as a gift, you have no contract with the retailer and don't have the same rights. In practice, most retailers will oblige the user of the goods but this is a gesture of goodwill, not a legal requirement.

Your rights under the Act also apply to goods purchased at sale prices. They must be of merchantable quality, fit for their particular purpose and as described. If goods are being sold as seconds or shop-soiled, however, you cannot expect the same standard.

Insurance and the Law

Having read through the previous few pages, you can well imagine that business people seek to protect themselves from liability. They use a mixture of the following ways: firstly, by taking every available precaution to avoid accidents through proper training and proper risk assessment (both covered in the safety statement); secondly, by forming limited liability companies so that if things go badly wrong they are not liable personally; and finally, by taking out insurance.

Insurance provides financial compensation for the effects of misfortune. You take out an insurance contract with an insurance company, who for an annual premium (money you pay to them) will insure you against losses arising from specific events (e.g. a fire in your premises, a car accident). The terms of the contract are contained in the insurance policy. One of the terms is *uberum fides*, or absolute good faith – in other words, you are insured in good faith on the basis that what you have declared is true. For instance, if you declare you are using your car solely for private use, and you are involved in an accident whilst towing a trailer full of equipment for your lawn-mowing business, the insurance company will have an opt-out. They will keep accepting your money based on the answers you give on the proposal form, but will investigate the facts if they need to in the event of an accident.

It is possible to insure against practically anything, but it is not practical to insure against every possibility.

Some questions on insurance might make things clearer:

1. **What affects the cost of the premium?**
   The level of risk (e.g. using power tools, or working at height) and the level of past claims (acts as a deterrent).

2. **What insurances am I obliged to have?**
   Only motor insurance is obligatory, but if you have employees and work in public areas, then public liability insurance and employer's liability insurance are advisable and often required. Property and contents insurance is also important, and a personal accident policy is optional. Professional indemnity insurance is also required in some cases if you are giving professional advice to clients.

3. **Do insurance contracts provide a reward or profit to the policyholder for their misfortune?**
No, they provide indemnity, an exact financial compensation: repair, replacement, re-instatement, or money.

4. **What if my insurances overlap and my loss is covered twice?** You may not claim double compensation; the insurance companies will share the loss between them.

5. **Finally**: always shop around for insurance – it can greatly reduce cost.

Small Claims Court

The Small Claims Court provides an inexpensive, fast and easy way for people to resolve disputes without the need to employ a solicitor. The following types of claims can be dealt with:

- a claim for goods or services bought for private use from someone selling them in the course of a business (consumer claims)
- a claim for minor damage to property (but excluding personal injuries)
- a claim for the non-return of a rent deposit for certain kinds of rented properties.

See www.courts.ie for more information.

In Conclusion

Some people have legal minds, just as others have a great head for figures, so don't worry if you feel some of the legal issues are a bit beyond you. As with everything else, you can work at what you're good at (making money in the process) and simply hire the expertise of your solicitor as you need it.

Keep your mind open to the use of the company structure, as it can be useful in limiting liability, reducing taxation, and enabling you to take on bigger projects.

And finally, a disclaimer: these notes are a general guide in non-legal language; they should not be taken as a legal interpretation. Each case is different, and the law is never black and white.

With this in mind, be slow to resort to the law in sorting out disputes except when absolutely necessary, as the outcome can be uncertain and very expensive.

Exercise

Partnership Agreement

Unfortunately, a number of business partnerships have difficulties owing to the absence of a formal partnership agreement. A good partnership agreement safeguards trust between the partners.

In drawing up a partnership agreement, anticipate problems that may arise and write up a clause for avoiding or dealing with them in advance. The checklist below will give you some prompts. When finished, have it checked for comprehensiveness by your solicitor.

1. Members of the partnership (paid-up)
2. Period of the partnership: commencement, duration and termination
3. Name of the partnership
4. Business activities and location (limit)
5. Partnership premises including tenancy agreement/leases
6. Starting capital: sharing of, and interest payable thereon, risk premiums
7. Profit (and loss) sharing formula
8. Payments to partners, including wages, bonuses, overtime, expenses, etc.
9. Books of account to be maintained
10. Treatment of deposits or other client monies, if applicable
11. Accountants, bankers, solicitors
12. Responsibilities of partners, including holiday entitlement (job specifications)
13. Provision of transport
14. Outgoing partners' arrangements
15. Admission of new partners
16. Tax provisions
17. Covenants in restraint of trade
18. Dissolution of partnership
19. Expulsion of any partner
20. Partnership meetings and voting – arbitration.

Notes

Chapter 13   Health and Safety

Workplace Health and Safety

Prevention is better than cure.

A proper approach to safety helps prevent accidents and ill health, saving human suffering, lost time, lost productivity, and prosecution. Due to the number of deaths, serious accidents, and ill health suffered by employees during the course of their work, workplace health and safety measures have been given huge importance in recent years.

We are all familiar with notices on building sites such as 'Hard hat area', or 'Caution – wet floor' in public buildings when floor cleaning is taking place. Were the owners of these premises not to warn their staff and the public about the dangers involved, they would be liable to be sued for accidents arising from this 'negligence' – neglecting to warn people of danger.

So where do you start? As owner and manager, the starting point is your own attitude. If you put an emphasis on safety at work through identifying hazards and anticipating dangers, this is a great start. Everybody has a right to go home from work as healthy as they went in to it, and that of course also includes you. Many small businesses that operated quite profitably went out of business because of an accident happening to its owner.

After an accident, people will always be wiser and say 'If only I did this or stopped doing that'. Accidents do not happen by chance – they usually happen because somebody neglects to do something the right way. It is often not the culprit themselves, but somebody else, who gets hurt.

The Legal Position

Overall responsibility for the administration and enforcement of health and safety at work lies with the Health and Safety Authority. It watches for compliance with health and safety law in the workplace, and can take enforcement action (including prosecutions) against law breakers. Its officers have a right to talk to employees, take photographs and samples, and impound dangerous equipment.

Its main brief includes:
- Promoting good standards of health and safety at work.
- Inspecting places of work to ensure compliance with the law.
- Investigating accidents and causes of ill health.
- Publishing guidance notes and advice.

The Safety, Health and Welfare at Work Act (2005) requires you to ensure, so far as is reasonably practicable, the health and safety of yourself and others who may be affected by your work activities. The notion of 'reasonable' is a commonly used standard of the law in general.

The 'others' to whom you have a duty include:
- Anyone who works for you (part-timers, trainees, and subcontractors).
- Anyone hiring a premises from you.
- Anyone allowed to use your equipment (ask a carpenter for the loan of his power-saw or ladder and see what you'll be told).
- Anyone visiting your premises (note the signs at the entrance to most building sites).
- People who may be affected by your work (e.g. your neighbour).
- People using your products or professional services.

In summary, the health and safety legislation applies to all work premises, work activities, and everyone at the place of work.

Managing Health and Safety

The evidence strongly suggests that effective workplace health and safety actually contributes to business success, whereas accidents and ill health cost the business dearly. Workplace safety is a key component in the overall management plan. Managing health and safety involves a simple strategy – being aware of the hazards in your place of work, then putting safety measures in place to eliminate, or at least minimise, those hazards. The management tool that is used to list these risks, and to identify the steps required to avoid them, is the Safety Statement.

Because it is a statement about the risks to health and safety in your workplace and the measures you want to take to reduce these risks, you can write it up yourself. For most small businesses a responsible approach is for the owner/manager to write and actually implement a safety plan themselves. Only where things are more complex will you usually need a consultant to prepare a Safety Statement. Creating a safe environment involves thinking about safety in the first place (thought), writing it up as the second stage (word), and most important of all implementing it in the third stage (action).

80% of your accidents will be caused by 20% of your people.

So where do you start? There are **six simple steps** to be followed in the drafting of the statement:

1. State your safety policy.
2. Identify the hazards.
3. Assess the risk – who might be harmed by these identified hazards, and how might they be harmed?
4. Decide what precautions need to be taken.
5. Record your findings.
6. Update the statement as necessary.

Having fully recorded all this information, you must then bring the Safety Statement to the attention of all employees in a way that is easily understood. Other people coming onto your premises should also be made aware of the Safety Statement and have access to it.

Let's look a little closer at the six steps involved in drawing up the statement.

1. State Your Safety Policy

A 'policy' is a course of action or a system of administration. You need to spell out your system of administration with regard to Health and Safety matters. Following is a sample policy that you may choose to include in your Safety Policy.

"This Safety Statement is aimed at protecting our employees, contractors, and any visitors to our premises from workplace accidents and ill health. It is our program for managing health and safety.

We will provide a safe workplace for employees, the necessary protective equipment, and information, training and supervision.

We will update this statement as necessary, and review it once a year. Staff and others are encouraged to put forward constructive suggestions for improvements to the statement.
Safety at work is fundamental to our operation, and our standards of Safety, Health and Welfare will be maintained at the highest level that is reasonably practicable.

The Safety, Health and Welfare at Work Act (2005) requires the organisation, the employees, and others to take reasonable care for their own safety and other persons affected by their acts and omissions. Towards this end they are required to co-operate with their employer's safety procedures, and to use the protective equipment provided.

It is only with your active co-operation that good health and safety conditions can be attained. If anyone is found to have been seriously negligent in any matter pertaining to health and safety, or contributed to an accident through personal neglect, then that person may be subject to dismissal.

A hazard is anything that can cause harm.

In so far as is reasonably practicable, sufficient training in the safety, health and welfare aspects of work shall be provided, to ensure that everyone is aware of the potential hazards and the action required to overcome them."

When bringing the Safety Statement to the attention of employees it must be in a form, manner and, if necessary, in language that can be understood. This should be done initially on recruitment, and thereafter any time there is a change made to the Safety Statement.

2. Identify the Hazards

A hazard is anything that can cause harm (e.g. electricity, working at height, a wet floor, etc.).

To compile the information for your Safety Statement you need to identify the potential hazards in your workplace. Walk around the workplace and really look for significant dangers, as the hazards in most workplaces are few and simple to spot. Don't be overcomplicated or trivial – use your common sense. Ask your employees for things they have noticed. Refer to manufacturer's instructions for dangers of and prevention of accidents using their equipment.

A checklist of **typical workplace hazards** in various employments:

1. Slips, trips and falls resulting from untidy workplaces, wet floors.
2. Falls of persons from height (chairs, ladders, shelving, machines, roofs).
3. Falls of material from height, e.g. badly stacked bales of material.

4. Manual handling of loads, be that lifting, pushing, pulling, carrying.
5. Hazards from plant and machinery (e.g. exposure to dangerous moving parts).
6. Mechanical handling, and not tying or securing loads properly.
7. The movement of vehicles and site transport, especially by untrained or inexperienced drivers.
8. Fire and explosion.
9. The use of hazardous substances (e.g. toxic, corrosive chemicals).
10. The use of compressed air.
11. Exposure to harmful levels of noise, and working without ear protection.
12. Exposure to dust and fumes without a proper ventilation system.
13. Hazards associated with electricity, and not using low voltage tools.
14. Exposure to harmful vibration, damaging bones and joints.
15. Entry into confined spaces.
16. Unsuitable lighting levels in the workroom.
17. Workplaces being too hot or too cold.
18. Work with visual display screens.
19. Human factors (for example, violence to staff, stress, bullying at work).
20. People under the influence of drink, drugs, medication, tiredness and exhaustion, illness, bereavement, etc.

Source: Health and Safety Authority

This list is not complete, nor is it ranked in order of priority. Circle any hazards that apply to your workplace; then add others that apply to your own particular situation and you'll have identified your workplace hazards.

See the Health and Safety Authority's website (www.hsa.ie) for more information.

3. Assess the Risk

Having identified the hazards, you now have to assess any risks arising from those hazards.

Assessing the risk involves using your best judgement to categorise the degree of risk (high, medium, low) for each hazard. Common sense suggests that the high risk hazards need to be dealt with as a first priority, the medium risk hazards next and the low risk last.

A risk is the likelihood of the harm occurring, and the severity of the consequences if it does.

As you assess risks be aware of who might be harmed, particularly if they have a disability (e.g. partially sighted or partially deaf), if they are pregnant, working alone or inexperienced/new to the job, or if they are visitors (especially unsupervised children). A hazard that might present a medium risk to an experienced employee (e.g. using a power saw) would present a high risk to an inexperienced person.

In general terms the risk assessment must address all significant hazards, apply to all aspects of the work (including production and office work), and cover non-routine as well as routine operations (e.g. occasional maintenance tasks).

It's generally true that two heads are better than one, so involve your employees in identifying the risks. Having completed an assessment of each hazard you are then ready to decide on the precautions to be taken.

4. Decide What Steps are Required to Avoid Injury

Having weighed up the risks you need to decide what precautions need to be taken to eliminate the hazards and, where that cannot be done, to reduce the risks. In other words, can you get rid of the hazard altogether, and if not can you change the way the job is done to make it safer? Following are some examples:

Hazard: Faulty electrical equipment
Risk: High – shock and severe injury
Steps required to avoid injury: Report defective electrical

equipment to manager; do not use until repaired or replaced.

Hazard: Manual handling of heavy boxes
Risk: High – back injury
Steps required to avoid injury: Manual handling training; use of sack trucks.

Many of the steps required to prevent injury will already be included on equipment manuals, printed on containers and packaging that comes with chemicals, or detailed in standards of good practice within your industry. In addition, proper training, use of protective clothing and equipment, and repair of faulty equipment are obvious preventative measures.

Your real aim is to reduce all risks to a minimum, so learn from near misses, and recall actual accidents you've seen and heard about, and this will help put the final touches to prescribing ways to avoid injuries and ill health. These practicalities are likely to be the most valuable in the long run.

5. Record Your Findings

Having gone through the above steps, you will now be in a position to fully write up your Safety Statement.

To organise this task you can mark some blank sheets of paper into three columns. In the first column list all the hazards that you've identified; in the second column opposite each hazard state what that risk is and rate it in terms of high, medium, or low. In the third column list the precautions to be taken to prevent injury from the identified hazard.

A casual attitude towards safety often results in a casualty.

Alternatively you can compile a list of individual hazards, risks and avoidance measures under the following headings (as per examples in step 4 above):

1. **Hazard**
2. **Risk**
3. **Steps required to avoid injury**

In addition to listing the hazards, listing the associated risks, and listing the preventative measures to be taken, the document must also:

1. Name those responsible for implementing and maintaining the measures (that's probably you as manager/owner).
2. Contain plans to deal with an emergency.
3. List the names of the safety representatives (if any).

When you've put all of the information in these five steps together, type it up in clearly understood English (and other languages as required) and you will have a completed Safety Statement.

6. Update the Statement as Necessary

Because workplaces constantly change, your Safety Statement must be updated as conditions change and new risks are introduced, e.g. a new machine/piece of equipment. In addition it is recommended that you review your Safety Statement at least once annually. It is also important that you keep detailed records of risk assessments carried out and any controls put in place.

The Safety Statement must also be reviewed when there is reason to believe that it is no longer valid (an accident, dangerous occurrence or a 'near miss' may prompt such a review). The Safety Statement must also be revised, within 30 days, if directed by an inspector from the Health and Safety Authority.

Duties and Responsibilities

Both employers and employees are responsible for creating and maintaining a safe and healthy workplace. Following are the principal duties of each:

Employers' duties include:
- Managing and conducting all work activities so as to ensure

the safety, health and welfare of people at work. This includes the prevention of improper conduct or behaviour likely to put employees at risk (e.g. horseplay and bullying).

- Designing, providing and maintaining a safe place of work that has safe access and exit, and uses plant and equipment that is safe and without risk to health.
- Prevention of risks from the use of any article or substance, or from exposure to physical agents, noise, vibration and ionising or other radiations.
- Providing and maintaining welfare facilities (e.g. washing facilities) for employees at the workplace.
- Providing information, instruction, training and supervision regarding safety and health to employees, which must be in a form, manner, and language that they are likely to understand.
- Cooperating with other employers who share the workplace so as to ensure that safety and health measures apply to all employees (including fixed-term and temporary workers) and providing employees with all relevant safety and health information.
- Providing appropriate protective equipment and clothing to employees (at no cost to them).
- Appointing one or more competent persons to specifically advise the employer on compliance with the safety and health laws.
- Ensuring that reportable accidents and dangerous occurrences are reported to the Health and Safety Authority.

Source: Health and Safety Authority

Workers' duties include:
- Comply with relevant laws and protect their own safety and health, as well as the safety and health of anyone who may be affected by their acts or omissions at work.

- Ensure that they are not under the influence of any intoxicant to the extent that they could be a danger to themselves or others while at work.

- Cooperate with their employer with regard to safety, health and welfare at work.

- Not engage in any improper conduct that could endanger their safety or health or that of anyone else.

- Participate in safety and health training offered by their employer.

- Make proper use of all machinery, tools, substances, etc. and of all personal protective equipment provided for use at work.

- Report any defects in the place of work, equipment, etc. which might endanger safety and health.

Source: Health and Safety Authority

Other people's duties

Persons who have control over a place of work have a duty to ensure that the place of work and any equipment or substance provided is safe and without risk to health. For example, a person in control of an office has to ensure that a visiting window cleaner is provided with safe access and exit and, in particular, that any permanent window cleaning equipment is safe to use (of course, the employer of the window cleaner also has duties in relation to his or her employees).

Others who have duties include:

- Manufacturers, importers and suppliers of equipment, machinery, articles, or substances used at work have the duty of ensuring safety and health concerning the use of the materials that they produce or supply.

- Those who design or construct a place of work must ensure that it is designed and capable of being constructed and maintained without risk to safety and health.

The Role of the Competent Person

As an employer, you should appoint one or more competent persons to assist you in following these steps, and to play a key role in the management of safety and health. In this context, 'competent person' means someone who is able to give informed and appropriate advice on safety and health to management (rather than a person who has specialised technical knowledge). You should select someone for the role on the basis of his or her training, knowledge and experience, or you may appoint yourself to the role if you consider that you have the necessary capabilities. However, if you do not have the appropriate range of expertise in-house, a combination of external and internal competence may be advisable.

'Reasonably Practicable'

Some of the general duties placed on employers under the 2005 Act are qualified by the term 'reasonably practicable'. It is based on the concept of the 'reasonable man' in law, and is essentially a matter of balancing the degree of risk involved against the time, trouble, cost and practicality of the measures necessary to avoid it.

Consultation with Employees

Employers must consult their employees with regard to safety, health and welfare at work and must provide them with certain information on these matters.

As part of the consultation process, employees have the right to select safety representative/(s). Employers must provide certain information on safety, health and welfare at the workplace to employees or their safety representative/(s). These arrangements require the employer to:

Have the courage to act, instead of react.
- Oliver Wendell Holmes

- Consult with employees or their safety representative on any proposed measures likely to substantially affect their safety, health or welfare at work.
- Provide employees or their safety representative/(s), or both, with the results of the risk assessment and consult with them on the preparation of the Safety Statement.

- Refrain from penalising any employee for acting in accordance with safety and health laws or for reporting complaints regarding safety and health matters at work.
- Recognise that safety representatives have various rights, including the right to:
    1. Inspect the place of work.
    2. Investigate accidents and dangerous occurrences (as long as this does not interfere with an investigation being carried out by an inspector).
    3. Investigate complaints made by employees (after giving reasonable notice to the employer).
    4. Be given time off from work, without loss of remuneration, to receive appropriate training.
    5. Accompany an inspector carrying out an inspection at the workplace.
    6. Make representations to the employer on safety, health and welfare.
    7. Make representations to, and receive information from, an inspector.
    8. Consult and liaise with other safety representatives in the same undertaking.

Source: Health and Safety Authority

Enforcement

The Health and Safety Authority is responsible for enforcing and promoting safety and health at work. For the most part, health and safety inspectors give advice and information during the course of an inspection. However, they have a wide range of enforcement powers that are used in appropriate circumstances.

"Effective leadership is putting first things first; effective management is discipline, carrying it out."
- Stephen Covey

1. An inspector may serve a direction for an improvement plan requiring the submission, within one month, of an improvement plan setting out the proposed remedial action for dealing with a specified risk.

2. Enforcement notices may be served to deal with a failure to comply with the law. An Improvement Notice gives a

period of time for the matter to be remedied, while a Prohibition Notice requires the immediate cessation of the activity that has created the risk. The Authority may also apply to the High Court for an order prohibiting or restricting the use of a place of work.

3. Following prosecution, the courts may impose fines or prison sentences (or both), depending on the seriousness of the offence. The Authority also has the right to publish the names and addresses of those subjected to a Prohibition Notice, High Court order or a penalty following a court conviction. The 2005 Act provides for the specification in Regulations of on-the-spot fines of up to €1,000 for certain offences.

Hazards, Risks and Precautions

List obvious hazards in your place of work, assess the risk of them happening and identify how you can prevent them from happening.

HAZARDS Anything that can cause harm	**RISK** State the risk	**PRECAUTIONS** Steps required to avoid an accident
Faulty electrical equipment	**Risk:** shock and severe injury	• Report defective electrical equipment to manager • Do not use until repaired or replaced

Notes

Chapter 14   Employment Issues

Introduction

As a business succeeds there comes a time when a decision has to be made about recruiting additional people. When thinking about employing a person or people (including contract or temporary staff) you need to consider the following points.

Have you Counted All the Costs?

Employees are costly – that's stating the obvious; but of more importance is the fact that many of the employment costs are hidden. It takes time to manage an employee, to train them, to organise work for them, to quote for extra jobs and to collect money on these jobs. All of this extra administration takes a lot of time, which means that your own work output will go down. This is the first cost of employing someone – the reduction in your own output.

The second area in which your costs will increase is your overheads. If the employee is office based they will be using a PC and internet, a phone, paper and ink, occupying expensive floor space, etc. If they are out and about the indirect production costs will increase, including transport, phone, insurance, hire of equipment, additional equipment, basic supplies, etc.

The worst mistake an employer can make is not to say "well done".

Be aware that you will also need more working capital in taking on a heavier workload. If, for instance, it takes €6,000 to keep yourself working on various jobs and waiting to get paid, it will cost up to double this to keep two of you going.

And finally there's wages (if paid weekly) or salary (if paid monthly). There's the direct cost of what you pay staff (in their wage packet and as PAYE/Employee's PRSI) but there's also Employer's PRSI (10.75%). Don't forget that your employee is entitled to six weeks paid holidays per year (21 days holidays plus 9 bank holidays) during which time they are earning nothing for your business. Add in the additional administration attached to these wages, including monthly returns.

Do you Really Need an Employee?

The biggest employment jump in percentage terms that most businesses usually take is from one person to two – a 100% increase. Going from two people to three only entails a 50% increase, and so on.

Even if you are currently working 60 hours a week, that doesn't justify taking on an extra employee – you may end up creating a full job for someone else but leave yourself short of work! If you can avoid taking on a skilled staff member by doing extra hours yourself, and by improving other staff performance and general efficiency, you can save up to €34,000 (the average industrial wage). This would service a property loan of c. €500,000 (and if replacing existing rents would service a much larger loan). Thus the 'opportunity cost' of that extra staff member can be huge. Remember, staff costs are usually the biggest overhead cost for any business, and so require productivity-based management.

Are you (and your staff) working to maximum output? There are three elements to this. Firstly, there's time management and working to targets (an hour lost per day is a day a week) so eliminate all slow time. Secondly, are you equipped as well as possible? Equipment may seem like a big investment, but you'd never feel paying out, for example, €6,000 in wages plus employer costs – about ten to fifteen weeks! And if there's anything worse than working under-equipped yourself, it's several people working without the right gear, thus multiplying the inefficiency. Finally, there's the possibility of working extra hours yourself, which may be twice as productive as those of an unskilled staff member.

Having sorted out the basics of efficiency first as outlined above, there will then come a time where the only remaining route to expansion is through employing someone. At that stage it is important that you stand back and take an overall view of the business. Where is it at now? Where is it going in the next few years? And how will staff contribute towards this? This will help in drawing up a job specification for the kind of person that will be of greatest benefit to you.

Compare the Cost to the Benefit

Before you employ anybody (either directly or on a subcontract), always ask the basic question 'Will this person make money for me or cost me money?' When you add it all up, it costs at least double what you pay an employee to cover all the costs of employing them. After you add in a profit margin you should aim for two and a half to three times wages as a revenue target for each employee. If you're tendering for tightly priced work you can charge labour at twice wages, but be careful about unforeseen delays as the margin for error is small.

Given the basic business equation (take in more than you let out) you have to figure out how much extra money you will make (per day/week) by employing this person. In other words you must set targets for extra work to be completed – at two-and-a-half times wages. Thus a wage of €30,000 translates into an additional sales target of €75,000 per year, or €6,800 for each of eleven working months. Regularly ask yourself 'How much extra money am I making by employing this person'?

If the need to get in sufficient work to keep unnecessary staff paid means you have to start quoting for lower priced work and messier jobs, then you'd need to stand back and re-evaluate the situation. Decide whether or not you'd be better off as a smaller operator concentrating only on higher priced work.

What Kind of Person are you Looking for?

You cannot possibly hire the right person for the job if you haven't thought out clearly what the job is. The most important exercise to carry out prior to hiring anyone is to write up a job specification, i.e. a basic list of all the things you need them to do (essential), followed by a wish list of what you'd like them to do (optional). Will they need to drive; to lift; to sell; to price work; to supervise; to deal with people; to work alone; to take responsibility; to show initiative; to take orders; to have computer skills; good administration skills, etc.?

Thereafter there are two main evaluations you must make with regard to recruiting staff: firstly, do they have the necessary technical work skills; and secondly, do they have the required personal qualities? Do out a list of interview questions under these two headings (even for an informal interview) and you'll sharpen your awareness of what to look out for.

Will the person you recruit bring experience, additional knowledge, new contacts and possibly some new clients? Will they have a set of skills that will complement yours, and from which you can learn? As a general approach to employing others, if you can recruit someone better than yourself it should mean you'll build a good business; recruit less capable people and the business will go down in quality. Needless to say, you want to keep control of the business so stay close to your customers and maintain the key assets and processes yourself.

Employees will not have a neutral effect; they will either cost you money or make you money.

Apart from recruitment, a job specification is important because it outlines to staff precisely what they are supposed to do in their job. Staff are not mind readers, so you need to define the job you want them to do. Whilst as a one-man-band there is no doubt as to what you must do (everything), when there's more than one person working in a business it's important to take the time to divide up the workload fairly evenly, according to ability. That's the whole purpose of a job specification – to divide out the workload. Otherwise too many cooks will spoil the broth, and everybody might end up doing the 'nice' jobs, and the 'not-so-nice' ones get ignored.

Employ skilled staff if at all possible, and they'll most likely be valuable contributors from the first week. But above all watch out for a negative attitude – a person with low skills you can train, but you'll be unlikely to turn around someone with a negative attitude as they have a lifetime of training gone into acquiring it. In your overall assessment of anyone you are considering taking on, there is one key assessment that you must make – will this person bring your business forward or bring it back? Hiring the right or the wrong people will have a bigger effect on your business than you can imagine – so pick your staff very carefully.

Supports for Employment

Work Placement Programme

The Work Placement Programme facilitates your business to take on a person for a work experience placement for a maximum of nine months. While the person is gaining valuable work experience they are also contributing to your business. You have the opportunity to see how they work and if you are in a position to recruit you will have had ample opportunity to determine if they are suitable. Visit www.fas.ie for more details.

Short Time Working Training Programme

This FÁS Programme allows people who have had their hours of work reduced to improve or add to their skills. It provides two days training per week for employees who are on systematic short-time working for three days a week and getting an SW payment for the two days they are not working. Each placement lasts for 52 weeks. Training is flexible to allow people complete courses if they return to full time work. Visit www.fas.ie for more details.

Employer PRSI Exemption

An employer who creates a new job and employs a person who has been on the live register for six months or more will be exempt from employers PRSI for the first 12 months of that employment.

The Employer Job PRSI Incentive Scheme may save an employer in the region of €3,000 from the annual cost of employing an additional worker.

Interviewing

Good interviewing is critical because:

1. It reduces employee turnover. A high rate of employee turnover causes hassle; wastes the time given in training; lowers both customer loyalty and customer service; puts remaining staff under pressure; lowers their morale and wastes the time and money required to re-hire.

2. Bad employees mean bad business. Customers remember bad service, bad manners, and bad treatment. Bad employees make for hard work on the manager in just holding the fort. There is also the danger of unfair dismissal claims etc. when it comes to trying to rid your business of its problem, which can sap your enthusiasm.

Benefits of Getting the Right Person for the Job

1. The main benefit of getting the right employee is that they cause you less stress. You can delegate a lot of your work to them, in the confidence that it will be done correctly.

2. In addition to getting the job done the right person will get through more work, thus earning you more money (even if they cost a little more).

3. They may bring extra skills to the work situation, thus improving your product offering, and will be more responsive to your customers.

There's no point having a dog and barking yourself.

4. They will require a shorter training period and be up to productive speed faster.

A final point: In order to get the right person it is critical that the interviewer sell the business and the opportunities it presents to the employee. An interview is a two-way process, and just as the interviewee has to sell themselves to you, you have to sell yourself to them. That way everybody gets their needs met.

Delegation

Delegation is the art of getting someone else to do the work properly and profitably. Having recruited the correct person there is no point keeping them under your thumb; you have to allow them to use their own talents and initiative. Obviously these are to be applied to the work as outlined under their job specification. Make clear the extent and limits to which they are authorised to make decisions without referring back to you, particularly in the early stages until they have proven themselves.

How do you know if you are delegating too little?
- A constant backlog of work to be done; never a minute to spare.
- Unfinished or part-finished work, often at a cost to your business.
- Ending up with a lot of routine or technical tasks.
- Making all or most of the decisions in the business.
- Constant pressure and stress.

A typical self-employed person is often too busy, too stressed and too tired to take the additional opportunities that are there in every business. Many owner/managers find their workload becoming increasingly heavy. However, good delegation is a critical skill that every owner must learn in order to allow the business to move on to the next phase of growth.

In delegating any project or piece of work, there are a few simple steps:

1. Define exactly the work that needs to be done and highlight how you want the final job to look, drawing attention to any particular techniques or quality issues you want complied with. Ask a few questions to ensure that communication is good.

2. Ask the worker to explain how they intend to go about the work.
3. Clarify anything you are unclear about, and correct any aspects you are unhappy with.
4. Agree a time for completion, and any times for an interim review, if necessary.
5. When completed, review the work in line with the directions you gave at the start, compliment good work, and insist on bad work being brought up to the required standard.

Failure to delegate properly will cause mistrust, poor quality, delays and frustration. Stand back from the business and see which jobs can be safely delegated. If you can delegate or subcontract it, and there's still a good profit margin left for you, then be slow to do this work yourself.

When delegating work, always try to get rid of the work you don't like – and ideally hand it to somebody who does like it. Recruit staff with this consideration in mind. Good delegation – getting others to do the work properly – is the ultimate skill in good employee management and good time management.

Motivation

The difference between what an employee can do and what they actually will do depends a lot on motivation. This is one of the main reasons why some people use more of their skills than others.

By knowing and understanding what motivates an employee, what 'makes them tick', you can then organise a system of work which will get the best out of that person. Find out what they are particularly good at (i.e. their strengths – therefore they enjoy doing it) and give them plenty of that to do. That makes for high productivity and satisfaction all round.

"People, like nails, lose their effectiveness when they lose direction and begin to bend."
- Walter Savage Landor

Generally it is understood that motivation refers to forces within and outside a person that push them to try to satisfy needs or wants, be that a need for survival at the bottom of the scale or a need for self-fulfilment at the top. Some people love responsibility, need to be in charge, are driven to achieve, and need praise – others just want to work away quietly on a project. Every human being is unique, so your job as manager is to find the unique motivators in each, not to apply a 'one size fits all' approach.

Various studies have been conducted by industrial psychologists on what best motivates people, and one of the best known is the Douglas McGregor 'Theory X and Theory Y' scenario. In this he presents two common sets of attitudes that managers bring to bear on their employees.

Theory X suggests that people:
- Are mostly lazy and have a dislike of work
- Lack ambition and need to be forced to work
- Avoid responsibility
- Feel no desire to achieve
- Do not care about organisational needs
- Cannot be trusted or depended on
- Avoid decision making
- Resist change
- Need money and rewards to motivate them
- Do not change even when they mature.

Theory Y suggests that people:
- Work hard to achieve what they are committed to
- Assume responsibility
- Are self-directing in their work
- Desire to achieve
- Are aware of organisational needs and want it to succeed
- Prefer making decisions about their own work
- Can be trusted and depended upon

- Are motivated by challenges and tasks
- Want support and help at work
- Want to change and progress themselves.

Your management style will tend to lean towards one style or the other whilst having some elements of both. A Theory X manager will tend to compensate for their lack of confidence in their employees by controlling their work very closely. A Theory Y manager believes in the unused potential of people, and tends to act as a coach and facilitator. On assessing your own style, which type would you say you are?

These are extremes of course, and even though in some circumstances either Theory X or Y attitudes have been adopted, it is suggested that a combination of the two works best, depending on the unique individual you are working with. One management style does not fit all employees, so you must tailor your style to maximise the abilities of each individual. As an exercise you can go back through the attitudes listed, and with a particular person in mind tick the ten that you think most apply, taking a number of attitudes from each theory.

Dealing with Discipline

It is important that you keep a professional distance from all of your employees, maintaining good boundaries. You are there to manage, not to make friends or have favourites, and this professionalism pays dividends when it comes to issues of discipline.

Everything will not always go smoothly; sometimes you may need to deal with non-performance or misconduct. When an issue requiring discipline comes to your attention, remember to apply the four F's – get the Facts; then be Fair, Firm, and Friendly.

Facts: Investigate carefully and thoroughly in a calm, sensitive and reasonable manner.

> **Fair**: Take exceptional human circumstances into account (e.g. relationship difficulties, financial pressure, etc); don't show favouritism; be reasonable and consistent with sanctions.
>
> **Firm**: Make sure you're in charge and that what you require to be done is done.
>
> **Friendly**: Keep perspective, don't get stuck in the moment. These things settle down if dealt with properly, and you need to maintain a good working relationship for the future. You'll earn respect for it.
>
> If there is gross misconduct, e.g. an assault, or damage to equipment, never fire someone on the spot – the 'You're fired' Alan Sugar/Bill Cullen line. In this situation ask the person involved to take the rest of the day off, cool down, get perspective, and get legal advice before doing anything further. Unfair dismissal costs a lot of time, energy and money.

Labour Law – the Basics

A comprehensive guide to all aspects of labour law is available from the Department of Enterprise, Trade and Innovation at www.deti.ie. Following is an outline of the most common legal issues that arise.

Employment Contract

If you employ someone you are required by law to give them an employment contract within four weeks of starting. Anyone who works for an employer for a regular wage or salary has a contract automatically, whether it is in writing or not. It must include:

- Name and address of employer
- Job title/description
- Date of commencement
- Temporary or permanent contract
- Hours of work/overtime
- Pay conditions/maternity/holiday/sick leave, etc.
- Pensions/injury

Wages

Every employer is obliged to pay wages (at least the minimum rate of €7.65 in 2011) to an employee. Employers are obliged to give a wage slip itemising all deductions made along with the wage packet.

The only deductions allowed are:
- PAYE or PRSI.
- Any that were stated in the contract, e.g. uniforms, breakages.
- Health contributions and pension schemes (with written consent).

Hours of Work

The normal working week is fixed at 39 hours per week.

Breaks
- One hour between 11.30am and 2.30pm unless otherwise agreed.
- One half hour between 4pm and 7pm.
- No employee is obliged to work more than six hours without a break for a meal.

Holidays

Most employees are entitled to 21 days holidays from the 1st April to 31st March the following year.

In addition, there are nine Public Holidays:
- New Year's Day
- St. Patrick's Day
- Easter Monday
- First Mondays in May, June, August,
- Last Monday in October
- Christmas Day
- St. Stephen's Day

If any of these days are worked, the employee is entitled to one day's holiday with pay, or an extra day's pay in lieu.

Minimum Notice

By law you are required to give a substantial amount of notice before ceasing employment.

Time worked	Notice required
13 weeks – 2 years	One week
2 – 5 years	Two weeks
5 – 10 years	Four weeks
10 – 15 years	Six weeks
More than 15 years	Eight weeks

The employer or employee can terminate employment at any time without notice if misconduct of either party has taken place.

Redundancy Payment Scheme

An employee between the age of 16 and 66 who is expected to work more than one day a week and whose employment has ceased because of redundancy (e.g. workplace closes down due to financial difficulties) is entitled to redundancy payment, if they have been employed by the business for two years or more.

A lump sum is calculated at half a week's pay for each year employed with the company between the age of 16 and 41, and one week's pay over the age of 41.

Employers are entitled to a rebate of 60% from the Department of Enterprise, Trade and Innovation as long as the employees have received at least two weeks' notice.

Protection of Employment Act

If an employer is planning to make several people redundant he must first supply the employees with the relevant information regarding the decision and consult with those involved at least 30 days before the first person is made redundant. Employers must also notify the Minister for Enterprise, Trade and Innovation at least 30 days in advance.

Transfer of Undertakings

When one owner transfers ownership of a company to another, the obligations of the original owner to each employee should automatically follow.

Dismissal

The law provides protection against employees being unfairly dismissed. Every dismissal is regarded as unfair unless the employer can show that it resulted from one of the following events:

- Employee misconduct
- Employee was incapable or unqualified
- Redundancy of the employee
- Another substantial reason for dismissal.

If an employer dismisses an employee he must produce the dismissal in writing within 14 days after being requested to by the employee. Dismissals are considered to be unfair if they are based on involvement in trade union membership or activities outside the normal working hours.

Other unfair dismissal issues include: religion or colour; person's political opinion; sexual orientation of the employee; pregnancy; a person wishing to have time off for protective leave or natal care; age; being a member of the Travelling community.

Children and Young Persons

Even though law does not usually allow for the employment of a child under 15, a person over 14 years is allowed to work part time during school holidays as long as it does not interfere with school or affect their health.

When employers are employing persons under the age of 18 they are required to look for a copy of their birth certificate. People between the age of 15 and16 are not allowed to work more than eight hours in a day or 40 hours in a week. People between 16 and 18 are not allowed to work more than nine hours in a day or 45 hours in a week.

Safety, Health and Welfare at Work

Employers, employees, and self-employed alike are obliged to ensure that their workplace and systems at work are safe. Every employee has a right to come home from work as healthy as they went in, and the management tool for health and safety is a 'Safety Statement' as outlined in Chapter 13.

Exercise

Job Specification

Draft a job specification for an employee or subcontractor that you may need for your business during the coming year, by outlining all the different types of work they will have to do.

Chapter 15   Time and Stress Management

Time Management

Introduction

The time in each day is the one thing we all have equally. How we use it, however, is our own choice. We can waste it, or we can use it wisely; we cannot save it; once it is gone it is gone.

Our length of time on earth is not the same for everybody, but on philosophising with an old person they will often comment on how fast it went. We know that time flies when we're enjoying ourselves, but drags when we're having a hard time, so there's a mental dimension to time – it's not just something a clock measures. Time waits for no one, so it is important to manage it as best we can. If we stand still whilst time flies by we will find ourselves in the same position years later, just older.

"And then one day you'll find ten years have got behind you, no one told you when to run: you missed the starting gun."
- Pink Floyd, Time (Dark Side of the Moon)

In terms of time management the past is irrelevant because it is gone, and no-one has yet invented a way of changing the past. The future hasn't arrived just yet, so we can only plan to do things differently then. However, the difference between what we plan to do and what we actually do can be quite large. The best real indicator of what we will do in the future is what we are doing in the present, because the future is really just a continuation of the present.

The present is the only time there is. If you want something done, do it now. A large project like starting a business needs to be broken down into its separate tasks. These tasks need to be put in the correct order, and if completed as presented one by one, the basis of a business will present itself.

Time Management Wisdoms

- **Work expands to fill the time available**
Are you always 'too busy working' to manage your business, e.g. to advertise and quote for jobs; collect cash; write up your

books; organise the work for the week ahead? You must **make** time for these vitally important management tasks in addition to 'working'.

- **If you need a job done, ask a busy person to do it**
Why? Because they're sharper and more efficient, and can't afford to be wasteful with their time. They get in and out fast, and do quality work.

- **Early to bed, early to rise makes a man healthy, wealthy and wise**
Burning the candle at both ends means it will burn out a lot faster. You may keep going, but the vital management tasks will be the first to get ignored. When you're tired your whole business is tired, and who wants to deal with a tired business? And if you can't get out of bed early in the morning, then forget about self-employment before you ruin yourself.

- **Thou shall keep holy the Sabbath day**
There's only so much you can do in a week. It is possible to maintain a six day working week indefinitely, but once you start working the seventh day, burnout and bad judgement are just around the corner.

- **An hour a day is almost a day a week**
A day a week is 48 days in the year (allowing four weeks for holidays/bank holidays) or nearly ten working weeks wasted. This is the way time gets wasted (an hour per day), leaving you with no time for days off, holidays, etc. – always half working, always time wasting.

- **You make time for what you value**
There's no point saying 'I didn't **have** time' – just be honest and say 'I didn't **make** time'. You always make time for the things that you feel are important.

> - **To be on time you have to aim to be early**
> On an average job or journey, there are a whole number of things that can hold you up. Allow for them in advance if you want to be on time.
>
> - **Do all you can today, and let the rest wait**
> There is only so much you can do in a day. If you are happy that you've done your best on the most important jobs, then sometimes the rest will just have to wait.
>
> - **The early bird catches the worm**
> If you are asked to quote for a job, the sooner you get the quote in, the better. Someone else might get there before you if you delay.

Why Bother with Time Management?

Because time is our scarcest resource, to not manage it would be to waste much of it. Our lives are made up of time, so to waste our time is to waste our lives. Our lives are short because time flies.

The story of Tír na nÓg from the old Irish legend looks at man's attempt to escape from time into a land of eternal youth. Man has always dreamt about stopping time but it's impossible, because even if you succeed for yourself, everybody else will have moved on. Even though Oisín remained young, when he returned from Tír na nÓg all his family and friends had passed on. Time waits for no man, not even the great Oisín. When we sit back in our retirement we will reflect on whether or not we managed our time well, i.e. whether we managed to spend our time on the things that were important to us. It would be better if we made that evaluation now, whilst we still have time to make changes.

A new business should come with a health warning – running it badly can seriously damage your health.

It takes less time to succeed than to fail, so the best way to waste time is to fail repeatedly. Building a profitable business will save you a lot of time, and you'll be able to buy even more time with these profits and can then choose to live a fuller, richer life.

Work expands to fill the time available, states Parkinson's Law. Consequently, the average self-employed person works longer than they intend to, often for much less money than their counterparts in employment. Guard against this happening by valuing your time, and consciously managing it properly.

Thinking about how you use or lose time has several benefits:

1. It forces you to consider whether you are using your time properly by focussing on what's important, or just squandering it by working on what seems urgent (but isn't that important).
2. No-one has enough time, yet everyone has all there is. As a manager, time spent working **on** your business is more important than time spent working **in** your business.
3. Your time is your life. What you do with your time determines what you do with your life, so deciding what you want your life to be about gives you clear direction on how to spend your time.
4. If you mistreat yourself by constantly putting yourself under time pressure, then you are less caring towards family, friends, and yourself.

In order to get a better perspective let's look at your usage of time through three different time frames.

1. Life Time View

From time to time you need to take an overview of your life from the cradle to the grave, and ask what is valuable to you. Is this value reflected in the amount of your life-time you spend living these values? Will it be helped or hindered by self-employment? Let's consider the issues.

Working time

For instance, what age and stage of your life are you at now? How many years have you been working? How many more productive years do you intend to work before retiring? How many hours do you work in the average week, and how does it compare to the standard 39 hour week? Do you get to take holidays every year? Are you happy with the way you are spending your time or is it just something that happened through habit?

Lifestyle

What sort of a lifestyle do you live? Do you want a big house and a big lifestyle with big bills and long working hours to pay for them? Or would a more modest house and modest lifestyle, with more family and leisure time, be better? Have you finished your education and training, or do you intend to do more on a part-time/full-time basis? Will this be possible whilst running a business, or would a regular job with a career break be more suitable?

Retirement time

If you assume you will live until you are 80, how many years will you spend in retirement? What do you want to do during retirement and will you have enough money to do so? What sort of a pension plan or investment plan do you need to put in place now in order for this to be possible, or will you settle for mere survival and not bother with a pension plan?

2. Week Time View

Just as your money is more easily managed by dividing it into three accounts, you also need to open time accounts for the things you consider important. If you don't allocate specific time to important areas you'll find one or more of them gets neglected – how could it be otherwise if it doesn't get its fair share of time?

Time spent working on your business is more important than time spent working in your business

Following are three suggested time accounts that you could operate weekly:

1. **Business time/work time**. A business is a greedy thing for time, absorbing all you make available to it. This problem is

even more acute with a home-based business (the majority of business start-ups) where there is no clear boundary between work time and home time. You need to be disciplined about the amount of time you let it take – because if you don't set clear boundaries it will take more than its fair share.

2. **Home time**. Needless to say, it will cause hassle if you're never there for your family. You need support, not hassle, but you need to earn that support by keeping the home fires burning. A single person has fewer demands on their time from a family perspective, but anybody in a relationship or with children has family needs that require time to be spent on them.

3. **Social time**. 'All work and no play makes Jack a dull boy' is a well-known phrase of old. It is important to be able to get away from work and home and unwind. This may take the form of going to a football match, going fishing, going for a few pints, visiting friends and family or doing whatever interests you.

3. Day Time View

It's not a delay to stop and sharpen the scythe.

When Charles Schwab was president of Bethlehem Steel, he presented Ivy Lee, a consultant, with an unusual challenge. "Show me a way to get more things done with my time," he said, "and I'll pay you any fee within reason."

Handing Schwab a sheet of paper, Lee said, "Write down the most important tasks you have to do tomorrow and number them in order of importance. When you arrive in the morning, begin at once on number 1 and stay on it till it's completed. Recheck your priorities; then begin with number 2. If any tasks take all day, never mind. Stick with it as long as it's the most important one. If you don't finish them all, you probably couldn't do so with any other method and without some system you'd probably not even decide which one was most important. Make this a habit every working day. When it works for you, give it to your men. Try it as long as you like. Then send me your check for what you think it's worth." Some weeks later Schwab sent Lee a check for $25,000 with a note saying that the lesson was the most profitable he had ever learned. In five years this plan was largely responsible for turning Bethlehem Steel Corporation into the biggest independent steel producer in the world.

Summary of the Ivy Lee Method

1. At the end of the day make a list of all the jobs you want to get through the next day
2. Number that list in order of importance
3. Start at number one on the list, and stay at it until it's completed; then move to number two, and stick with that until completed, and so on.

If you don't get it all done, at least you get the most important things done, and you still get more tasks completed than if you were skipping from task to task – remember you can only do one thing at a time.

Consider the opposite to the above strategy: 1. Don't bother making a list at the end of the day; 2. Do any job that suits you, instead of the most important ones; 3. Jump from job to job instead of getting jobs finished. Is this the way you sometimes find yourself managing your time at present?

In Business Time is Money

Time is one of our scarcest resources. From a business point of view we can clearly argue that time is money, and we all sell time to other people for money, buy time from other people for money, share time with family and friends for free, and spend time doing things we want to do. Whilst there is a limit to the time available to us, there is an unlimited supply of money. This makes time management more important than money management, yet people often show more respect for money than for time.

Customers buy time so that they can spare their own, and spend it doing something they put more value on. Thus a customer may buy something they could do themselves, for example, a mowed garden, a cooked dinner or an ironed shirt, in order to spare their own time to do something they enjoy, for example, play golf, earn more money, read a book. A phrase you may have heard about people during the Celtic Tiger era is that they were 'Cash Rich, but Time Poor'. In other words, they may have had two incomes coming into the house, but very little time to spend on living at their ease. This has resulted in a whole range of time-saving businesses, like cleaning, laundry and ironing, online shopping, pet care and dog walking, etc.

Good time management ties in closely with maximising your profitability. Remember the profit-ability formula – 'reduce costs, increase prices, sell more stuff'? If you waste money through bad pricing or unnecessary costs, you will have to spend more time earning money to pay for them. If you are selling your time for money then it is important that you get the best possible price for it.

It follows that good profitability is a key factor in good time management. A poor, struggling business can be an awful waste of time. Don't tolerate unnecessary hard graft and time-wasting, as they deny you your deserved rewards of time and profit abundance. Imagine that – an abundance of both time and profit!

Think about this observation – often the people that make the most money are the people that work the least hard, and vice versa. The profitable business owner will generally have the most of both time and money – because they make the most efficient use of both their time and their money. Needless to say, this should be one of your key business objectives.

Time Management Techniques

Set time budgets and deadlines

Once you decide on the main areas you want to spend your time on each week, how do you make each area stay within its time allocation? Remember Parkinson's Law – 'Work expands to fill the time available'. Because of this universal law it is common business practice to apply deadlines to limit work expansion. A deadline for starting and finishing work every day. A deadline for every project at work – getting the work out the door and paid for instead of striving for unattainable perfection (and getting on to the next job).

Avoid over-optimism – use accurate project management

Whilst optimism is a positive quality, over-optimism is where your optimism overrules your level-headed judgement and you ignore the problems and the hidden difficulties. Always allow yourself sufficient time to cover emergencies and contingencies when organising your week's work. Otherwise you'll become one of those who can never finish a job on time, and get a name for being late, slow and unreliable.

Even worse – you'll most likely under-price jobs, because they take longer to complete than you estimate. Inaccurate material estimates can be cured with a factual quantity survey of materials, and inaccurate time estimates can be cured with good project management techniques which calculate time deadlines.

Plan ahead

Take time out on a Friday evening to plan a schedule for the week ahead in your diary – what you must get done, and which days you plan to do it. Then every weekday evening compile a detailed task list for the following day, and adjust as necessary. This is a key skill in good management – developing an accurate ability to estimate the time and money needed to get work done.

The creation of a prosperous future through accurate time planning is one of the key changes to be made in switching from being employed by someone else to being self-employed.

Make time for the family – either morning or evening
Because people are busy with work it is practically impossible to have time for the family in both the mornings and the evenings. Depending on which suits your partner, it is best to choose the morning or the evening for family time. As a self-employed person it is generally best to get up early (around 6am), get out the door, and get stuck into travel and work. Then get home by six in the evening for family time; housework, homework, shopping or sports runs. Maintain these healthy time boundaries. Don't let the home time interfere with your mornings – let it wait until early that evening; likewise in the evenings don't let the business interfere – let it wait its turn until early the following morning.

If your children have been used to you spending more time with them, try to involve them in some aspect of your business. Posting letters, loading the van, going with you on short deliveries, even a small amount of involvement in your business builds up a respect for your work. Also, travel time on these runs can be great talking time, about school, sport, family, etc.

Putting Things Off

A stitch in time saves nine.

Procrastination or putting things off has been described as 'the art of keeping up with yesterday'.

It takes not one drop of sweat to put off doing anything, but it becomes very tiring. You don't really put it off – simply, you either do it or you don't do it. Guilt from feeling you 'should' have done it, and giving out to yourself afterwards represents crazy behaviour. It's an example of not working in the present moment as fully or as efficiently as possible.

You can do anything you set your mind to accomplish, but by putting things off for a future moment you are giving in to self-doubt, and most significantly, self-delusion. You're hoping that things will magically improve in the future; 'I'll wait, and it'll get better'.

Action is a much better measure of what you are than words. What you are doing is the only indicator of what you are as a person. 'Do not say things. What you are hangs over you all the time, and thunders in my mind so that I cannot hear what you say to the contrary.' So don't put it off – do it now!

Here are some tips to tackle procrastination:

- Get started on something you've been postponing.
- Make decisions quickly. Slow decision-making eats up time.
- Tackle what you don't like first; don't leave it 'till last!
- Get rid of problems as soon as possible – don't let them hang around for too long.

Losing Time – Some Causes

A lot of time is wasted through misdirection, miscalculation, and disorganisation.

Misdirection is where you get involved in things you should have avoided, often because it suited someone else and they convinced you. Exercise your judgement first, and try to avoid getting into things that don't suit you. They may not suit you because they do not fit in with your plans and goals, or because you don't have a natural ability with them. A little word called 'no' can be your best ally in these potential time-wasting situations.

Miscalculation is where you get into something that may suit your abilities and goals, but you mis-calculate the time resources it requires, i.e. it takes a lot longer than you thought it would. To under-estimate your time means to under-estimate your price. Keeping a close count on what time it takes to complete every job is the key to solving this problem.

Disorganisation is seldom a case of not having enough ability, but usually results from not paying enough attention to the need to organise yourself properly. Organise yourself with a system that will **S**ave **Y**our **S**elf **T**ime, **E**nergy and **M**oney, as much time is wasted in purposeless activity, 'going around in circles'. If you add in starting late, bad equipment, and talking too much, you can see how time-wasting can become a big problem.

The cost of this type of time wasting includes the financial cost, time-pressure stress, damage to reputation, and poor creativity.

Summary: Time Management Tips

1. Fix deadlines for all jobs, and stick to them. Anything can only take the time that you allow it to take.
2. Learn to say 'no'. Get used to asking 'Am I the right person for this task?' and don't take on work that you shouldn't.
3. Do not postpone important matters that are unpleasant. Tasks rarely get more pleasant by being postponed.
4. Do one thing at a time. Keep an overview of the next jobs to be done.
5. Analyse your interruptions. Take steps to eliminate them or to reduce their effect.
6. Plan your telephone calls. Make a brief note of what you want to say and what you want to find out.
7. Organise your time in one place – your diary.
8. Make it a rule to regularly check your use of time. Keep a close watch on your diary for a full week every few months, and ask yourself what time-wasters have crept in.
9. Put off everything that seems to be urgent, but is not important. Many so-called urgent problems have a tendency to solve themselves if you ignore them for a while, because they weren't really your problems in the first place.
10. Don't take on other people's problems.
11. Encourage employees to come to you with solutions, not problems. Force them to think their way through to a solution rather than stopping and complaining at the problem.

	Exercise
	Time Management

The true test of living is to be able to look back after a long life and to be able to say, "Yes, I have done what I wanted to do in my lifetime." Visualise yourself in ten years' time, and answer the following questions.

What have you accomplished in the past ten years?

1.
2.
3.
4.

What lifestyle have you enjoyed?

1.
2.
3.
4.

What advice would you give to others starting off?

1.
2.
3.
4.

Stress Management

Introduction

Stress is a major time-waster, as well as a major cause of ill-health. Increasing levels of stress reduce your effectiveness in the medium term, and are proving to be a silent killer in the long-term. The World Health Organisation is predicting that by 2020 stress will be the major cause of workplace ill-health. Symptoms of stress include disturbed sleep, fatigue, increased alcohol consumption, headaches, loss of concentration and short temper.

In order to make progress towards your goals you have to stretch yourself a little, but avoid over-stretching. The right amount of pressure brings speed and high performance; too much and things go wrong, with serious consequences.

By 2020 stress will be the major cause of workplace ill-health.
- World Health Organisation

Self-employed work can be open-ended and never-ending. You may find yourself on the phone at any time of the day or evening, so my advice is to have a dedicated phone for work and let it go on to message minder outside of work hours. If you have done a good day's work, then draw a line under it until the following morning.

Determining your correct pace is also very important. You must aim to strike a sustainable pace that you can maintain every week, and not be stop – go – stop – go, alternating between bursts of work and exhaustion. We all have a pace that is right for us. Finding this pace is a combination of experience and common sense. Working below this pace for too long (i.e. under-employed) or exceeding this pace (i.e. under constant pressure) will cause stress. Finding your own natural pace is the best option for the removal of unnecessary stress.

Typical Stressors and How to Counteract Them

Financial concerns	• For your business, aim to maintain a minimum of 2 months' working capital. • For your personal finances, put a savings nest-egg together by reducing expenses (smoking, phone, food, socialising, etc.) and saving the difference.
Irregular income	• Secure some regular weekly/monthly contracts if possible. • Supplement income with a regular part-time job (either you or your partner). • Maintain sufficient working capital to allow a regular weekly wage independent of week-to-week business cashflow.
Employees	• Keep employee numbers to a minimum by working longer hours yourself. • Employ staff on a part-time basis and subcontract work at keen rates. • Learn to delegate properly and profitably.
Frustrational stress	• Review your goals for their realism and timeline. • Talk to a good mentor regarding the cause of your frustration.
Collecting money	• Set out clear terms and conditions with your quotations. • Look for regular stage payments. • Stop work/supplies on first default.

Failing physical or mental health	• Maintain good habits of diet, exercise and sleep. • Maintain a positive attitude, and talk with family or friends about your concerns. • Pray, learn relaxation techniques such as yoga or meditation.
Bank repayments	• Avoid all unnecessary borrowing. • Avoid credit cards; if in place, cut them up and reduce balance as quickly as possible. • Lower repayments by extending loan periods.
Overwork	• Don't work seven days a week except in exceptional circumstances. • Take a break every holiday season. • Work hard for 5½ days per week, maximum 3 late evenings; then forget about work!
Conflict	• Avoid difficult people. • Avoid difficult jobs. • Maintain good boundaries, keep your side of the bargain and insist on others doing likewise.
Seeking perfection	• Don't play God. • Work to agreed specifications, not perfection.

Develop a spirit of thankfulness for all you do have rather than a feeling of lacking about what you don't have.

Losing a major contract	• Maintain a broad customer base and a diversified product offering. • Be prepared in advance to scale back costs immediately.
Falling sales	• Reduce costs immediately. • Provide a better product for less money.

Sharpen Up

Ask yourself the question: which is easier, to slog away with a blunt instrument, or take out some time to sharpen and maintain your tools?

The importance of self-maintenance can be illustrated by the following story from **'The seven habits of highly effective people'** by Stephen Covey.

You are walking through the woods one day and come upon a man struggling to cut down a tree. He looks exhausted and is drenched with sweat. 'How long have you been at this?' you ask. He replies, 'Over five hours! This is hard work; no end is in sight, and I'm about to collapse!' You reply, 'Well, why don't you take a break for about five minutes and sharpen your saw? I'm sure your job would go much faster then.' 'I don't have time to sharpen the saw,' the man says emphatically. 'I'm too busy trying to cut down this tree!'

All work and no play makes Jack a dull boy.

It is important for us to keep our "saws sharpened" – to make time to do maintenance activities that revitalise us. If we do not take the time to recharge our batteries, we will waste even more time struggling to keep on top of things. Remember, 'It takes less work to succeed than to fail'.

Overwork is overwork, which is not sustainable in the long term. The German attitude is that you should always complete your work in the allocated time, and come in ready and sharp for work the next day; putting in long, slavish hours is seen as inefficient. On the other hand, the Japanese approach is to apply yourself totally to your job, at the cost of work/life balance. There are advantages and disadvantages to both approaches. Decide on your own individual pace. But as the old saying goes, 'Even a good horse can't keep running forever'.

Worry and Anxiety

Both have been described as the thief of time. Two observations that might put worry into perspective:

1. The things we worry about happening usually never happen anyway, so they're a waste of time and life.
2. Even when they do occasionally happen, we are able to handle them.

It is therefore critical that we take a strategic decision to eliminate worry as the useless activity it is. Practicing a personal routine in the areas of physical, mental, emotional and spiritual health as outlined below all help to eliminate worry.

We can safeguard our **physical health** by eating properly, sleeping enough but not too much, taking exercise and not abusing ourselves with drink, drugs or cigarettes. Our **mental health** is reliant on maintaining a good mental diet of positive thoughts, and guarding against the negative creeping in. Our **emotional health** is safeguarded by respecting ourselves, maintaining good self-esteem and a good opinion of ourselves generally, and respecting and maintaining good friendships. Our **spiritual health** is improved by making a spirited effort to reach the full potential of our God-given talents, and through meditation and prayer. All of these states of health are undermined by continuous stress.

Business can be very stressful at times. It is therefore important that you build into your lifestyle a number of different stress relieving measures. Hobbies like golfing, fishing, and sport are widely used and adopting a regular exercise routine is also critical.

Remember the children's story about the golden goose? Whilst initially delighted with a golden egg a day, the little boy got greedy and wanted more of them. So he decided to open up the golden goose and get them all together but the goose dies. You know the moral of the story – if you kill the goose that lays the golden eggs (i.e. if you ruin your health), you will soon run out of golden eggs (i.e. money).

Conclusion

Much of the discontent people suffer is because of the huge expectations they have of life, fuelled in part by the advertising industry and by Celtic Tiger greed. A much more enlightened philosophy is to develop a spirit of thankfulness for all you have, not regret for what you don't have. This simple philosophy alone can completely turn around one's attitude, increasing happiness and reducing useless anxiety and stress.

And finally, a Quotation to Consider

"Those who think they have no time for bodily exercise
will sooner or later have to find time for illness."
Edward Stanley, during an 1873 address to Liverpool College

Stress Management

A simple approach to managing stress is by identifying what factors cause it in the first place, and figuring out how you might eliminate these stress factors.

What causes you stress?	What are the symptoms?	What is the cure?

Chapter 16   Goal Setting

Introduction

If you don't know where you are going, it will be almost impossible to get there. Before you waste time and energy on hard work that leads nowhere, make sure to sit down and figure out where you want to get to. Deciding on your goals is the simplest and best-kept secret of success. There is no point in working just for the sake of it – you need to be working towards something, towards a 'goal'.

Life tends to give us what we believe we deserve, so our expectations of ourselves and of life are very important, often becoming a 'self-fulfilling prophecy'. Many of these expectations and goals are ingrained in our national culture (e.g. home ownership) or imparted through our schools (e.g. career ambitions), not to mention our families who largely shape our value system and our view of how the world works.

Goal setting is the best-kept secret of success.

As people go through the different stages of life, their goals and expectations change. Starting off as young people small goals are set – like buying a music system, going on a foreign holiday, buying a car; later on it becomes houses, weddings, etc.; and later again it's pension plans and other savings and investment.

Once you become self-employed you have to create an additional set of goals – your business goals. This makes good goal setting all the more important, firstly because you have more of them to set (personal and business goals); and secondly because if you miss your business goals (e.g. no profit) you may also miss your personal goals (e.g. pensions, investments) as you won't have the money to pay for them.

Dreams or Goals?

'Follow your Dream' is a line we have all heard, so are dreams goals, or what's the difference? Dreams take very little effort, often occur whilst still in bed, and if not translated into definite actions can become nightmares. Dreams are illusions which, when not realised, will create a state of disillusion.

Goals, on the other hand, require a vision of the future, hard work, deadlines, sacrifices, focus with time and money, ongoing measurement, realism, and courage.

A goal may be inspired by a dream, but it must have goal-achieving discipline imposed. However they arise, goals are inspired by your vision of the future. Creating a mental vision and a wholesome, emotional reaction to achieving them is critical to success. This practice of 'visualisation' is a well-established technique that comes naturally to us and is also used by sportspeople and high achievers in all fields. The clearer you can see a goal, the more likely you are to reach it. Successful goal scoring is more about being clear and less about being clever.

Fears and Goal Setting

Every dog fights a good fight on its own doorstep.

Reflect for a few minutes on the many wisdoms presented in the following passage, delivered by Nelson Mandela on his release from prison:

'Our deepest fear is that we are powerful beyond measure. It is our light, not our darkness, that most frightens us. We ask ourselves "Who am I to be brilliant, gorgeous, talented, fabulous?" Actually, who are you not to be? You are a child of God. Your playing small doesn't serve the world. There's nothing enlightened about shrinking so that other people won't feel insecure around you. We are all meant to shine as children do. We were born to make manifest the glory of God that is within us. It's not just in some of us; it's in everyone and as we let our light shine we unconsciously give other people permission to do the same. As we are liberated from our own fear, our presence automatically liberates others.'

- Nelson Mandela

Why are some people afraid to set goals?

1. 'I might bring too much pressure on myself.'

Taking on too much all at once certainly brings on too much pressure and is a recipe for failure. But the whole point of setting a number of clear goals is to avoid putting too much pressure on yourself. You consider what's most important for you to achieve in this short life, then go for that and don't worry about the rest! By concentrating on a few important and manageable goals you avoid the pressure caused by spreading yourself too thinly over too many.

2. 'If they're too high and I don't achieve them it will only cause feelings of failure and disappointment.'

If you don't bother setting goals at all you're much more likely to suffer feelings of failure and disappointment, because you are seriously reducing your chances of success.

Obviously if they are too high and you cannot hope to reach them, then you are setting yourself up for failure. Instead be realistic, give yourself a clear direction, stretch yourself a bit but avoid overstretching, and you'll find that your efforts will take you a lot further in the right direction straight towards your goals.

Unconscious Symptoms of Fear of Success

People often assume that the reason they try is because they are afraid of failure, but equally it is true that people are afraid of success, because success changes the whole way they relate to the world. How might fear of success manifest itself?

1. **Setting too many goals, thereby diluting your energy amongst several**

   This is regularly referred to as 'spreading yourself too thinly.' In terms of physics, a comparison with a shotgun and a rifle illustrates the point. A shotgun blast sends numerous pellets a short distance, and a few extra yards is achieved with a stronger cartridge. Likewise with too many goals, all of them take energy to progress a little distance, but even with huge effort they can only go so far. On the other hand, a rifle shot concentrates its effort on one bullet, sending it a distance of several miles.

Concentrating on one major project allows for faster progress, and enables you to achieve deeper understanding of the problems and solutions on hand. Spreading your resources of time and money over too many projects slows down your progress with them all, and results in gaining only a superficial ability with them, becoming a 'Jack of all trades, master of none'.

2. Not finishing things

Weak desire brings weak results.

Making an optimistic and enthusiastic start on several projects is fine and well, but it doesn't produce any worthwhile results unless each project is completed, and the lessons learned are carried on to benefit the next task. Going on to a new project before the previous one is finished means the same mistakes will be brought to bear – it won't be finished either. But more importantly, you are denying yourself the feelings of success that come from a job well done. All the hard work is done but the success is denied, and your subconscious fear of success is strengthened.

In striving to reach any goal it is not the start that hurts, as one is fresh and full of enthusiasm. It is when the goal is in sight that muscles and nerves become strained. Knowing this, it is important that you double your efforts when you get near your goal in order to make sure it gets finished properly.

3. Self-sabotage, once success appears

If the subconscious belief is that you don't deserve the success resulting from your goal, then you will blow it. This

> tendency is commonly referred to as 'Grabbing defeat from the jaws of victory'. Examples would include Alex Higgins, George Best, various politicians, and numerous business people and bankers. They may take reckless chances and self-destruct because, subconsciously, they felt they didn't really deserve the success they seemed to have.

Prepare to Set Goals

1. **Exercise your judgement first**

   It is vital to decide on goals that suit you. Getting involved in projects that don't suit your natural, innate abilities but 'seem like a good idea' can be very wasteful. Don't just get 'stuck in', before you map out the route to your destination. Whilst enthusiasm, raw determination and sheer hard work will get any business started, and even sustain it when it's small, these qualities alone are not enough when you move on to stage two growth, playing for bigger stakes.

   Having carefully decided on what you stand for in terms of goals and achievement, you must weigh up the price you have to pay for achieving them (discipline, work, sacrifices) with the cost of not reaching them (lack of fulfilment, regrets, damaged confidence).

2. **Get 'turned on'**

   How do you feel about your goals? Do you feel anything? Feelings are a much better indicator of what will happen than thoughts. Thoughts just involve your head, but feelings also involve your heart, your motivation, your desire and your courage.

   Do you trust yourself to deliver? At the back of your mind are there doubts about your own resolve, or a steely determination to do whatever it takes? 'To your own self be true' said Shakespeare (Hamlet) so be true to your self and your goals. Get yourself really turned on by finding the reason why you deserve success with these goals, remembering that strong desire produces strong results. Most successful goals are based on your values (core beliefs), but it takes the emotional guidance system of your desire, emotion and passion to really energise them.

3. Give yourself permission to succeed

Your mind operates on both the conscious and the subconscious levels, with the majority (c. 90%) being subconscious. The subconscious is there but you cannot get at it too easily. That's the way it's designed, to make access to it fairly difficult. So whilst you can quickly change your conscious mind, your subconscious thinking is not changed quite so quickly. It needs a little more work in order to be sure this isn't just the latest fanciful notion that the conscious mind has come up with. Although you may consciously be all up for starting a business and making plenty of money, you may, at a deeper level, come up against subconscious blocking beliefs.

Not knowing where you want to get to before setting off will result in a lot of wasted effort.

Successful people give themselves permission to succeed, and have the confidence to fully believe that they are worthy of their success. They have a conviction that they deserve success, and a compulsion to work towards achieving it.

A practical aspect of giving yourself permission is developing a prosperous vision of yourself having achieved your goals. The magnetic power of thought, sometimes called 'the law of attraction', will then enable your subconscious to spot the many pieces in the jigsaw needed for you to achieve your full vision.

4. Affirm your right to succeed

Affirmations are a type of brain strengthening, whereby you repeat a short message 30 times, at three intervals each day. The original one, developed by Dr Émile Coué was 'Every day in every way I am getting better, better, and better'. For success in business it can be adapted to 'Every day in every way I am becoming more and more successful'. If you have difficulty in setting or reaching your goals you could try 'I achieve my goals easily and enjoyably.' Try it for a month or two and you'll see that what started as your own self-suggestion becomes an automatic way of thinking.

Whatever the mind can conceive and believe, the mind can achieve.

You can make up affirmations yourself to address any area of your thinking that needs a boost, but always keep the statement in the present tense. If you wish for something in the future your subconscious will keep it in the future, just like you're telling it to.

'I can, I will, I knew I could' is a tried and trusted confidence boosting affirmation. The 'I can' affirms that you have the ability to do it; the 'I will' affirms that you have the determination to do it. 'I knew I could' puts you mentally in the position of already having achieved your goal. It acknowledges that there is a major difference between getting to the line and getting over the line successfully.

5. Commit yourself fully

We defined commitment earlier as 'being prepared to do whatever it takes'. It certainly requires a steadfast focus on the benefits arising from your goals – it may even mean an obsession with them. Let's look back on a memorable quote:

'Until one is committed, there is hesitancy, the chance to draw back, always ineffectiveness. Concerning all acts of initiative (and creation), there is one elementary truth, the ignorance of which kills countless ideas and splendid plans. That the moment one definitely commits oneself, then providence moves too. All sorts of things occur to help one that would never otherwise have occurred. A whole stream of events issues from the decision, raising in one's favour all manner of unforeseen incidents and meetings and material assistance, which no man could have dreamed would have come his way. I have learned a deep respect for one of Goethe's couplets:

Whatever you can do or dream you can, begin it. Boldness has genius, power and magic in it.'

Excerpt from *The Scottish Himalayan Expedition* by W H Murray

Setting Goals

There are three main goal-setting techniques which we will examine in detail below.

1. Basic Goal Setting

We know that the future is not just something that happens to us but something we have a major role in creating. Like any act of creation, goal setting involves the three-step process of thought, word and action. Let's keep it simple and confine ourselves to business goals only. Set goals that represent real achievement and will stretch you, but aren't so big that they are unattainable.

1. **Thought**. Think about where you would like to see yourself in the future. What is your grand vision for yourself, free from the usual negativity but based on confidence and good self-worth, yet realistic? 'Without a vision the people perish' says the Bible, and it is generally accepted that if you intend to go anywhere you need to have a picture in mind of what and where this place is. For ease of comprehension we can look at the future in terms of the short-term future (up to one year), the medium-term future (up to five years) and the long-term future (up to the end of our lives). What sort of a timescale are you comfortable with?

   Within this future there are certain things that you may wish to have: a new car/van? A healthy savings account, equipment, plant and tools? Shop fittings? A workshop? An investment property or holiday home? A retirement plan?

2. **Word**. Writing out your goals in a SMART (**S**pecific, **M**easurable, **A**ttainable, **R**ealistic, **T**ime-related) way serves two main purposes. Firstly, it makes you think about them more, replacing woolly thinking with specific words.

Secondly, it makes them available for rewriting several times until you are happy with your results.

In addition to writing out your goals and putting a time frame and a value on them, outline one or two critical moves you need to make in order to achieve them.

3. **Action/visualisation**. See the outcome clearly in your mind's eye – burn the image into your brain. The clearer you can see yourself in possession of these goals, the better the chance of them becoming your reality. Then get into action. Action speaks louder than words, so get started on doing things that need to be done to bring you closer to your goals.

2. Treasure-Mapping Your Goals

Many a ship was lost close to the harbour.

A second method of goal setting that is very effective is the technique of treasure-mapping. It is one of the simplest techniques, and on thinking about it, one of the most obvious. It works by gaining direct access to your subconscious mind.

It is simply a matter of putting a smiling picture of your own face super- imposed on the goals that you wish to achieve. Thus if it's a new car, it's a case of putting your own smiling face in the centre of a brochure for the car. Likewise if it's a house or a business premises, it's a case of putting a smiling picture of you into a larger picture of this property. Have the final product look colourful and bright. Put this image in a place where you will regularly see it, e.g. in your wallet or inside a door in your bedroom, that's also reasonably private, as visitors will probably be ignorant about your goal-reaching techniques.

This simple technique works by getting the attention of your subconscious mind, which will then strive to achieve it. The subconscious mind is highly perceptive and picks up on details that we normally wouldn't give a second glance to. This is the basis on which subliminal messages were included in advertising, a practice which is now illegal. Scientists have proven that every experience is recorded in high-fidelity detail in our brains, including taste, touch and smell in addition to sight and sound.

This technique is a variation on the 'Blue Ford Escort Theory', which states that out of streams of irrelevant information we notice the bits that have meaning for us. Stop your conscious mind dismissing it as a load of nonsense; at the very least it can do you no harm. The effort involved in getting the pictures of the goals, and a smaller, smiling picture of yourself to paste onto them, will get your thinking more focused. But the real power is in accessing your subconscious.

Goal setting requires real effort, unlike dreams of a better future which take no effort or courage. Yet people put great faith in their dreams and hopes. Better to get down to setting goals, even if it takes you out of your comfort zone for a while. Like everything else it gets easier with practice, at which stage you will have a simple and strong goal-setting technique added to your business skills.

3. Six Ways to Turn Desires into Gold

Following is an extract from the book 'Think and Grow Rich' by Napoleon Hill, one of the best-sellers of all time. It outlines an alternative goal-setting and goal-achieving technique consisting of six definite, practical steps:

1st: Fix in your mind the exact amount of money you desire. It is not sufficient merely to say 'I want plenty of money.' Be definite as to the amount (there is a psychological reason for definiteness...).

You see things and you say 'why?' But I dream things that never were and I say 'why not?'
- George Bernard Shaw

2nd: Determine exactly what you intend to give in return for the money you desire (there is no such reality as 'something for nothing').

3rd: Establish a definite date when you intend to possess the money you desire.

4th: Create a definite plan for carrying out your desire, and begin at once, whether you are ready or not, to put this plan into action.

5th: Write out a clear, concise statement of the amount of money you intend to acquire, name the time limit for its acquisition, state what you intend to give in return for the money, and describe clearly the plan through which you intend to accumulate it.

6th: Read your written statement aloud, twice daily, once just before retiring at night, and once after arising in the morning. As you read, see and feel and believe yourself already in possession of the money.

It is important that you follow the instructions described in these six steps. It is especially important that you observe and follow the instructions in the sixth paragraph.

Reference: Think and Grow Rich, Napoleon Hill.

If you followed these steps, and completed step six every day for a year, would it have a big effect on your thinking? It is self-suggestion, so of course it would. Hill only gives you the technique, you decide the details, so don't aim for anything you don't want.

Notice a few things about the technique which are common to all goal setting. He asks you to be specific, which we have come across with the SMART approach. He wants you to be specific as to the amount and the time frame within which you will have attained this amount.

He also asks for your commitment to this goal in terms of what you are prepared to give in return, on the basis that there is nothing for nothing – you have to pay a price to deserve this money.

He asks for a plan of action and a written statement, so the process of creation of Thought gets confirmed in Word, and achieved through twice-daily Action.

He asks for a twice-daily repetition – which is the same type of reinforcement that all affirmations which try to implant a new idea into the subconscious use, getting past the judgement of the conscious mind by sheer repetition.

He asks that you practice this repetition on awakening in the morning and again at bedtime – just like when you were asked to say your prayers (to pray is defined as 'to ask earnestly'). These are the two times during the day when your subconscious is most open to suggestion, i.e. as you enter and exit from the unconscious state of sleep. This gives the message a better chance of sinking in.

He also asks that you see and feel and believe yourself already in possession of the money – and this is very important. To the subconscious it is a reality which it will strive to fulfil, because it accepts everything it is told at face value. If you wish for something in the future it will keep it in the future – so be very careful to stay present.

Which Technique?

Of the three techniques, which would you be most comfortable with? Which would be the most powerful? Which would you adopt as part of your efforts to build a profitable business, and why? Complete an exercise on all three, try them out, then decide.

General Observations on Goal Setting

- Before goal setting became an accepted technique, good old-fashioned ambition was the approach; ambition to be someone of note, to do something worthwhile, to own something of value.
- If you create a clear mental picture of the result of your goal, it provides light at the end of the tunnel on a large and difficult project. Create positive feelings about this picture – feel deeply what the success feels like.

- Goal setting is necessary to keep you on track even on a daily basis, not to mention how 'out of direction' you can get on a yearly basis.

- A well planted goal, long forgotten about, often emerges fully completed several years later! Just goes to prove the power of the subconscious, which doesn't forget.

- Goals represent your higher, full-filled vision of yourself. This is your truest self, more true than the small, belittled self you may feel like when worn down by life.

- Be resolute in your determination to always do your best, knowing that your best will vary from day to day; forgive yourself the bad days provided it was your best effort.

- Some people set and achieve goals, whilst others dodge out by constantly making excuses for themselves. The day progress really starts to happen is the day you stop making excuses.

- Goal setting is the difference between mere survival and real, noteworthy achievement.

- Self-help books often dangle dreams, but don't deliver results; adopting a goal-setting technique that you are happy with is a far more reliable way of focussing your efforts on real results.

- Taking the time to set goals really saves time. It saves years.

- Goal setting gives you a road map for where you want to get to. Once your overall destination is decided you can concentrate on the day-to-day work. Like on a long car journey you can only drive the section of road directly in front of you, but if you're on the right road you'll get there.

- Give your goals a special place in your heart. Don't weaken the energy surrounding them by telling other people, as others may be cynical and jealous. Action speaks louder than words, so let your results do the talking.

- Life passes by quickly. When you're older and you look back on life, you will want to be able to say that you achieved what you set out to achieve.

Positive Mental Attitude

People often ask, 'What is the right attitude?' The right attitude is a positive mental attitude. Skills may not be necessary as they can be acquired or bought in, but a positive attitude is necessary from the very start.

The right attitude is looking for the best opportunities, looking to create the best. How else did people learn to fly, to build skyscrapers, to improve their standards of living?

A positive thinker always looks for change as a means of moving towards improvement. If we keep on doing the same things, we'll keep on getting the same results; to expect a better result without changing and improving our approach is stupid, to say the least.

The negative comes in without an invitation, like weeds in your garden; the positive needs to be planted, nourished and kept free from weeds until it gets well established and strong.

How do you strengthen your attitude? Andrew Carnegie once said 'Give me a man of average ability but with a burning desire and I will give you a winner in return every time'. Really ask yourself why you are striving to build your business, and keep asking until you find your motivation.

A heartfelt, true, solid motivation will see you clear of nearly any obstacle that comes between you and your goal. People regularly question their ability. But instead of doing this, they'd be much better off to question their desire.

Being able to master the bad times is also very important. As professional business people you cannot leave your attitude down in the dumps. It will cost you too much, maybe even put you out of business. We all have ups and downs, but how do you get out of a negative rut?

Whenever you're faced with a crisis, whatever that crisis may be, look at it with a positive thinking approach, and ask 'How can I turn this to my advantage?' Face any major disaster with that mental approach: 'How can I turn this?' If you can handle and turn around the bad times, the good times will take care of themselves.

Are you becoming negative or positive?

1. Check what you say! Is it mainly positive or negative?
2. Check what you think, as it will eventually come out. You can't possibly be fully successful if there is much negative in there.
3. Visualise a 'bullet-proof screen' to deflect the constant negativity that is thrown at you.
4. Mix with positive people and avoid negative people, because attitudes are contagious.

Avoid Negative People

Smile
Be happy
Be positive
Talk positively
Look positive

Remember, no monument has ever been erected to a critic; monuments are erected to those who don't criticise, but who achieve. Avoid people who are constantly criticising, condemning and complaining. There's very little about criticism that is constructive; condemning only gets people's backs up; and complaining gives away your personal power. You must become aware of the negatives in yourself and eliminate them, and become aware of them in others and avoid them. It takes no conscious effort to be negative. So stick by the positive, and reinforce it regularly.

If someone emptied a dustbin on your kitchen floor, what would you do? After getting annoyed about it you'd clean it up, which might take about ten minutes. But what if they dumped their negativity, whinging and complaining into your brain for a whole evening? Does it not matter if they regularly dump their rubbish in your mind, which takes a hell of a lot longer to clear out?

If you want to stay positive and goal-focussed, hang out with positive, goal-focussed people. They will support you in moments of weakness, not drag you down to a lower level.

A Small Change in Direction

There is a thin line between success and failure, between profit and loss. It only takes a small change to shift from one to the other. Most of what you're doing is right – it only takes a small change to turn break-even into profit. That last little bit of focus that's achieved through goal setting makes all the difference.

Picture this: you are crossing the street towards two doors which are side-by-side. Veer slightly to the left and you end up going in the front door of a bar. Veer slightly to the right and you end up in the bank. In terms of a life-plan, the consequences of this small change in direction are huge. It depends on which destination you set your sights on.

When you have a vision for what you wish to achieve in your life, not only will others stand aside and let you pass, but they will join you in your quest as well. When you speak of your passion in life, your definite major goal, they will see the intensity of your desire, and they will respond with encouragement and assistance or they will stand aside. It will be apparent to all who know you that you will succeed.

You may get by in life without a clear goal, but you will never get far ahead. Clear goals are the starting point for all noteworthy achievements.

```
┌─────────────────────────────────────────────────────┐
│                    Exercise                          │
│                                                      │
│                 Five Year Goals                      │
│                                                      │
└─────────────────────────────────────────────────────┘
```

What are your five main business goals to be achieved over the next five years?

1.	
2.	
3.	
4.	
5.	

How will you go about achieving them? What strategic moves do you need to make?

1.	
2.	
3.	
4.	
5.	

Notes

Chapter 17   Networking for Business

What is Networking?

The Oxford English Dictionary describes a network as '... a group of interconnected people or things'. We are all familiar with the idea of computer networks and the internet, but of more importance to us are our people networks – the groups of people we interact with.

'Birds of a feather flock together' is an old wisdom, because like-minded creatures tend to hang around together. This happens throughout nature with schools of dolphin, herds of cattle, and packs of wolves. Humans, birds and animals tend to 'network' for a variety of reasons, be it for company, protection, joint undertakings (e.g. hunting), information, or learning new skills. Because of this it can be argued that networking is the most natural thing in the world.

Tell me who your friends are and I'll tell you who you are.

The modern world is full of a range of groupings, be they family, work-related, sporting, religious, social, professional, etc. As people we belong to certain such groups; as business people we need to belong to some more.

In business it is vital to understand the value of networks, and to commit both time and resources to growing your network and maintaining your contacts. Networking in a business sense is the **work** of making and maintaining a **net** of contacts.

Promotion (definition: to put forward) is one of the P's of marketing, and networking is simply a means of putting yourself and your business forward in a low-key, friendly way. This makes it an efficient and cost-effective way of advertising what you can do.

Why Network?

'Why do people bother networking?' Did you ever try to get a 'ticket' for an all-Ireland final? If you don't have a network, you don't get one. Likewise with a top rugby or soccer international. The same applies to getting business. For successful business people, getting to make good contacts is not left to chance. It is not a vague thing requiring luck, over which they have little control. It is approached in a methodical way by creatively building a whole series of networks and relationships with people.

Starting a business is not simply about changing the way you earn your living, it is a life-changing experience. How and where you work, who you meet, when and where you socialise will all change to a greater or lesser degree. Effective networking will enable you to build a new support system of advice, information and resources that can help you build a profitable business. Being new to business it will help you develop a business-like attitude, much of which is absorbed and reinforced by associating with other business people. Networking gives potential clients an opportunity to get a sense of your true character and enables trust to develop. Trust is a key ingredient in securing work from practically everyone.

A typical response to the idea of networking which prevents many people from developing a network is the mistaken view that it is somehow devious or underhand. It smacks of 'jobs for the boys', the 'old school tie', 'unfair influence' or 'getting too big for your boots'. This is often followed by 'that's the way it is in this country'; well, that's the way it is in every country.

It's both what you know and who you know that counts.

Maybe you can afford not to bother building relationships with people if you are satisfied with what you have. However, if you want to reach your goals quickly, getting involved with relevant associations or groups of people makes for faster progress.

The reality of life is that people hang out in like-minded groups, talk to each other and about each other, and make decisions. It is people, not organisations, that make decisions; and all other things being equal they will decide in favour of the people they know and trust rather than strangers. You need to try to influence these decisions in your favour by getting the inside line. If you want to get on in business you need to 'push yourself' to mix with people, even though this means leaving your comfort zone, rather than hiding at home in your office or workshop.

Main Benefits of Networking

1. Simplify the world of business

All the advice and information you need is in somebody's head. Nobody knows it all, but if you know the right people you can quickly get the necessary information. This will simplify getting around the many obstacles you'll face in business.

At a basic level it may enable you to quickly solve a problem (through a phone call or two) that might otherwise take a couple of days. A good network can make it easier to source reliable suppliers, get trade credit or a bank loan, access advice, hear about events and gain valuable information on 'the grapevine'.

2. Make sales and personal contacts

Networking puts you in contact with people that will help you in different areas of your business – getting various contracts, building your customer base, etc. Generally you will find people in your network will encourage you and be willing to help.

Think back to selling – it's a type of advance sales. Before people will buy your product they have to buy you. If they get an opportunity to get to know you and like you over a period of years, then it's likely you will get business from them, and that they will refer others to you. It's that simple – you are selling yourself in advance. Sales is a numbers game – the more people that know you and think well of you, the more sales you will make.

3. Exchange and develop new ideas

You can increase your business creativity by exchanging ideas with others. Many business people tend to focus their attention on their competitors, and self-obsessed people focus on (you've guessed it) themselves. This type of focus can be very narrow and may blind you to new opportunities. Networking enables you to listen to other people's ideas and to bounce your ideas off other people, particularly those who have different experiences and are in a different line of business. This gives you a new angle or perspective on things and awakens your creative thinking.

Networking is about mutual benefit – there must be something in it for everyone.

4. Identify opportunities for co-operative action

You can complement your business activity by forming business alliances with others, maybe even taking on some joint ventures. Joining forces with others to perhaps enter a new market, tender for larger contracts, or distribute your goods and services more efficiently could prove very beneficial.

5. Learn to adapt to new thinking and practices

The business environment undergoes continuous changes and businesses must always be ready to learn and adopt new practices. Networking with others will help you keep abreast of new thinking and to learn from others. Adaptability is key to survival in a fast-changing business world, so keep tuning in to others' observations, adaptations and visions of the future.

6. Minimise isolation

'It is not good for man to be alone' says the Bible. Self-employment by its very nature can be isolating, because unlike a regular employee you don't have workmates to confide in. This isolation leaves you vulnerable when difficulties arise. Your network can act as a support system where you will find others with whom you can seek advice, solutions and friendship.

Building contacts will also open up new opportunities for your personal and family life – access to clubs and organisations for you or your family members and invitations to parties or social gatherings.

7. Does it really work?

Try to think of some personal examples of when you've actively used networking yourself. For instance, did you ever try getting work abroad? As a student I had the opportunity to work in London and Chicago. I knew nobody on arrival, so I plugged into a network – the Irish pubs. They acted as an informal network, where the subcontractors met the lads looking for work. Many years later and self-employed, I still find that I get most of my work through referrals and networks.

You can learn an awful lot through your involvement in a local community development group, if they are a strong, go-ahead group. The young chairpersons of two different groups I worked with put a lot of their personal success (both self-employed) down to the various contacts made and business skills learned during voluntary time with local community groups.

How do You Network?

Networking is not a new concept, so you already know how to do it. People have been going to the funerals, christenings and weddings of family and friends for as long as man can remember. Sports clubs have been organising memberships, dinner dances and fundraisers since they were first formed. People have been sending Christmas cards to family and friends for years. It's all networking, just mainly centred on family and community. Business networking is the same thing, with a slightly different focus.

For many people it involves little more than handing out their business cards at a conference or trade meeting; for others it involves going to all the funerals in the area, and being seen at local events, be it a wedding, a football match, at church, community functions, etc. And not just to be seen there but to get around and chat to the maximum number of people.

When networking it is necessary to have a good grasp of human relations. As always, the golden rule is to have respect for everyone, regardless of their baggage and peculiarities, and for yourself. Thereafter, listen, be friendly, show kindness, decency and generosity of spirit, be positive, be humorous, have a good word to say, show character, volunteer, and sing a song if you can! Don't ram your opinions down everybody's throat, bore people, whinge, be pretentious, be too loud, lick up to or look down on anyone.

A lot of organisations require voluntary effort to keep them going, and it is noted and appreciated if you give your time and talents. Volunteer for a job or a committee in a local organisation and you will get value for your efforts in terms of a good reputation.

Remember that networking is about mutual benefit – there must be something in it for everyone. It is important for you to understand what you can do for other people. Good networking is about building relationships with people who can vouch for you, and all relationship building involves both give and take. You must be prepared to give of your time, work and expertise if you expect others to do likewise in return.

And don't forget to enjoy it rather than take it too seriously! Networking and good socialising are similar; it's just that networking has a business focus in addition to maintaining friendships.

Where Can I Network?

Most people's networking strategy takes a two-pronged approach: firstly in a **group** setting, and secondly on an

individual basis. A bit like fishing with a line or a net – they are both ways of fishing, and each has its place depending on the type of fish you are trying to catch.

Following is just a short list to get you thinking about group networking:

Sporting: fishing club, hurling, football, soccer; rugby, tennis, bridge, golf, boat club, gun club, motorcycle club, hill-walking, etc.

Business: Chamber of Commerce, Rotary, Lions, Masons, Knights of Columbanus, Round Table, trade associations, trade shows, etc.

Community organisations: Political parties, residents' association, community group, IFA, ICA, school meetings, charities, Tidy Towns, etc.

Over-seriousness is the curse of the modern age – don't become a social bore.

In addition to group events, there are an endless number of ways in which you can meet people for individual networking:

Social/recreational: pubs, restaurants, dinner parties, musical societies, church, prayer meetings, etc.

Educational: Primary school, secondary school, third level, training courses. Are any of your old school mates doing well? Were there any school re-unions? Could you organise one?

Work: All the previous jobs you worked on. Referrals from satisfied clients you have worked for can be a major source of work. Also former employees and workmates.

Just in case you're wondering, it's not practical to participate in every possible network. Join the ones you enjoy, plus the ones that are good for business. Where both of these measures are satisfied in the one event, you're on the pig's back! Plan your socialising so that you don't always get stuck in the same corner of the same bar talking to the same people about the same things! Networking involves getting out there and putting yourself about a bit. That means variety, which is the spice of life.

When?

In order not to waste working time, most of this aspect of business is done whilst you are socialising – during the evenings and at the weekends. Many formal networks arrange their meetings during dinnertime, once a week or so. Friday evening after work has been a traditional time for informal networking, as people finish off their working week having a pint or two with their friends/associates within their network.

Thinking back to Chapter 15 on Time Management, we need to make time for what we consider important. Relaxation time is certainly important, and doubling up relaxation time with informal networking time is ideal.

'If you want to gather honey, don't kick over the beehive.'
- Dale Carnegie

When starting off a business people may complain that they do not have enough time for networking, as they put every spare hour into getting their business off the ground. However, in terms of stress management it is not good to spend all your time working, because the quality of the work goes down and the level of your stress goes up. Can you thing of any better form of stress relief than going to a match on a weekend, getting involved in the play and roaring your head off? If you can get family members involved it can also be great family time.

It is important not to get caught up in an expensive socialising circle – overspending through acting 'Mr. Big' has cost many a person their business. Having said that it costs very little to go to a match, and because of drink driving regulations the most you can have is a pint and a coffee or two afterwards anyway.

Do not leave your networking or building of friendships until the wolf is at the door, i.e. until you desperately need to make contact; rather do it well in advance on a regular basis. It is also one of the best strategies to recession-proof your business, as people you have solid relationships with will tend to stand by you in hard times, regardless of the general economic climate.

Start small, but start, and grow your awareness and networking skills over time. As you get more established with a bigger business to run and with more staff to do the work, you will need to become more and more of a front man or woman. Starting off in business you may well struggle to find time for it, but as your business grows networking becomes a much more important activity.

Fears About Networking

Like many things in life, between you and your goal there may be a big obstacle – fear. 'People won't like me', 'I'm not good enough' and various other stuff. Like most fears these are usually unfounded, although there are some insecure people who try to exclude others from their 'exclusive' set. Ignore them, and deal with the decent, solid people in every group.

Probably the biggest obstacle for most people is the fear of being seen as a social climber. There are two aspects to this: firstly, there's the 'external' fear of what your present associates might say, because they may feel you are leaving them behind, which makes them uncomfortable about their own situation. A true friend would want you to be the best that you can be, so it's only the negative knockers that will react this way and you should disregard their view.

Secondly, there's the 'internal' fear of becoming a fickle, shallow, superficial person, of losing your integrity. Never lose your integrity in any situation, always remembering that the highest standard is 'to thine own self be true'. If a network seriously undermines your value system, leave it straight away. On the other hand, if under-performing on the bottom rung of the ladder is not your true position, then you need to quit it also. Your true fulfilment lies somewhere between being stuck in the muck and being a social climber.

As people go through life both they and their circumstances change and grow. How many of your friends from primary school do you still hang out with? Your 'inseparable' friends from secondary school? Your buddies from your first job? The reality of life is that a fully alive human being is changing and growing all the time. Starting a business and developing a business network is just another part of this.

In conclusion, far from fearing good networking, you need to realise that people admire those who voluntarily give of their time, energy and goodwill for a good cause. Provided they are not doing it to hog the limelight, it shows that they are not self-obsessed in their own little world. It shows that they live in abundance, with the spare time and energy to give to others.

Start Making it Happen

Seek first to understand, then to be understood.

You need to make regular networking a key part of your business strategy. As mentioned earlier, building your networks must be approached in a methodical fashion and shouldn't be left to chance, so here's a suggested approach:

1. Make a commitment to networking

Like most things in life, if you feel it doesn't matter then it doesn't – to you – but that doesn't make your opinion right! Assess your commitment to the practice of networking, because, if you don't believe in it, it won't happen. Many people are uncomfortable with the idea of networking – either they don't find it easy to engage in or they consider it a waste of time and a distraction from 'real work'. It is important to understand that promoting your business is essential work. You must be prepared to put in the time and recognise that networking is 'real work'. If your networking is effective, the time and effort will be well rewarded.

2. Document your networks and identify gaps

Take a sheet of paper and write out your existing 'group' networks (e.g. clubs, associations, schools, church, etc.), listing people and organisations within each group with whom you are in contact. They, in turn, can make personal introductions to other group members that you may need to know. Remember, business is a combination of both what you know **and** who you know.

After mapping your 'group' networks, work on identifying individuals or organisations who are not in these groups but who are potential contacts, customers, allies, or 'friendly advisers'. If you need to meet them for possible future business then figure out how, and act when the opportunity presents itself.

3. Take definite steps to build your network

Decide on what new clubs, associations and other groupings you are going to join in the coming year. Decide on what social scenes you wish to partake in, be they sporting, theatre, church, political, etc. and make these a social priority rather than just going to the usual gigs. Join, and then get actively involved. But on a final word of caution, don't get heavily involved in too many — far better to make haste slowly.

Summary Tips for Networking	1. **Invite** other business people to events and activities you organise.
	2. Join clubs or associations that will open up new opportunities to make new contacts.
	3. Utilise every opportunity to promote your business – ask people what line of work they are in and tell them what you do.
	4. Carry business cards with you at all times and give them to people when they ask 'what do you do'.

5. Accept invitations to formal and family events and use the opportunity to network.
6. Try to tune into the other's wavelength as quickly as possible – 'seek first to understand...then to be understood'.
7. Realise that networking is a life-long process, not a quick-fix solution.
8. Don't wait until you need something to get involved – people will read this as shallow. Network in advance, when you don't need to.
9. Become an interesting person to talk to. Read, and develop your hobbies.
10. Return favours. Give as well as receive, otherwise people will see you as greedy and cut you out.
11. Don't expect favours and information from people before you have established a solid relationship with them.
12. It is important to periodically evaluate how well your networks are performing.
13. Observe the way politicians network, and get their pictures in the paper – it's all to promote themselves.
14. Social skills and good networking abilities are very important in sales – watch the way professional salesmen network.

Social Networking Websites

Internet and web behaviour has changed significantly in recent years, and rapid changes are occurring every day. The early use of the web concentrated on provision and consumption of information, basic communication and commerce. People used the web to research information, helping them to make decisions and choices. They also used the web to purchase goods and to communicate with others, both personally and professionally. Most content was generated by professional organisations, companies and governments.

With the advent of Web 2.0, user behaviour has changed and

'ordinary' people are now using the web to express themselves, to publish their own content, to network and communicate with each other in a more widespread and integrated way. Social networking sites have enabled people to reconnect with old friends, meet new friends worldwide and influence the choices and decisions of others without third party or authority channels. Commercial organisations and companies have realised the impact of this unlimited and unfiltered communication on traditional marketing, and advertising online and viral marketing are the fastest growing channels in the marketing world.

There are a wide range of social networking sites and platforms on the internet. However, Facebook (www.facebook.com), Twitter (www.twitter.com) and LinkedIn (www.linkedin.com) are the most popular.

In the same way that one can establish a profile as an individual, many businesses, organisations and interest groups have established profiles or communities to communicate with target customers, colleagues and industry contacts, etc.

As with most web applications, initial set-up is relatively easy and straightforward. However, ongoing maintenance requires a certain amount of time and commitment to keep content fresh, to engage new users and to make the profile/page dynamic and relevant.

Facebook also allows integration and hosting of other applications and acts as an information aggregator, so it can also be used as the platform to introduce file sharing channels such as Flickr or Picasa for photos, YouTube for video, iTunes for podcasts, Twitter for micro-blogging, etc.

Blogs
A blog (which comes from the words 'web log') is a website usually maintained by an individual, with regular entries of

commentary, descriptions of events, or other material such as graphics or video. Bloggers typically make rich use of hypertext, to connect to what others have written on a topic or to resources on the Web. Blog entries are normally followed by a comment button, allowing readers to write a reaction, which is then logged and linked, along with all other comments, into the original text. While most blogs are created and managed by individuals, group blogs are also possible.

Many businesses and organisations successfully use blogs to promote their products and to increase traffic to their company/corporate website or to increase the sale of products and services. While many of these are selling something, lots of blogs are simply vehicles to convey information, share thoughts and ideas and connect with people around the world.

Blogs are, by their nature, very personal. Even those written by and for a commercial audience tend to take an informal tone and part of their attraction is the sense of sharing on a human level, without the conventions and formality of traditional business websites. Some companies have been caught out by producing blogs purported to be by company CEOs and senior executives but which are actually 'ghost written' by others. These 'flogs' or fake blogs often do more to damage a company's reputation than enhance it. Genuine blogs require a high level of information sharing, often not just about the core subject but about life in general, and blog readers are usually attracted to genuine, simply written, honest blogs with passionate people behind them.

Exercise
Networking

Make a list of people you know that can help you with your business. These may be drawn from sports clubs, community associations, social connections or business/professional associates.

Name	Work role	Can advise/assist with
1.		
2.		
3.		
4.		
5.		
6.		
7.		

Notes

Chapter 18 Investment and Retirement

Introduction

Investment involves applying money or time to create future profit. Some people don't want to invest in the future. Let's look at some of the comments they make:

'Why not live for the moment?' Definitely live for the moment – but living for the moment doesn't exclude putting aside for the future! Why not aim to do both? If you create abundant circumstances, you can do both.

"An asset is anything that makes you money; a liability is anything that costs you money."
- Robert Kiyosaki author of Rich Dad, Poor Dad.

'We're here for a good time, not a long time.' Absolutely, we're here for a good time – but retiring at 65 and living until 85 on a very small pension won't feel like such a good time, and may feel like a very long time.

'There are no pockets on a shroud'. Not usually anyway, and you cannot take it with you – but can't you leave some of your abundance to someone else? What's wrong with that, provided you've had plenty for yourself?

'You're only young once'. A phrase often used to justify messing around at whatever we fancy – but it can also be interpreted as referring to missed opportunities in youth that may never be recovered.

'You could get hit by the next bus that comes along'. Yes, but you probably won't. If you do then it doesn't matter anymore, as long as you've provided for your dependents. If you don't, then you might live to be a ripe old age!

Investment – What and How?

What?
The quote at the top of the page answers the question about what type of investments to make. Quite simply, invest in things that make you money, and avoid the so-called investments that cost you money.

You may want to invest in things for a range of personal reasons, but never forget the basic rule above. The main things most ordinary people invest in are: cash, homes, businesses, education, savings certificates, investment policies, property for business or for rental, shares and pensions.

How?

The 'how' question is really a question of the amount of 'return' you get on your investment, and involves a few questions: How much money will you make from this investment? How long until you get your money back? How much money will you get back? How sure are you? Are there guarantees/security on offer?

There's always a trade off between risks taken and the potential reward. Even money left under the mattress loses its value through inflation – it will not buy as much in a year's time as it will today if there is inflation in the economy (on the other hand, it will buy more if there is deflation). The best strategy is not to put all your eggs in the one basket, and over time to have a mix of a few different investments. If you can afford to you'll eventually have a few going at the same time – e.g. mortgage, business, investment policy for children's education costs, pension for retirement, etc. Don't overstretch yourself, and maybe the pension can wait until the mortgage is under control, or other investments can wait until the business is built.

The Foundation – Saving

A good indication of Irish people's attitude to saving was the uptake of the governments' saving scheme (Special Savings Investment Accounts) in which 1.2 million people participated, with 1.1 million seeing it through to completion five years later in 2006. In addition to this scheme people invested in homes, property, businesses, pensions, shares, etc., indicating quite a strong saving culture.

To save is 'to reserve for future use'. Because things won't always go smoothly (health, recession, old age) and sometimes you'll need savings to save you. In terms of weather there are the seasons; in economic terms there's the 'boom/bust' cycle; likewise business fortunes vary, and in a lifetime there's the working/retirement cycle. No more than the farmer must save hay during summer to feed his cattle in the winter, people must save money to carry them through their quiet seasons.

Any fool can earn money but it takes a wise man to save it.

Whether or not you will save depends to a great extent on the attitude you attach to it – is it painful or pleasurable? If you consider it painful not to be able to spend all your money, then you'll spend it all. On the other hand, people who decide that they deserve more out of life than mere survival will organise themselves with regular and reliable savings plans. If you don't consciously organise a reliable method, Parkinson's law ('expenses rise to meet the income available') will apply.

If you're having a problem in this area, the statement 'A tenth of all I earn is mine to keep' is a good affirmation to start with, and can be increased as profits increase. It may be OK to give away most of what you earn, but surely you deserve to hold onto some of it? As you start to practice that statement you will be practicing abundance. This fundamental shift in your thinking will lead initially to short-term savings, which can then be used as the key to open a long-term door – a deposit for a mortgage, for example.

Strategy – Expenses to Investments

Here's a critical point to understand in developing an investment strategy: It's not just about making money that you don't have – it's also about how you spend the money you do have. If you can transform something that has been making you poorer (an expense) into something that will make you richer (an investment), this will automatically create a large turnaround in your fortunes.

Owning equipment instead of hiring it, and making interest on savings instead of paying interest on borrowings, are examples of this turnaround. As always, it takes money to make money, so until you get some initial savings together as outlined in the last section, you may find it hard to make this transformation. Once you can contribute to the original purchase price, **the investment should pay for itself**, i.e. cost you nothing extra in the short term, and once paid for will then make even more money for you.

Following are some typical annual costs and their equivalent investment:

Costs	Amount	Investment
Home rental	€9,600	Mortgage
Equipment hire	€1,500	Purchase/lease
Unnecessary phone	€1,000	Saving certificates
Hire purchase	€500	Straight purchase
Loan interest	€1,000	Deposit interest
Smoking	€4,200	Investment policy
Excess entertainment	€2,600	Investment policy

If you could change even half of these costs into investments, you'd transform your wealth. The message being promoted by much advertising is 'enjoy now, pay later' which has resulted in a borrowing culture that has put many people into financial slavery. Moving from financial slavery into financial mastery is the reward for transforming expenses to investments.

Investment Options

There are several investment options, some of which we explore in detail below.

1. Your Business

Your business represents a major investment of your two scarcest resources: time and money. If it's properly developed it will give you a wage every week, and additional profits as a return on your investment. As a business person you are a natural investor, with your initial investment being in your own business as you build up stock, equipment, a workspace, a customer base, and goodwill.

However, there comes a time when you must demand a fair

financial return, as cash and time inputs are investments, not gifts. A business can be a greedy thing, but the deal has to be 'if you make the business, then it has to make you'. This new 'return on investment' attitude is a subtle psychological shift, and most experienced business people can tell you about when they became aware of the need for it.

You will have great difficulty making investments if you're not making profits. Your first goal may be just to break even, but thereafter you will want to make profit. The basis for a healthy business beings profits, the question which then arises is what to do with these profits? An investment that you'd really like to make can act as a real incentive to make profits.

Aside from the profit you get from the business, remember that it has the potential to become a valuable asset in its own right, and may have a decent sale value when you decide to leave it or retire from it. Alternatively, it may provide you with an income into your retirement years, working a few days a week as it suits you, which would reduce the need for a large pension. Given all these benefits it should be fairly clear that a good business is indeed a very valuable investment.

On a note of caution the process of investing in your business should be a phased, gradual one, particularly if it is your first time in business. If you had access to all the finance you required, and spent it all in the first month, you would invest in a lot of things that were unnecessary. Thus it is recommended that you adopt the following approach:

1. Make a list of all the investments (equipment, premises, transport, stock) that you need or want.
2. Organise this list in order of importance in terms of income-generating potential.
3. Stick to this order regardless of salesmen or ego temptations.

This will help ensure that your investment decisions are made in a logical sequence based on maximum return.

2. A Regular Lump Sum Strategy

Wouldn't it be nice to have a cash lump sum coming to you every few years? A lump sum you can do something with, something between ten and fifteen thousand? It's very possible if you set up a system of small investment policies that mature every few years. These policies invest in a mix of property, bonds, shares and cash (see 'managed funds' later in the chapter). Now is not a bad time to start investing in them, as share values are low, and most likely to increase in value over the period of your investment.

Depending on how often you want the lump sums, you can organise three or four different savings schemes for an affordable amount of c. €70 each per month, being €210 for three – less than what an average smoker spends each month. These saving schemes could be a mix of An Post saving certificates (choice of three-year or five-year and six month); National Solidarity Bonds (four-year or ten-year) also available from An Post; and investment policies with any of the financial companies. To have a regular flow of lump sums you can cash in your policies over time, and replace each encashed policy with a new one to maintain continuity.

Sense does not come before age. There is many a wise youth and many an old fool.

In general you are better to spread your investment across a few top companies, i.e. if you had €300 per month to invest, you would be better to put €100 into three different policies. This diversification gives you a good chance of getting the best return on at least one of the policies. More importantly, it means that if you need to cash in a policy, your total investment fund isn't finished as two-thirds of it would remain intact.

One advantage of an investment policy is that it is paid by direct debit, which systematises your saving. Secondly, it is easy to get into a managed fund and commit, say, €70 a month, the kind of money that gets wasted on 'silly spending' if it's lying around, but that builds up nicely if committed to savings. Finally, there's usually a penalty in the form of a reduced return if you withdraw your funds early, making you more inclined to leave them there as planned.

You can invest in a managed fund through an insurance salesperson, bank official, broker, or company sales representative. In general you get the widest range of choices from a broker, but always ask 'Why are you recommending this plan? Why this company? What are my top three options, and I'll consider all three?'

3. Investing in Your Own Home

Robert Kiyosaki's and Sharon Lechter's book *Rich Dad, Poor Dad* suggests that investment in a home isn't really an investment at all because it just costs money, therefore it is an expense! Nonetheless, providing ourselves with shelter is a necessary expense, whether we pay rent or pay a mortgage. From an investment perspective, over-spending on your home represents bad value. Up to a point it represents a saving on rent, but after that it shows a poor return, and investment in interior décor isn't an investment at all!

A journey of 1,000 miles begins with a single step.

Buying your home is still one of the biggest investments you will make, and with the collapse in the property market, 2011 onwards may present some good value. If you can buy a property that will also accommodate your business you will have killed two birds with the one stone. A workshop out the back, or an office in the house, can save the need to lease a separate property. Watch out for planning permission issues arising, particularly if there is noise, dust, or a lot of extra traffic involved.

The situation with raising a loan for the purchase has changed quite a bit with the credit crunch, and if you are hoping to borrow on a self-employed income you'll have a tough time, especially for the first few years.

Don't forget that in addition to the purchase price there are other costs associated with home purchase: application or arrangement fees, legal and valuation fees, administration fees, indemnity bonds and stamp duty.

A useful website is www.consumerproperty.ie.

Stamp Duty Update

The rates for stamp duty changed in Budget 2011, with a reduction in the rate for transfers of residential property to 1% on properties valued up to €1 million, with 2% applying to amounts over €1 million. Various reliefs were also abolished, including first time buyer relief against stamp duty, exemption for new houses and exemption on residential property transfers valued under €127,000.

Types of Mortgage

A principal and interest mortgage is the safest and simplest mortgage with which to finance a home purchase, with monthly payments consisting of interest and some of the principal of the loan. If you go to pay it off after the first few years you will find that the principal (the amount borrowed) has hardly gone down at all, because most of what you're paying in the early years goes on interest, with only a small portion used for reduction of the principal.

An endowment mortgage (not recommended) combines the home loan and a life assurance policy. Under this method you pay the lender interest only for the entire term, while at the same time paying monthly premiums into a life assurance investment policy. If all goes well with the investment markets there will be an investment fund large enough to pay off the mortgage at the end of the term. However, if there is a shortfall in the fund value, it is your problem. It is best not to mix up these two types of product (a mortgage and a life policy), when you can take both out separately if you so choose.

Another question that arises is whether you should arrange your mortgage on a variable interest rate basis, or fix the interest for a period of years. A fixed interest rate is set slightly higher, but can provide considerable peace of mind and protects the borrower from large increases. It makes most sense to fix when interest rates are low.

In addition to the mortgage payment you will also have to take out a mortgage protection policy, which will clear the mortgage if either of the borrowers die. Mortgage protection is compulsory, as is a buildings insurance policy in case of the building being destroyed by fire, etc.

Mortgage Interest Relief

Tax relief for home mortgage interest is not paid through the tax system but through the bank, with mortgage repayments reduced by the amount of the tax credit due. Relief is due at the standard rate of tax (20%), with a maximum tax credit on a first mortgage of €800 p.a. for a single person and €1,600 for a widowed person or married couple (available for seven years at time of writing but due to be reduced in upcoming budgets).

An empty house is better than a difficult tenant.

Choosing a lender that offers the best long-term interest rates is very important. By carefully shopping around, you may be able to save yourself a considerable sum of money over the term of your loan. In general the shorter the term of the borrowing the better the value you get, as you pay less in interest. However, your monthly payments become lower the longer the term you go for. It's important to strike the right balance between the two, and if you have to go for the longer term of 25–30 years initially, make sure there's no penalty for restructuring the mortgage to a shorter term later on.

Local Authority Loans

Affordable Housing and Shared Ownership Schemes are operated by local authorities and for many they offer the first step in purchasing a home of their choice. You need to raise a mortgage of between 40% and 75% of the value of the house from the local authority, who will then rent you the remaining share of the property for up to 25 years. Contact your local city/county council office for details, or check out www.affordablehome.ie.

4. Buying an Investment Property

Initially when you start in business you may find that you are making everybody else rich! You may be paying interest to the banks on borrowed money, hire to the hire companies for equipment you cannot afford to buy, and rental to a landlord for a space to work in. As already outlined, a key part of your work in the early years will be transforming these costs to investments, thereby making you wealthier. A much longer-term investment is the purchase of a commercial property – so how might you organise the finance?

Many people concentrate on building up their business for the first few years, increasing profitability to a point that they may be able to invest in their own premises. If mortgage repayments cost much the same as rent, they are then in a position to make a good case to any bank. With commercial properties falling in value, if rental doesn't fall then it may become cheaper to pay a mortgage than to pay rent.

Borrowing for a commercial property is more difficult than for a home, as people will do everything possible to repay their homes, but may not go to quite the same lengths to hold onto a commercial property. As a consequence a bank will normally require a 20% to 25% deposit on a commercial loan. Planning ahead to get a deposit together makes good sense. The purchase deposit might be financed from your savings, an investment plan that is maturing, or a re-mortgage on a home or other property.

On an unknown path, it is better to be slow.

Making your case to the bank for a loan will require you to put together some information in support of your application, including the following:

- Present rental outgoing (if relocating to purchased premises).
- Valuation on property to be purchased.
- Accounts, plus bank statements for the past year.
- Potential additional rental income.
- Business plan.
- Amount of deposit.

The cost of the property will depend on a few factors, including the state of repair of the property and the location. The market for commercial property continues to fall, which means there may be bargains available for those with the means to buy.

If you are letting all or part of the property you will need to be collecting rents, which can be a headache if you get the wrong tenants. Repairs and maintenance also cost money, as does having the place vacant for extended periods. Property transactions can be slow and costly – from planning permission to legal and auctioneering fees, stamp duty, etc.

On the positive side an investment property is a long-term investment, and if you are prepared to put up with some of the hassles involved, you will have someone else paying for your property as your mortgage gets paid off.

If you can buy at the right price and borrow at a low interest rate, rental income can match interest payments, leaving any capital appreciation to you as investor. Capital depreciation may also occur but is less likely if you're buying in 2011 or later as the market will already have fallen quite a bit. Even if it falls further once the rental income pays the borrowings you should be OK.

5. Retirement Pensions

It takes no great foresight to plan for a known future event. In this case the known future event is the onset of old age, unless we die in the meantime.

Unless you plan to work until the day you die, you need some kind of a pension income in your retirement. Increasingly warnings are being issued to make private provision for a pension in the future, and it's planned to raise the retirement age from 66 to 68 years of age. The reason for pressure on state pensions is a combination of the reduction in average family size throughout the country (with fewer children being born to look after a growing number of pensioners), and an increase in life expectancy (resulting in longer retirements).

It is important to take a balanced view of what you will need in retirement. Generally your costs will decrease as mortgage and travel costs reduce, so you can afford to take an income reduction.

Don't panic - it's never too late to start a pension. Even starting at

58 you'll probably have 10 years saving if your health holds; and retiring at 50 isn't all it's cracked up to be. Take a sustainable approach, based on the stage of life you are currently at (e.g. mortgaged with childcare costs?) and your distance to retirement (10/20/30 years?), assuming you retire at 67 or 68.

A pension is a part of your just reward for working.

But don't ignore the issue completely. Even starting late and creating a modest pension is worthwhile; an extra €100 each week can make a big difference as a pension top-up when you're retired.

Whether or not you conceive of a good pension as being a bonus or as a fair return for your hard work is a key perception. If you think of it as a bonus then it is possible that you will deny yourself this privilege. If you think of it as a fair return for your work then you will make definite provision for it – and organise your business to pay for it.

Like most things it's a question of attitude – if you believe you deserve it, you're right; if you believe you don't deserve it, then you are also right. The same attitude applies to your pension – if you consider you deserve it you will make provision for it, and not stop until you succeed.

What if you were a well-paid, risk-averse, job-for-life public servant? In addition to your wage you'd also be earning a five star pension. That's not to say that the public servant is wrong in negotiating a good pension for their retirement years, but that you are wrong if you don't develop one for yourself.

But there's a key difference – as an employee of a good company a pension would be organised for you (like many other aspects of your work), but as a self-employed person you will have to organise it for yourself. This will take the form of either a personal pension (if you're a sole trader) or an occupational pension (if you are an employee of your own company).

Pension Options

As a self-employed person, there are three basic pension options:

1. **Social Welfare Pensions**. As an Irish citizen you are automatically entitled to a pension – either a contributory pension (€230.30 single, €446.60 married, both over 66) if you pay PRSI, or non-contributory (€219 single, €363.70 married) if you haven't contributed enough PRSI. As a self-employed person your PRSI payment is submitted along with your tax payment on an annual basis.

   With a contributory pension you are not means tested, so you can add to it with any other income. A non-contributory pension is reduced by any other income, making it less valuable if you do have any such income (e.g. rental income, deposit interest, part-time work, etc.). It is critical that you try to qualify for a contributory pension by paying enough years of PRSI; check with your social welfare information officer for an exact update on your situation as a matter of urgency if you have any worries.

2. **Personal Pension Plans**. You may take out a personal pension in order to increase your pension entitlements – for instance as a self-employed person wishing to top-up your contributory pension. Quite simply they are savings plans which can only be used for your retirement, with your monthly/yearly contributions tax deductible up to certain limits. Also, profits earned by the investments within these plans are not liable to any tax, so they should grow faster than other savings plans. Their main disadvantage is that they vary with the stock exchange, and if they mature during low market values they might not be as valuable as hoped.

3. **DIY Pension**. You might create your own pension by investing in property, shares, etc. in order to provide real/dividend income in your retirement. The main

disadvantage is that the DIY option attracts no tax relief. The advantages include more control over your funds, and the property remains after your death for your next of kin, whilst your pension dies with you/your spouse.

The best option for a good pension is a mix of all three, starting with no. 1 as an essential, no. 2 as very important, and no.3 as an optional extra.

A self-administered pension fund can combine the tax relief of the personal pension (no. 2) with the control of the DIY pension (no. 3). However, it requires costly supervision by the pensions industry making it inappropriate for smaller pension funds, but check it out if you have c. €100,000 in your fund.

When Should One Start?

The earlier the better, but it is never too late to start a pension.

Whenever it's appropriate. If you have a big mortgage, car repayments and childcare bills, you don't need the added pressure of pension contributions. During your productive phase of middle age it is important to prepare for retirement; it's never too late, but the later it is the more urgent it becomes.

The amount of time you have to make a pension provision depends on three things: your age now; your planned retirement age; and your age at death. Your age at death is unknown – so we'll assume it to be 85. If you plan to retire at 65, that leaves 20 years in retirement, without an income. The only calculation left is the number of years before retirement at 65. If you're 35 today that's 30 years, and a work-life to retired-life ratio of 3:2. If you're 45 today, that's 20 years, and a work-life to retired-life ratio of 1:1. If you're 55 today, that's 10 years, and a work-life to retired-life ratio of 1:2. Depending on the proportion of work-life to retired-life, you need to make appropriate provision.

What will my Private Pension be Worth?

There are two elements to this question:

(a) the **value of your pension** fund

The value of your pension depends on a number of factors:
1. The value of the contributions paid into the fund.
2. The growth rate achieved by the pension fund.
3. The administration charges levied by the fund manager.
4. The amount of the fund you withdraw as a lump sum on retirement.

(b) the **'pension for life' or annuity you buy** with this fund

Given the same fund, you buy a better pension at 70 than at 60, because it won't have to pay you for as many years. The value of your annuity pension depends on
1. How early you retire.
2. Annuity rates at the date of your retirement.

When choosing a pension plan there are a number of other issues to consider, including: entry charges and commissions (which will reduce the value of the amount invested in the early years); finding the right mix of investments (high, medium or low risk); assessing the performance of different pension companies' investment funds; and ongoing administration charges which eat into the fund value (c. 1% is the maximum you should be prepared to pay).

Investment Company Jargon

- **Managed funds**

Managed funds are simply money investments that are managed on a daily basis by full-time fund managers. The size and the risk strategy of each fund are decided by the investment company involved (e.g. New Ireland), and you can choose to invest in a safe or an aggressively managed fund.

- **Investment companies**

There are more than ten investment companies with managed funds in Ireland. Some are better than others, without question. Make sure to examine the previous growth rates of the company you are considering investing with before doing so. Put it to you this way – would you put the spare cash you needed for your retirement on a horse without checking out how many top three finishes it had? No more than you'd shop around before buying a new car, it's even more important with a cash investment. Otherwise you might end up with a low-growth policy when you could have a good one. Check the financial section of the Sunday papers for fund performances.

It's better to thrive late than never do well.

- **What about inflation?**

Inflation is always a threat to savings and investments. Put simply, inflation is the rate at which your money loses its value in terms of what it can buy. Ten years ago ten pounds had a lot more buying power than its euro equivalent has today, and looking forward ten years the same will be true. The best way to provide protection against inflation is to maintain a balanced portfolio of investments.

What do these Funds Invest in?

If you decide to contribute to a 'Managed Fund' administered by one of the banks or insurance companies, they will employ a fund manager to do the investing on your behalf. Fund managers usually go for a balanced investment, spreading the money under their control over a number of investment types, as follows:

Cash is quite simply a deposit account, paying interest at the going rate. Returns from cash have been just ahead of inflation over the longer term.

Equities (also known as shares) give you a share of/part ownership in a company or number of companies. The return on share ownership comes from either the income the company pays in annual dividends or from the growth in the share price, but share prices also fall in value making them much riskier than cash. Equities have tended to be the best performing of all investment types in the long term, but looking at the stock market performance during 2008 wouldn't inspire confidence. Having said that, buying while share prices are low wouldn't be a bad idea as values should start to recover and you'll get the benefit over the coming years.

Bonds are loans to governments and large companies. You get a fixed interest rate and are almost guaranteed your money back at the end of the term. As such, a bond can be viewed as somewhere between cash and equities in terms of security and return but there is always a risk that the issuer of the bond will default on repayment.

If you wish to purchase some Irish government Bonds, it is proposed to introduce a new, four-year, National Solidarity Bond to complement the ten-year National Solidarity Bond which was launched in 2010. The bond will pay a coupon each year and a bonus for those who hold it to maturity. The bond will be sold by An Post on behalf of the National Treasury Management Agency (NTMA).

Property is probably the investment we can most easily identify with. However, the falls in property prices since 2008 have left a lot of investors exposed to serious losses.

Property is one of the easiest investments to 'gear up' (i.e. borrow against) but it is also relatively 'illiquid' (i.e. it cannot be bought and sold as quickly as other investments).

Return on Investment

Remember, there is no magic formula that will multiply small money into a massive return – it's nearly impossible to catch that Leprechaun with his pot of gold! What you receive at maturity will usually be closely related to what you put in as you go along using a regular savings system.

If you are looking for an exceptional return, the best investment is usually an investment of time and money in your own successful business. If it provides an income and some profit over ten years on a small initial investment, that's a good return on investment.

References

www.itsyourmoney.ie

www.pensionsboard.ie

1. Savings Certificates – Short-Term Savings

Visit your local An Post office or the website www.anpost.ie. There are a range of savings options outlined on the 'Savings and Investments' page (use the search facility on the home page). Assess one or two options that are of most relevance to you.

2. Managed Savings Funds – Medium Term

Visit your local insurance broker with a view to choosing a medium-term savings policy that will suit your needs.

Also check out your investment options at www.itsyourmoney.ie

3. Pension Calculation – Long Term Investment

Go to www.pensionsboard.ie and click on 'Pension Calculators'. The calculator allows you to estimate the amount of money you would need to contribute to your pension in relation to your age and current yearly salary, to end up with the level of pension you expect in retirement.

Calculate one or two scenarios for your retirement.

Some useful websites

Affordable Homes	www.affordablehome.ie
Arts Council	www.artscouncil.ie
Business Access to State Information and Services	www.basis.ie
Bord Bia	www.bordbia.ie
Central Statistics Office	www.cso.ie
Chambers of Commerce	www.chambers.ie
Citizens Information	www.citizensinformation.ie
Companies Registration Office	www.cro.ie
County Enterprise Boards	www.enterpriseboards.ie
Crafts Council of Ireland	www.ccoi.ie
Data Protection Commissioner	www.dataprotection.ie
Department of Enterprise, Trade and Employment	www.deti.ie
Department of Social Protection	www.welfare.ie
Domain Registration	www.domainregistry.ie
Enterprise Ireland	www.enterprise-ireland.ie
Fáilte Ireland	www.failteireland.ie
FAS	www.fas.ie
First Step	www.first-step.ie
Government Public Tenders	www.etenders.gov.ie
Health and Safety Authority	www.hsa.ie
IBEC	www.ibec.ie
Irish Credit Bureau	www.icb.ie

Some useful websites (continued)

Irish Exporters Association	www.irishexporters.ie
Irish Franchise Association	www.irishfranchiseassociation.com
Irish League of Credit Unions	www.creditunion.ie
Irish Management Institute	www.imi.ie
Irish Pensions Board	www.pensionsboard.ie
Irish Small and Medium Enterprises	www.isme.ie
LEADER Programme	www.pobail.ie
Marketing Institute of Ireland	www.mii.ie
Money Advice and Budgeting Service	www.mabs.ie
National Consumer Agency	www.nca.ie/ www.itsyourmoney.ie
Patents Office	www.patentsoffice.ie
Revenue Commissioners	www.revenue.ie
Revenue Online Service	www.ros.ie
Seamus Caulfield	www.seamuscaulfield.ie
Small Firms Association	www.sfa.ie
Shannon Development	www.shannon-dev.ie
Teagasc	www.teagasc.ie
WESTBIC Business and Innovation Centre	www.westbic.ie
Western Development Commission	www.wdc.ie